The excellence of play

The excellence of play

2nd edition

Edited by
Janet Moyles

OPEN UNIVERSITY PRESS

Open University Press
McGraw-Hill Education
McGraw-Hill House
Shoppenhangers Road
Maidenhead
Berkshire
England
SL6 2QL

email: enquiries@openup.co.uk
world wide web: www.openup.co.uk

and Two Penn Plaza, New York, NY 10121-2289, USA

First published 1994
This edition published 2005

Reprinted 2006 (twice)

Copyright © The Editor and Contributors 2005

A catalogue record of this book is available from the British Library

ISBN 10: 0 335 19068 5 (pb)   0 335 19069 3 (hb)
ISBN 13: 978 0 335 19068 3 (pb)   978 0 335 19069 0 (hb)

Library of Congress Cataloging-in-Publication Data
The excellence of play / edited by Janet R. Moyles
    p. cm.
   Includes bibliographical references (p.) and index.
   ISBN 0-335- 19069-3
   2. Play. 2. Early childhood education - Curricula.   1. Moyles,
Janet R.
  LB 1140.35.P55E93   1993
  372.21 – dc20   93-25317
                                                       CIP

Typeset by RefineCatch Limited, Bungay, Suffolk
Printed in the UK by Bell & Bain Ltd, Glasgow

Contents

Figures and photographs

Notes on the editor and contributors

Lesley Abbott is Professor of Early Childhood Education in the Institute of Education at the Manchester Metropolitan University and director of the English government project *Birth to Three Matters: A Framework to Support Children in their Earliest Years*. She also directed the earlier research project *Educare for the Under Threes*, which resulted in the training and resource materials *Shaping the Future: Working with the Under Threes*. She has a background in primary and early childhood education. She has served on a number of government committees and contributed to conferences nationally and internationally. She has published widely in the early years field. Publications include *Working with the Under Threes: Training and Professional Development* (Open University Press 1997) and *Working with the Under Threes: Responding to Children's Needs* (Open University Press 1997), both with Helen Moylett. She co-edited with Gillian Pugh *Training to Work in the Early Years* (Open University Press 1998).

Siân Adams has a background totally rooted in the early years. Following a period of teaching in primary schools, she was an early years advisory teacher in the Midlands. She then moved to Leicester to study for her PhD on teachers' reflective practice within the context of playful learning. This was followed by a move to Anglia Polytechnic University where Siân was engaged in several research projects with Janet Moyles and other colleagues relating to effective, playful pedagogy in the early years, including *SPEEL (Study of Effective Pedagogy in the Early Years)* (DfES 2002) and *Recreating the Reception Year* (ATL 2004). She has also published a number of articles on early years practices. Her latest book, co-authored with Janet Moyles, is *Images of Violence* (Featherstone Publications 2005), which explores the challenges for practitioners of responding to children's expressions of violence in society.

Angela Anning is currently Emeritus Professor of Early Childhood Education at the University of Leeds. She has a background in teaching early years education at class teacher, headteacher, lecturer and researcher levels. Her current research interests include the curriculum for young children (in particular art and design education), the professional knowledge of those who work with young children, and multi-agency teamwork in delivering services to young children and their families. She is an investigator within the National Evaluation of Sure Start team based at Birkbeck College. She has a strong belief in the key role of creative play-based activities and high-quality experiential learning in promoting young children's learning at home and in early years group settings.

Pat Broadhead is Research Professor for Education at Northumbria University. She has worked at Leeds University and York University and as an early years teacher. Her main research interests are how young children become sociable and cooperative and how young children learn through play. She has several publications in these areas including *Early Years Play and Learning: Developing Social Skills and Cooperation* (RoutledgeFalmer 2003). She has also extensively researched school development planning in primary schools, with associated publications.

Tina Bruce is a Professor currently at the University of Roehampton. Tina was a member of the working parties that developed *Curriculum Guidance for the Foundation Stage* (QCA/DfES 2000), now enshrined in law and part of the National Curriculum. She was also part of developing the *Birth to Three Matters* Framework (DfES 2002) and is a member of the Ministerial Early Education Advisory Group. She is widely published and is best known for *Early Childhood Education* (Hodder Arnold 2005), *Time to Play in Early Childhood* (Hodder 1991), *Developing Learning in Early Childhood* (Paul Chapman 2004) and *Learning through Play: Babies, Toddlers and the Foundation Years* (Hodder and Stoughton 2001) – plus many more.

Tricia David is Emeritus Professor of Education at Canterbury Christ Church University College, having officially retired in 2001. She was a Professor of Education at Canterbury Christ Church University College for seven years and prior to that worked at Warwick University for ten years, having been a headteacher of both nursery and primary schools earlier in her career. Tricia's research and writing is mainly concerned with the earliest years (birth to age 6). Her publications include 15 books (single authored or edited by her) and over seventy journal articles and chapters in books. Tricia is known internationally for her work with *l'Organisation Mondiale pour l'Education Prescolaire* (OMEP) and the OECD. Her first research experience concerning play and learning was as a member of Corinne Hutt's team on the *Play, Exploration and Learning* project in the early 1970s.

Dan Davies is Principal Lecturer in Primary Education at Bath Spa University College. He is also leader of the Primary PGCE course. He has taught the 4–7 age range in London primary schools and published widely in the fields of science and design and technology education, including *Teaching Science and Design and Technology in the Early Years* for David Fulton Books with Alan Howe (2003).

Bernadette Duffy originally trained as a teacher and since then has worked in a wide range of settings over the last twenty years. She is Head of the Thomas Coram Early Childhood Centre in Camden which has been designated as a Children Centre by the Sure Start Unit at the Department for Education and Employment. The Centre offers fully integrated care and education for young children and has a tradition of involvement in the arts. Bernadette has contributed to a number of publications and is the author of *Supporting Creativity and Imagination in the Early Years* (OUP 1998). Bernadette was part of the Foundation Stage working party which devised the Curriculum Guidance and had a particular input into the section on creative development. She is Vice-Chair of the British Association for Early Childhood Education, a fellow of the Royal Society of Arts, a member of the DfES Early Education Advisory Group and the Primary Education Study Group.

Aline-Wendy Dunlop has taught in the university sector since 1993, first at Moray House Institute of Education in Edinburgh, then from 1996 at the University of Strathclyde where she is a Senior Lecturer in the Department of Childhood and Primary Studies. She has had a very varied teaching experience over 23 years in schools and the community, which has included home visiting, training education staff in residential childcare, teaching SNNEB students, working with parents, special educational needs and mainstream early education. Her main areas of current research interest are leadership in early education, special needs, social interaction and understanding in autism, the empowerment of families of very young children, continuity and progression for children in educational transitions and training for professionals in the field of autism. She is an invited keynote speaker at a range of conferences, and is published both in early education and in autism.

Carey English has worked as actor, writer and director in theatre for children since 1978. A joint artistic director of Quicksilver Theatre, she has specialized in theatre for 3 to 5-year-olds since 1988. She strongly believes that theatre for the very young can function as a potent form of communication which can affirm emotions and inspire ideas and feelings, as well as entertain. Recent plays include a trilogy about family relationships *Baby Love, All By My Own, The Mamas and the Papas. Upstairs in the Sky* is the product of two years of research at Mapledene Early Years Centre. She is also a primary school governor.

Hilary Fabian is Head of Education and Childhood Studies at the North

East Wales Institute. She has taught young children in the London Boroughs of Hillingdon and Harrow, in Buckinghamshire, in Shropshire and with the Service Children's Education Authority in Germany. Since 1991, she has worked in the university sector, first at the Manchester Metropolitan University where she was course leader for the Early Years Continuing Professional Development programmes, then at the University of Edinburgh and, since 2000, at NEWI. She has an MSc degree in Education Management where her dissertation explored staff induction. Her PhD thesis, books and journal publications reflect her interest in the transitions that people make in their lives, particularly children starting school, and the way in which induction is managed.

Rose Griffiths is Lecturer in Education at the University of Leicester where she is responsible for initial and in-service education in primary mathematics. Starting as a mathematics teacher with a particular interest in working with children who find maths difficult, she was head of mathematics at a comprehensive school, and later worked extensively with young children and their parents, including through Sure Start. Her publications include several books for parents and teachers and she also enjoys writing books for children. The latter include the *Oxford First Book of Maths* (Oxford University Press 1999), *Simple Maths* (Heinemann 2005), and a series of books called *Number Connections* (Heinemann 1996 to present).

Nigel Hall is Professor of Literacy Education in the Institute of Education at Manchester Metropolitan University. He is the author, co-author or editor of over twenty books for teachers about young children's language and literacy. The most recent is the *Handbook of Early Childhood Literacy*. Publications 2003), co-edited with Jackie Marsh and Joanne Larson. He is the author of over fifty journal articles about literacy and language, and over forty chapters in other people's books. He is co-director of *The Punctuation Project* and is an editor of *The Journal of Early Childhood Literacy*.

Stephanie Harding is the Pedagogical Team Leader at an early excellence centre in Norfolk. Since completing her MA in Early Education and Care she has used a Best Practice Research Scholarship and a Leadership Research Bursary to support practice at her Centre. She is also a distance learning tutor on the Early Childhood Studies Scheme at London Metropolitan University.

Jane Hislam lectures in primary education at the University of Leicester. Her research is broad-ranging, and includes a study of the use of song and oral story with under-fives and how trainee teachers at Key Stage 2 develop knowledge of grammar. Jane has published both articles and chapters about oral story, children's literature and knowledge of grammar. Her teaching includes work with PGCE primary students, teaching assistants and teachers on continuing professional development courses.

Alan Howe is Senior Lecturer in Science, Design and Technology and Education Studies at Bath Spa University College. Previously he taught in primary schools in Hertfordshire, Harrow, Bristol and Bath. He has published in the fields of science, technology and creativity in education, including *Teaching Science and Design and Technology in the Early Years* (David Fulton 2003) with Dan Davies.

Helen Jameson is a practising teacher with over twenty years' experience. She has taught throughout the primary age range in both the maintained and independent sectors, working with very able/talented children as well as those with emotional and behavioural difficulties. She developed a special interest in learning through play whilst involved in research at Homerton College, University of Cambridge. Her paper on 'The effect of play upon oral and written storytelling in able 5 to 7-year-olds' was presented at the Jean Piaget Society 33rd Annual Meeting in Chicago in 2003.

Neil Kitson was previously a Lecturer in Education at University of Leicester with special interests in early years development and the role of drama in early childhood learning. He is currently involved with the reorganization of schools in Northamptonshire. Having started his career working as a primary teacher, his interests in this area were further developed through his work as an advisory teacher for drama. He has lectured extensively both in this country and abroad on the area of drama and its function in early childhood development, and has written books, chapters and articles on drama and other primary issues.

Ann Langston is currently a Research Fellow at Manchester Metropolitan University. Ann has a background in educational consultancy, teaching, teacher and nursery nurse training, and management of under-fives provision. A major contributor to the development of the *Birth to Three Matters* Framework (DfES, 2002) she also managed the *Birth to Three Matters* Training of Trainers Programme on behalf of MMU and the Sure Start Unit. Formerly a local authority Early Years Adviser, Ann has also written extensively on early years issues, including management in the early years and curriculum guidelines, and most recently has co-edited with Professor Lesley Abbott *Birth to Three Matters: Supporting the Framework of Effective Practice* (DfES 2002).

Janet Moyles is Professor Emeritus at Anglia Polytechnic University. She has worked as an early teacher and head, and also run early years initial and in-service training courses for teachers and other early years practitioners on play and learning and effective/reflective pedagogy as well as supervising a number of PhD students. She has directed several research projects including *Jills of All Trades?* (ATL 1996), *Teaching Fledglings to Fly* (ATL 1997), *Too Busy to Play?* (Leicester 1997–2000), *SPEEL – Study of Pedagogical Effectiveness in Early Learning* (DfES 2002) and *Recreating the Reception Year* (ATL 2004). Janet has also published widely in journals and books, her main publications being *Just Playing?* (OUP 1989), *Organising for Learning* (OUP 1992), *StEPs* (with Siân Adams: OUP 2001), *Beginning Teaching: Beginning Learning* (OUP 2002), *Interactive Teaching in the Primary School* (with others: OUP/McGraw Hill 2003) and *Images of Violence* (with Siân Adams: Featherstone 2005).

Theodora Papatheodorou is Reader in Early Childhood in the School of Education at Anglia Polytechnic University. Theodora has long teaching experience in early years, bilingual and special educational needs settings. She has undertaken research in a broad range of areas (including behavioural aspects for her PhD) and published her work widely in national and international journals. She is the author of the book *Behaviour Problems in the Early Years* (RoutledgeFalmer 2003). Theodora is committed to, and interested in, early childhood provision that is inclusive and offers equal opportunities to prevent and/or minimize any potential risks for young children.

Linda Pound has a lifelong commitment to young children and their families. She has been deputy head of a primary school, a nursery headteacher and a local authority early years education inspector. She has worked at three universities, most recently at London Metropolitan University where she was responsible for early childhood courses. She is currently working as an early years consultant – writing, training and supporting practitioners. Her publications include *Supporting Mathematical Development in the Early Years* (1999) and *Supporting Musical Development in the Early Years* (2002), both with Open University Press.

Sacha Powell is a Senior Research Fellow in Education at Canterbury Christ Church University College. She works on a range of local, national and international projects, recent examples of which are the *Birth to Three Matters* Research Review (2002), the development of a play strategy and children's play council for Canterbury (2004), developments in ECEC provision in Shanghai (2003–6) and in Beijing (2004–5). Her interest in how play is shaped by cultures has been influenced by living and working in France, Spain, China and Taiwan, by her doctoral research on early childhoods in Shanghai and by her own children's play and play narratives.

Iram Siraj-Blatchford is Professor of Early Childhood Education and has been working at the Institute of Education, University of London for over a decade. She is visiting Professor at a number of universities including Beijing Normal University and the Institute of Education in Hong Kong. Her current research projects include: the major DfES ten-year study on Effective Preschool and Primary Education 3–11 (EPPE 3–11) Project (1997–2008), and the Evaluation of the Foundation Phase in Wales. She is particularly interested in undertaking research which aims to combat disadvantage and to give children and families from these backgrounds a head start. She was on the StartRight enquiry and provided evidence on early education to the National Commission on Education and the House of Commons Select Committee. She is the co-author of over thirty books, monographs and major published research reports and over one hundred articles, chapters and reports.

Peter K. Smith is Professor of Psychology, and Head of the Unit for School and Family Studies, at Goldsmiths College, University of London. He has researched extensively on children's social development, play, school bullying, and grandparenting. Two of his recent books are *Understanding Children's Development* (with Helen Cowie and Mark Blades), (Blackwell 2002) and the *Nature of Play: Great Apes and Humans* (edited with Tony Pellegrini) (Guilford Publications 2005).

David Whitebread is a developmental cognitive psychologist and early years specialist. His research interests are concerned with children's cognitive development and implications for early years and primary education. He is currently involved in research projects concerned with self-regulation, metacognition and the development of thinking skills in young children's learning. Other interests include children learning through play, the education of gifted and talented children, children's drawings, and the application of cognitive neuroscience to early years education. He is a governor of his local Early Excellence Centre, the book reviews editor for the journal *Early Years* and a member of the National Executive of Training, Advancement and Cooperation in Teaching Young Children (TACTYC). His recent publications include *The Psychology of Teaching and Learning in the Primary School* (2000) and *Teaching and Learning in the Early Years* (2003), both published by RoutledgeFalmer, and *Supporting ICT in the Early Years* with John Siraj-Blatchford (Open University Press 2004).

Acknowledgements

As with the first edition, the main people who are owed thanks and credit are those who have written the chapters and complied with deadlines with such good humour and commitment. The children whose play features so prominently in the photographs – and their parents/carers and practitioners – are also acknowledged, together with those who have supplied many of the photographs which so add that practical touch to any book.

One of the chapters which I would have liked to include in this second edition was the one by Vicky Hurst on observation of play. Sadly, as many of you know, Vicky died very prematurely in 1998, a sad loss to the early years community. Her memory, however, is still very much with us. I'm sure she would approve of the second edition of any book on play.

Finally, I'd like to thank my very own special playmates, Jack and George, for allowing grandma to continue to be a player and to share their play! I hope they don't grow up too quickly! And I hope they can experience 'the excellence of play' in all their social and educational settings.

Foreword

This book offers exciting and wide-ranging understandings of play and learning within a myriad of contexts, be they areas of learning (curriculum) or cross-curricular components, such as creativity or culture. However, what is common within this massively renewed and revised edition is the importance of embedding learning within and from the child's interest and experience.

Emphasis is, correctly, placed on the affirming thrust of *Birth to Three Matters* and the *Curriculum Guidance for the Foundation Stage* in England as sound vehicles for promoting a play-centred curriculum. But we also have evidence that play-centredness is distributed quite unevenly across different types of providers and even the countries of the UK. For instance, the role of adults scaffolding play is so dependent on the competence and observational skills of pedagogues involved, be they playgroup leaders or teachers. Also, although English documents support the medium of play it is largely for the youngest age group, birth to 5; the only country in the United Kingdom that extends this right to children over 5 is Wales. The Seven Areas of Learning in the *Welsh Framework for the Foundation Phase*, which includes children aged 3 to 7, have separate guidance on child development, play, active learning and assessment. The curriculum is also expected to be delivered through these approaches outdoors as well as indoors. We are therefore moving in the right direction.

This edited collection makes a stunning contribution to the practice of a play-based approach. The authors are expert in their areas and apply examples of play generously, making this a sound volume for early years practitioners. Many of the authors use their own valuable research perspectives, offering insight through examples. What comes across strongly is the need to provide young children, age 7 and below in particular, with more time. The authors draw our attention to the damage caused by hurrying children through work *before* they have had sufficient hands-on experience or the opportunity to apply their own interest through their own initiation and extension of activities. The book will support pedagogues in their attempts to make education and care meaningful to children and, for children, it will also help to establish the foundations for the aims in *Every Child Matters*. I hope the book is widely read, applied and discussed across the full range of early years practice and for those training to work with young children. It deserves to be!

Iram Siraj-Blatchford

Introduction

Janet Moyles

Jack (6 years old) and George (nearly 3 years old) are playing 'safari' in the garden.

This consists mainly of chasing visiting cats, stalking various bird inhabitants, 'speaking' (in squeak language) to a couple of resident squirrels and generally stomping around the garden with magnifiers hunting a range of mini-beasts. They suddenly decide that this imaginative game is worth extending: Jack thinks they need a safari vehicle and George wants a picnic! Together they plan what they need and ask the adult to help them. The partially written and mainly oral lists consists of: a tent; compass; a safari vehicle; biscuits; chocolate buttons; jam sandwiches; orange juice and water; a camera; animal books; and paper and felt pens. Having acquired all the small items in self-selected old ice-cream tubs, they rush out into the garden again and requisition the upside-down garden table as a vehicle. Somehow, however, this doesn't suit the current mood and the adult is asked if she can think of a way of 'making this [the table] better'. The table is set upright and covered with two old sheets. Suddenly, transformation for the children: the table becomes both vehicle and tent. George now decides that inside needs some blankets and cushions to make it cosier. Jack decides on windows and, rather than draw on the sheet (which he could have done), he draws five windows and a front grille with name on the previously acquired paper and fetches sticky tape to attach his drawings. Once done, he helps George to count windows and they withdraw into the vehicle/tent, taking 'photographs' (with an old camera) through the gaps. There is a shriek when they find their very own 'animal' under the table with them – a spider! – which is carefully transported to the nearest bush on a spare piece of paper. Then after some more safari hunts around the garden they withdraw to the tent for a 'sleep'.

Jack can be heard encouraging George to 'read' the names of the animals in one of the books. The safari play, in various forms, lasts more than two hours, including becoming a space safari (more drawings made and attached).

That these children are 'playing' is in little doubt. But what are they getting out of it? Are they learning anything? Can such play be equated with anything that is 'worthwhile' in the twenty-first-century world?

It is surprising that some eleven years on from the first edition of *The Excellence of Play* these questions should still need asking, especially since so much has been happening around the education and care of birth to 7-year-olds in the intervening years both in the UK and internationally. *The Curriculum Guidance for the Foundation Stage* (QCA/DfEE 2000) and *Birth to Three Matters* (DfES 2002) in England emphasize the value of play for young children (generally perceived to be birth to 5+). More importantly, early years has generally acquired an impetus across the world with a range of local and national initiatives that has put young children and early years practitioners 'on the map' and offered a status not conceived of just a short time ago.

So does this mean that play is now accepted as 'the norm' for all young children, including those within Key Stage 1 (KS1) of the National Curriculum? Well, frankly, no! While the foundation stage years are securing *a* role for play in children's learning and development, those over 5 years of age in English primary schools have increasingly been subjected to fewer and fewer opportunities to play, in part because of such initiatives as the Literacy and Numeracy Strategies (DfEE 1999 and 2000) – with their emphasis on formal learning and target-setting (Moyles *et al.* 2003) – whose downward effects are even felt in Foundation Stage settings (Adams *et al.* 2004; Anning, Chapter 1 in this volume). For children over

Photograph 00.1   We're on a safari!

7, play in school is very much restricted to breaktimes (Blatchford and Sharp 1994). Yet, children have a natural inclination to play, alongside a natural instinct to learn and to be curious and inventive, which are characteristics of the human race in general. In a way, these are what make children, children! Perhaps this is one of our adult problems, especially in fast-developing societies – we don't appear to have time for childhood and its incumbent challenges and demands.

An analysis of the introductory cameo will give some clues as to why any curtailment of play in children from birth to the end of the primary years is, in my opinion, misguided. It was obvious that Jack and George, although very different in age, were adept at playing together and learning about each other's skills, abilities and tolerances. Both individually and collectively, they exhibited cognitive and physical abilities through their play vital for people in the twenty-first century. These include:

- making choices;
- generating decisions;
- negotiating;
- pursuing their own interests;
- using their own ideas and imaginations;
- showing independence in thought and action;
- exhibiting intrinsic motivation and persistence;
- being physically and intellectually active in a sustained way;
- operating from a basis of what makes sense to them;
- being confident and prepared for challenges;
- experimenting, exploring and investigating ideas and objects;
- setting their own goals and targets;
- operating in an open frame of mind in which everything is possible and engaged in 'what if' situations;
- learning new behaviours and practising and consolidating established ones;
- acquiring new skills and interests;
- using skills and knowledge already acquired for different purposes;
- showing themselves, in an age-appropriate way, to be socially adroit and linguistically competent;
- using a range of social and interpersonal skills;
- performing in a literate and numerate way;
- understanding rules and structures;
- functioning symbolically.

Such links between play and learning seem obvious to many practitioners and to some parents: yet the dilemma still exists as to whether play can provide any kind of 'excellence' in relation to 'real' learning for children, as current and future citizens.

This second edition of *The Excellence of Play* strengthens and extends the initial arguments for play as a principal means of learning in early childhood and in the light of contemporary developments. These arguments centre around a number of issues which it is worth examining briefly before I take up the issue of practitioners' values and beliefs in relation to play.

Play and play behaviours

Grappling with the concept of play can be analogized to trying to seize bubbles, for every time there appears to be something to hold on to, its ephemeral nature disallows it being grasped! As Smith (2005) suggests, because of its diversity, play continues to defy attempts at quantification.

Even examining general usage in English, play can be deemed to be a noun, verb, adverb, adjective – the play or a plaything, as in drama and toys; to play in relation to method or mode; to undertake something playfully; or to be described as a 'playful child'. Even at this basic level, it is not easy to distinguish any one meaning which might be attached to 'children's play': it makes more sense to consider play as a process which, in itself, will subsume a range of behaviours, motivations, opportunities, practices, skills and understandings, as we have witnessed in the initial cameo.

Broad descriptive works on play were produced in the late nineteenth century and continued into the early 1980s in various forms (see Figure 00.1).

As can be seen, it was only in the early 1920s that play was linked directly to children's development and this was short-lived as behaviourist theories were generally embraced. (For a fuller discussion see Ellis and Bjorklund 2005; Pellegrini and Smith 2005.) However, the writings of such early educationalists, amongst others, as Froebel, the Macmillan sisters, Montessori, Steiner, and Susan and Nathan Isaacs, sowed the seeds for play being the basis for early childhood curricula. In fact, Susan Isaacs perceived play as 'nature's means of individual education' (1929: 9). The tendency was to consider learning as a 'behaviour' in which learners (children and adults) engage. This has sometimes led to a notion that learning only happens when the learner is taught something and in some way responds, which is the basis of behaviourist theories over the years such as those promulgated by Skinner. Eventually, play supporters gained nurture and encouragement through the theories of Piaget, Vygotsky and Bruner – well documented in early years literature and also discussed in different chapters of this book. With the advent of these theories, it became clear that learning behaviour has more to do with a construction and reconstruction by the learner of actions which make sense to him or her and which can be guided and supported by more experienced others (later to find further strength in emerging theories from neuroscience, as we shall see).

From around the 1970s, various authors focused on identifying further the links between play and children's development (e.g. Schwartzman,

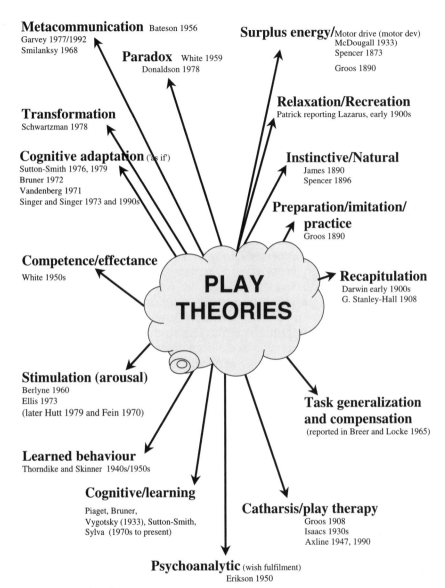

Metacommunication Bateson 1956
Garvey 1977/1992
Smilanksy 1968

Paradox White 1959
Donaldson 1978

Surplus energy/Motor drive (motor dev)
McDougall 1933)
Spencer 1873

Groos 1890

Transformation
Schwartzman 1978

Relaxation/Recreation
Patrick reporting Lazarus, early 1900s

Cognitive adaptation ('as if')
Sutton-Smith 1976, 1979
Bruner 1972
Vandenberg 1971
Singer and Singer 1973 and 1990s

Instinctive/Natural
James 1890
Spencer 1896

Preparation/imitation/
practice
Groos 1890

Competence/effectance
White 1950s

PLAY THEORIES

Recapitulation
Darwin early 1900s
G. Stanley-Hall 1908

Stimulation (arousal)
Berlyne 1960
Ellis 1973
(later Hutt 1979 and Fein 1970)

Task generalization
and compensation
(reported in Breer and Locke 1965)

Learned behaviour
Thorndike and Skinner 1940s/1950s

Cognitive/learning
Piaget, Bruner,
Vygotsky (1933), Sutton-Smith,
Sylva (1970s to present)

Catharsis/play therapy
Groos 1908
Isaacs 1930s
Axline 1947, 1990

Psychoanalytic (wish fulfilment)
Erikson 1950

Figure 00.1 Play theories

Smilansky, Sylva, Hutt, Sutton-Smith and Smith) with later research including tentative associations with curricular issues. The main forms of play identified have been essentially physical, object and pretence, all of which have been researched quite extensively over the last fifty years or so.

More recent work on brain studies indicates that learning is something that happens through the connections made within the brain as a result of external stimuli received through the senses (see e.g. Sylwester 1997; O'Shea 2002; Greenfield 2004). This knowledge facilitates thinking about how we unpick the early relationships between play and learning, especially through thought, problem solving and creativity. Though brain studies research is extremely intricate, it is not difficult to establish at a simple level that the human mind is seen to be a pattern collector and that young children are natural seekers after pattern and thence meaning. For meaning to be made, children's experiences should relate directly to them and involve first-hand experiences, as the basis for lasting learning through brain connections. This leads to questions about children's perceptions of formal learning contexts and how children begin to make sense of many of the activities presented to them.

One final piece of research is worth mentioning. It is the most significant early years longitudinal study to be conducted in England: *the Effective Provision of Preschool Education (EPPE)* by Sylva *et al.* (2003), the findings of which are leaving early years practitioners in little doubt about the value of high-quality play-based experiences in settings staffed with well-qualified staff. Such provision in nurseries and integrated settings offers children a better start to school as well as providing longer term intellectual and social/behavioural benefits. The study also found that warm interactions with adults are vital to children's intellectual development, as is 'sustained shared thinking' between adults and children. The researchers also found that where practitioners view education and social development as complementary and equal in importance to intellectual development, children make better all-round progress.

A plethora of other writing supporting play and curriculum has also been produced in the last ten years or so, much of it included within the various contributions to this edited book so it will not be repeated here. Suffice it to say, whilst the links between play, development and curriculum have yet to be established unconditionally through experimental research, there is more than enough evidence of children exhibiting their desire to play and the kinds of skills and abilities they are able to demonstrate in their play. Linked with the concept of child-oriented learning, for a majority of academics, writers and practitioners working within early years contexts there is no 'proof' greater than their own ongoing observations and analysis of children's play – which is where this chapter began! Whilst Jack and George's play was very much their own, a facilitating adult helped the process along.

The role of adults in providing for 'excellence' in play

As has been signalled, practitioners often express the view that they 'know' or 'feel' that play for children is, or must be, a valuable learning and developmental process; yet they are also aware that this is not often reflected in their curriculum planning or in their classroom management – let alone in the way they think about their roles in teaching and learning (Moyles and Adams 2001). Practitioners unfortunately show their values daily in the way they respond to children's play – 'You can play when you've finished your work'; 'Go out to play now and make sure you come back ready to work' – all give inherent messages about the purposes and processes of play as well as the lack of real value associated with it. Research doesn't always help as it is often presented in ways that make links between the findings and day-to-day practice very challenging: in a busy educational setting, there is simply not time. In any case, the findings frequently have to be interpreted in relation to those particular settings and those specific children. As has been emphasized, play is where children are; 'starting from the child' is enshrined in early years philosophy and is linked firmly with the early years play movement (Fisher 2002). Yet the ideology is exceptionally difficult for teachers to fulfil in practice (Bennett *et al.* 1997: Adams, Chapter 15 in this volume). Explanations presented by practitioners working with 4- to 8-year-olds include:

- Children need to learn, not to play.
- There is no time to let them play.
- Older children have grown out of that childish stuff.
- Parents don't want/expect to find their children playing in school.
- Children have plenty of opportunities to play outside school.
- We have to deliver the subject curriculum.
- Everything has to be documented for Ofsted.
- We don't have enough resources for all that active learning stuff.
- Children sooner or later have to learn to get down to work.

Some of these indicate restraints under which teachers perceive they work, for example, time, expectations of others and curriculum overload; others are related to possible confusions about play, work and learning. Yet others do not reflect the current world, e.g. children have less and less time for play outside school. More often than not, however, teachers' comments are tempered by other underlying views and beliefs, frequently with a hint of 'guilt' attached!

- Play is important for children but it's hard to justify to the head and other teachers.
- Children really get fed-up with the pressure – they do need to play more.
- They learn better through practical, first-hand experiences but . . .
- Children's social skills would be improved if we could provide more play.
- It's important to give them some choice when they've finished their tasks.
- Children do tire of sitting down and need something active.

- They love doing messy things and I know I need to achieve a balance.
- I do believe that children learn through play but the work provides the written record.

Yet those who operate a more play-based approach to planning would probably ask: 'Can we afford *not* to give children opportunities to play, given all that we know about the psychological bases of learning and teaching?' The National Curriculum and NLNS documents do give credence to children's active involvement in their own learning and assessment – by any other name, play! So we need to grasp the nettle for the sake of the children and, in so doing, make our teaching conceivably more enjoyable too.

The book – its rationale, structure and contents

The basic tenet of this book is that all human beings learn through the multifaceted layers of the range of activities variously subsumed under the heading 'play'. Each chapter is predicated around discussion of the playful nature of children, playful approaches to pedagogy and effective, playful curriculum practices. Play as a learning process and as a potential medium for teaching is explored and illustrated: perhaps this is best called 'playful pedagogy'. The book is intended for all practitioners across the 3- to 8-year-old age range: it constitutes an attempt to relate play theories to current practices in an ongoing, continuous and straightforward way. Those working with older children might also find much of interest. Throughout, examples of specific practices are given: play with the ideas and make them your own! It is possible to dip into the book at almost any point, for each chapter can be read as a discrete unit or viewed as part of a whole, the writers all operating from different but interrelated standpoints.

Amongst other aspects, we will explore how it is possible to play within designated curricular demands and how children in this age group (as well as older children and practitioners) can use a full range of play activities to implement and validate a broad, balanced and relevant education. Assessment of children's abilities, aptitudes and dispositions, through the important processes of observing, documenting and analysing play, are discussed. Various (playful) strategies will be used to provide opportunities for reflecting on, and articulating, play practices. Each chapter starts with a brief summary so that readers can get a feel for what it is about and ends with a few 'Questions to set you thinking', intended to generate increased reader interaction with the text and allow individual chapters to be used for continuing professional development purposes.

The title *The Excellence of Play* in itself indicates the main stance taken by contributors. Each of them, in very individualized ways, gives value to both the concept and reality of play and examines the concept from

several different stances, all drawing on contemporary res
strengthen their views. The result is a very powerful argument ~
'excellence of play', based on firm beliefs that practitioners themselves
must advocate strongly in support of a greater understanding of the direct
contribution of play to children's development and learning, whatever
the prescribed curriculum. The motivational qualities of play are
accentuated throughout this book, as is the concept that play in educational settings should have *learning* consequences. This is what separ-
ates play in that context from recreational play – practitioners need to
show quite clearly that, and what, children are learning through play.

Perhaps one of the greatest attributes of play is the opportunities it
affords us all for learning to live with *not knowing*, for it is readily recognized that we all learn more effectively through trial and error (Holt
1991): play is a non-threatening way to cope with new learning and still
retain one's self-esteem and self-image. Knowing children's learning
needs also enables adults to encompass the notions of Vygotsky (1978)
and Bruner (1972a) respectively in relation to the 'zone of proximal development' from which 'scaffolding' by the adult will enable progress in
learning to proceed from a point of current understanding. These proposi-
tions are extensively cited in the chapters of this book and practical
implications and applications discussed.

Anyone who has observed play for any length of time will recognize
that, for young children, play is a medium for learning, and practitioners
who acknowledge and appreciate this can, through provision, interaction
and intervention in children's play, ensure progression, differentiation
and relevance in the curriculum – and complete their assessments readily!
The sense of children as social and active agents in their own play and
learning, with a clear 'voice', is a strong feature throughout this second
edition, as is the importance of outdoor provision and the role of creativity. Meaningful self- and adult-initiated activities are integrated as a vital
aspect of an enabling education for all children but especially for those
with special educational needs. Links with all the recent English government initiatives are made powerfully and the role of observation in supporting assessment and profiling is highlighted throughout (instead of
occupying a specific section). These are just some of the changes since
the first edition. The book now has 18 chapters, only five of which were
part of the original edition, and these much revised. The remaining 11
chapters are all brand new and very much reflect current early years
curriculum practices and what we know about children's play and
development.

The chapters are arranged in four parts: the first explores a range of play
and curricular issues across the age range from birth to 7 years and
includes two new chapters on *Birth to Three Matters* and special educational
needs. In Chapter 1, Angela Anning has expanded her original argument
regarding the need for a review of curriculum practices in relation to what
the research now tells us about young children's learning. Most early

years practitioners will empathize with Angela's view that *children* are at the heart of the curriculum and that play-based, holistic learning opportunities must be central to early childhood learning and teaching. Angela emphasizes that the most recent initiatives in England for birth to 5-year-olds are going some way to supporting a curriculum based in play, but she warns of the need for appropriate continuity. Ann Langston and Lesley Abbott present their work on the *Birth to Three Matters* Framework in Chapter 2, highlighting the importance of play in babies' and young children's development and learning. The writers affirm that play and learning are inextricably linked and explore how, through the components taken from each of the four aspects of the Framework, adults can support children's play to ensure that they become strong, skilful at communicating, competent at learning and healthy. Theodora Papatheodorou outlines in Chapter 3 the nature of special educational needs, the importance of play to young SEN children as a major part of their education, and how play can be used effectively in ongoing assessments of need. Her chapter is illustrated with a story to which many practitioners dealing with SEN children will be able to relate.

Language and literacy are a vital part of all our lives and establishing motivation and skills early is essential for children's developing self-concept as readers, writers and story-makers. The second part of the book deals with play, language and literacy and includes a very diverse set of chapters ranging through storytelling, role play and drama to discussion of gender issues and story-making. Chapter 4 begins with David Whitebread and Helen Jameson's chapter in which they illustrate the power of playful approaches and activities in stimulating children's storytelling and creative writing, and the clear benefits of playful approaches shown by research. The examples show the use of *Storysacks*, highly effective in stimulating imaginative oral storytelling and high-quality creative writing with a variety of older children including some with special educational needs. This is followed by Pat Broadhead and Carey English's research (Chapter 5) that established a partnership between education and theatre to bring new insights to open-ended role-play situations. The links between creativity and social and cognitive development in children are emphasized and observation is identified as a central tool in understanding playful learning processes. In Chapter 6, Nigel Hall explores the relationship between play and literacy and shows how both provide opportunities for situated learning. He demonstrates the situated nature of the experience, which takes children into areas of world knowledge that are highly unusual in the education of young children. The issues of storytelling, story-making and gender surface in Jane Hislam's Chapter 7. She affirms that young children of both sexes act out roles, often as narratives, with great intensity and seriousness of purpose. As they do so, they develop language skills, try out behaviours and ways of being girls and boys and become more confident communicators and story-makers. Jane also stresses that adults are crucial in supporting and encouraging all children and must believe in their own capacity to do so. The final chapter in this section, by Neil Kitson, is also a revised version of his very popular chapter on role play, in which he outlines the important of fantasy play and socio-dramatic play in the cognitive, social and emotional development of young children. Like Jane, he asserts that practitioners within the socio-dramatic play situation can stimulate, motivate and facilitate the play, encouraging the children to work at a deeper level than they would if left to their own devices.

The longest section, Part 3, covers play within a range of other curriculum areas including science, maths, art and music and also begins with discussions about physical and outdoor play. In Chapter 9, Peter Smith reviews physical activity play which refers to playful activity that involves large body activity – particularly Exercise Play which includes running, climbing and other large body or large muscle activity, and Rough-and-Tumble Play, which includes play fighting and play chasing. The implications for practitioners in providing for indoor and outdoor play are also explored. This links well with the following new chapter by Stephanie Harding, a practitioner who has been part of the development of a 'pedagogical garden' at an early years centre. She shows how the impacts of the variation and diversity within the environment, the increased space, the flexibility and real tasks have supported the development of children's emotional, social, physical and cognitive skills. In Chapter 11, Alan Howe and Dan Davies propose exciting ways of developing children's science and technology skills through playful approaches. They focus on key ideas including the relevance of recent research into children's cognitive development, the role of the practitioner, science in the Foundation Stage and how assessment can inform planning of an appropriate play-based curriculum. Rose Griffiths offers more stimulating ideas for developing early mathematical learning in Chapter 12. She stresses how play can increase the child's motivation to learn by providing sensible and enjoyable contexts, and by allowing children to direct their own learning. Using and applying maths with young children can build the confidence of both children and the adults who work with them. In Chapter 13, Bernadette Duffy explores what is creativity and why it is important to the child and the wider society. She examines the links between creativity and the arts and explores ways in which the adults can foster creativity through their interactions with children and the environment they create. Planning, recording and documenting art experiences are discussed, alongside working with parents and carers to gain the richest experiences for all children. Chapter 14, written by Linda Pound, discusses the inclusion of playful music in the curriculum, including physicality as an integral part of music-making in young children. She reviews ways in which music can be made more playful by giving increased opportunities for improvization.

The final part broadens the scope yet further in scrutinizing the role of practitioners, examining the challenge of play in transitions and probing the value of play in different cultural contexts. In a thought-provoking

Chapter 15, Siân Adams reviews a research project in which nine early years practitioners had to challenge their own beliefs and values in relation to play. She questions whether the processes of adopting a reflective approach to practice – benefiting from informed support within a culture that values and celebrates pedagogical thinking – prompt the intellectual stimulation required to analyse playful practice critically. Such intellectual thinking is very much demanded of those involved in ensuring that transitions between home and schools/settings are smooth for children. This is the focus of the new Chapter 16, written by Hilary Fabian and Aline-Wendy Dunlop. The writers presents evidence to show that, amongst other helpful mechanisms to bridge curriculum transitions between phases, play provides important opportunities for children to make sense of the new and to achieve personal competence and progress in their learning. Cultural aspects of play are always fascinating. In Chapter 17, Tricia David and Sacha Powell discuss the ways in which culture shapes people's constructions of childhood and how, in turn, ideas about and policies and practices for provision for young children are influenced by these constructions. The chapter uses knowledge about China in order to consider if, how or why different cultures adopt particular views about play and learning, and what our answers tell us about that culture. The final chapter, as in the first edition, rests with Tina Bruce. In a revised chapter, she makes potential links between childhood play scenarios and future adult life, linking back with the very beginning of the book. She links her original twelve features of play with new knowledge about children's learning. Diversity and inclusion in play are shown to be of central importance, making a fitting conclusion to this wide-ranging book.

There is, of course, much more that could have been included had space permitted, for that is the divergent and flexible quality, indeed the excellence, of play.

Part 1
Setting the play context

1 | Play and legislated curriculum Back to basics: an alternative view

Angela Anning

Summary

The chapter traces the history of the introduction of a subject-based broad and balanced National Curriculum for 4- to 7-year-olds in English and Welsh primary schools in the 1980s. The subject focus sat uneasily with traditional topic and theme-based approaches to the infant school curriculum. The introduction of the Literacy Hour in 1999 and the Numeracy Hour in 2000 to primary schools in England, with related assessment for 7-year-olds, narrowed the curriculum to an emphasis on the 'basics' of English and mathematics. In the 1990s, the Foundation Stage curriculum and profiling intended to raise standards in literacy and numeracy but sat uneasily with the beliefs of practitioners in the value of play. Possible alternative approaches to designing a curriculum for young children and new insights into young children's learning are discussed which, in turn, offer us new understanding of appropriate pedagogies for promoting young children's learning, including the pedagogy of play.

Introduction

Every education system functions within a social context underpinned by a particular set of values and political imperatives. So it has been with the educational reforms in the legislated curriculum for early years education in England and Wales for the last twenty-five years.

The 1988 Educational Reform Act version of the National Curriculum (NC) and related assessment procedures, delivered in serried ranks of subject-based ring files to the staffroom shelves of primary and infant schools in England and Wales, had a particular genesis. It was constructed around concern to raise educational standards and deliver an effective workforce for the economic recovery in the UK. The ideologies underpinning the paper NC model were based on concepts of value for money in a market-led economy and a return to disciplined behaviour and competence in 'traditional' school subjects in classrooms in the maintained sector. The National Curriculum for 5- to 7-year-olds was designed to be broad and balanced. But the introduction of a Literacy Hour in 1999 and Numeracy Hour in 2000 to all primary school classrooms, along with the publication of results for 7-year-olds in Standard Assessment Tasks in language and mathematics at school level, reinforced an emphasis on the basics of reading, writing and mathematical development as the most important aspects of young children's learning at Key Stage 1.

In 1996 the unthinkable concept of introducing a statutory curriculum for under-5s (the statutory age for school attendance was 5+) was launched by the Department for Education and Skills. The curriculum became enshrined eventually in the *Curriculum Guidance for the Foundation Stage* with specified Early Learning Goals (QCA/DfEE 2000). These were linked to a baseline assessment system to be administered as children entered formal schooling at the age of 5. The CGFS consisted of six areas of learning: personal, social and emotional development; communication, language and literacy; mathematical development; knowledge and understanding of the world; physical development and creative development. Baseline Assessment focused on the first three areas of learning. The rather unwieldy *Foundation Stage Profile*, designed to record children's progression across all aspects of learning, was introduced in 2003. All settings (including daycare group settings, preschool playgroups and private nursery schools) who were claiming to offer education to 3- and 4-year-olds, and thus to qualify for government funding as providers of preschool education, have to demonstrate that they are delivering the FS curriculum. An early years branch of the Office for Standards in Education (Ofsted) inspects settings against this requirement.

The adequacy of these curriculum models for young children was always questionable. Before the introduction of the Foundation Stage to Reception classes in 1999, increasing numbers of 4-year-olds had been admitted into primary schools. Throughout the 1980s and 1990s many children not yet of statutory school age had by default been educated with a National Curriculum designed for 5-year-olds. The Guidance Notes to the FS curriculum (QCA/DfEE 2000) included references to the need to build on the knowledge and skills children bring to educational settings; to work closely with parents; to retain pedagogic strategies offering a mixture of adult-directed and child-initiated activities; even guidance about the value of learning through play. Yet the language of Early Learning Goals and Stepping Stones remained robust in relation to a prescribed curriculum with detailed attainments specified, particularly in language and mathematics. Moreover, the transition period from the Foundation Stage curriculum in Reception classes to the introduction of the National Curriculum Key Stage 1 subject-based curriculum in Year 1 of primary education became problematic for continuity and transition in children's learning from 4 to 7 years.

As I shall argue in this chapter, there are alternative models, which use play and creativity as the basis of an early years curriculum, which we might have been brave enough to consider in an era of educational reform in the UK. It was a radical change for English and Welsh schools to be subject to a nationally prescribed curriculum and associated testing regime. We accepted a watered-down version of a 'traditional' subject-based school curriculum. But where else might we have looked to design an alternative early years curriculum based on what we know about how young children learn – one which might encourage young children to gain positive dispositions to learning in their first years in school?

The existing framework

The value system of the dominant political power group of the 1980s – mostly men, mostly educated within the independent sector, mostly deeply uncertain about women – determined the policies for which they legislated under the terms of the Educational Reform Act. For them, play was a frivolous and low-status activity associated with the long hair, beads and hedonism of 'The Sixties Generation', or with women and children in church halls. Acceptable play took place only in competitive team games or on the golf course. A few comments from their public announcements during this period will serve to illustrate the point. Michael Fallon, a Minister within the Department of Education and Science (DES), criticizing the use of project work, said: 'At worst this kind of practice turns the primary school into playgroups where there is much happiness and painting, but very little learning.' Kenneth Clarke, in a brief period of opportunism, claimed that 'child-centred' education was failing to deliver: 'At its weakest there is a lot of sticking together of egg boxes and playing in the sand.' Finally, my favourite quotation comes from Tim Eggar, at that time minister with responsibility for women within the DES, trying to justify the lack of women in public positions: 'Women tend not to be in our networks; the chaps we know are not always women'!

Their appointees, the senior administrators at the now defunct National Curriculum Council (NCC), the Schools Examination and Assessment Council (SCAA) and now the Qualifications and Curriculum Authority (QCA), used a language of accountability, quality assurance, a market-led

economy, value for money and preparation for work. They espoused pub-
licly a morality based on the Puritan work ethic and discipline. Military
terms like 'troubleshooting' and sending 'commando-style' units into failing schools were designed to intimidate teachers. NCC and QCA working
groups designing the primary school curriculum were almost all drawn
from higher education or secondary school backgrounds. Representation
from the primary school sector was limited, and from early years education scandalously deficient. Consequently their understanding of how
young children learn was limited. I remember one senior official asking
me, 'Can children write at seven?'

Initially the messages from government were that, whilst they wished
to legislate for a statutory curriculum, they would not interfere with the
methods by which teachers were to deliver the curriculum. However, no
curriculum reform has ever succeeded without parallel reforms in assessment and pedagogy. By 1992 the so-called 'Three Wise Men' (Alexander
et al. 1992) were charged by the Secretary of State with reviewing available evidence about the delivery of education in primary schools. Their
brief was to make recommendations about curriculum organization,
teaching methods and classroom practice appropriate for the successful
implementation of the National Curriculum, particularly in Key Stage 2.
The authors strongly supported the view that primary schools should
introduce children to subject disciplines – 'some of the most powerful
tools for making sense of the world which human beings have ever
devised'. But they were critical, on the basis of empirical research evidence, of classroom organization in which children were working on too
many different activities in subjects simultaneously.

It is, of course, significant that their brief was to focus on Key Stage 2
(the education of 7- to 11-year-olds) but inevitably, since the Discussion
Paper was entitled *Curriculum Organisation and Classroom Practice in Primary
Schools*, it was assumed that Key Stage 1, though scarcely mentioned in
the text, was also included in the discussion. Key Stage 1 teachers, already
under huge pressure to cover the sheer volume of subject knowledge
specified in the KS1 curriculum, were alarmed at the incursion of central
government into how they should teach young children.

A critique of the discussion paper by 'Three Wise Women' (David *et al.*
1992) argued that the paper had neglected the specific needs of organizing
the learning diet of 4- to 7-year-olds. The authors were charged with
ignoring evidence from research (for example, Campbell and Neill 1991;
Pollard *et al.* 1994) that infant teachers had found ways of integrating
content from the Programmes of Study, continuing to use themes as a tool
for organizing the delivery of the National Curriculum, in ways which
were meaningful to young children, a point emphasized again and again
in this book.

In effect the government was able to influence the pedagogy of primary
schools directly by the introduction in 1999 of the Literacy Hour and in
2000 the Numeracy Hour. Under pressure to achieve the ambitious targets

for improvements in Standard Assessment Tasks at the ages of 7 and 11 years, primary school headteachers and teachers conformed to the tightly prescribed ways of teaching English and mathematics enshrined in the Literacy and Numeracy Hour boxes of materials. New teachers were trained to deliver the prescribed curriculum in formulaic ways. They were also trained to adopt 'interactive' whole-class teaching in primary schools. It became increasingly difficult for teachers to manage to cover other aspects of the English and mathematics National Curriculum or the rest of the subjects in the more informal, group-work approaches to pedagogy they had espoused up until 1999. Key Stage 1 classrooms began to operate more whole-class teaching and fewer practical, group activities (Moyles *et al.* 2003). Learning through play became sidelined. Children's choice of play-based activities was limited to perhaps a (tongue in cheek) 'golden hour' on a Friday afternoon.

Designing an alternative early years curriculum

Eisner (1982: 49) wrote 'The kind of nets we know how to weave determine the kind of nets we cast. These nets in turn determine the kinds of fish we catch.'

The 'nets' woven by those determining policy for the education of 4- to 7-year-olds in the UK seemed to bear little resemblance to those traditionally woven by the early years educators who were charged with the 'delivery' of a Foundation Stage and Key Stage 1 National Curriculum.

The value system espoused by practitioners emphasized beliefs in the

Photograph 1.1   What kinds of fish will we catch?

value of play as a powerful vehicle for learning, the importance of experiential learning, the education of 'the whole child' within both family and school contexts, the significance of physicality, the vital role of developing literacy and numeracy as tools for learning and the importance of fun and enjoyment as sources of motivation – themes reiterated by all the contributors to this book. Their nets were significantly different shapes, sizes and colours from those of the dominant policy makers. Practitioners felt deskilled and dispirited with the unfamiliar, brand new, 'official' nets, designed with scant reference to their established craft knowledge; merely thrust into their unwilling hands. These unfamiliar nets would not catch the kind of fish they valued.

Yet early years educators must accept equal responsibility for what happened. As a female-dominated profession, we had been socialized into taking a passive role in public decision-making. By inclination we had chosen to sit back and wait for 'them up there' (usually men) to tell us what to do, and then struggled to make models, designed without grassroots knowledge, work effectively. We had a poor record in researching, documenting and articulating our professional thinking (see Siân Adams' comments in Chapter 15 of this book). We lacked the confidence to engage in public debate and offered no convincing alternative to the NC framework for the education of young children.

Where might we have looked for materials to weave alternative nets? New research into how children think and learn has given us insights into what such alternatives might look like. But we need a boldness of vision to argue for a radical reappraisal of what constitutes 'basics' for the education of young children. So it is to some of the more visionary research and scholarship that we need to turn for inspiration. We have little opportunity to explore such visionary ideas in the mechanistic initial and in-service training for teachers required by government policy (although Broadhead and English report in Chapter 5 of this book on an innovative play and theatre initiative).

Brain development and functions

Early years educators have always argued the case for educating 'the whole child' and for the importance of recognizing links between the emotions, the intellect and the body in learning. Recent research into brain development and functions has alerted us to the importance of understanding the biological basis of learning processes (for example Gopnik *et al.* 1999), though there are caveats about the application of medical research to classroom contexts (Bruer 1997).

However, we do know that information comes to the brain via the five senses: sight, hearing, touch, smell and taste. Information is taken on board visually, auditorily or kinaesthetically (i.e. physically experienced or related to feelings). There is a processing system to prevent information overload, a sort of switchboard system, within the brain. Information that invokes an emotional response, or with content relating to

Photograph 1.2   It is important to recognize the links between the emotions, the intellect and the body in learning

self-preservation, ranks high in the editing process for selective attention. All information is processed through the left or right hemispheres of the brain. Both are capable of similar functions but they have particular propensities. The left-brain emphasizes language, logic, mathematical formulae, linearity, and sequencing: in general, analytical aspects of thinking. The right hemisphere emphasizes forms and patterns, spatial manipulation, images, things of the imagination, rhythm and musical appreciation. The right hemisphere appears to have the capacity to process faster more holistic aspects of thinking and learning. When the right side of the brain is processing data, it triggers pleasurable responses and chemicals are released which give the learner a sense of heightened awareness and well-being. This positive feedback encourages the learner to repeat the action.

Csikszentmihalya (1979, 1996) likened the absorptions and sense of total involvement that characterizes children involved in sustained bouts of play to a 'flow' state. Adults can recapture this 'flow' state – characterized by a loss of self-consciousness but at the same time an awareness of being in control of one's absorption in an activity – through highly motivating activities which may be work- or leisure-related. But for the adult and the child, a play context allows the learner the freedom to experiment without the fear of expensive or potentially embarrassing error. As Bruner wrote: 'Play provides an excellent opportunity to try combinations of behaviour that wouldn't be tried under functional pressure' (Bruner 1972a: 82).

Such research can help us to understand what we instinctively know about the power of play as a vehicle for young children's learning and to legitimate proper attention being paid to resourcing and supporting play-based activities in educational settings. Yet many early years practitioners feel under pressure to justify time spent in interacting with children engaged in play. They feel guilty about being seen to be 'wasting' time; about being seen to have fun. Yet we have more and more evidence of the power of the affective aspects of learning, including that emphasized within this book particularly in Parts 2 and 3.

In the past five years radical services offering young children and their parents opportunities to learn together through fun activities such as drama, music, dance, art or play, have been pioneered outside school and preschool settings in Sure Start Local Programmes. Sure Start (www.ness.bbk.ac.uk) was designed to be a radical anti-poverty initiative. However, hopefully lessons learned about the power of parents and children learning through playful activities together will be rolled out into the mainstream through the establishment of Children's Centres throughout the country.

Alternative forms of intelligence
Early years practitioners talk about the need to educate 'the whole child' and take the argument forward as a justification for an integrated approach to curriculum planning based on topics or themes. In the US, Gardner (1983) has argued for twenty years that a curriculum should be designed around the need to educate 'forms of intelligence'. He defines them as:

1 linguistic – dealing with language and words;
2 logical/mathematical – abstraction and numbers;
3 musical/auditory – rhythm and sound;
4 visual/spatial – patterning and imagery, knowing the environment;
5 kinaesthetic – physical skills, reflexes and timing;
6 interpersonal – sensitivity to others' emotions and needs;
7 intrapersonal – self-knowledge and inner focusing;
8 intuitive/spiritual – flow states and feelings.

These are the kinds of domains of 'the whole child' of which early years educators are aware, but which they find hard to define. For audiences of early years practitioners in the UK, Gardner's work resonates with their experiences of young children learning. His work has been taken up and packaged by the influential Accelerated Learning movement (Smith 1998). In the USA there are schools where the curriculum is designed around the eight forms of intelligence and three modes of learning: auditory (learning by listening), visual (learning by looking) and kinaesthetic (learning by 'hands on' doing).

Gardner argues that the education system of the Western world concentrates too narrowly on the first two forms of intelligence – the linguistic and logical/mathematical. Moreover, in the context of schooling most information is passed on through the auditory mode. Little emphasis is placed on the visual mode and, as the child progresses through the education system, even less on the kinaesthetic mode of learning. Gardner cites evidence that some people have a natural propensity to learn through verbalizing, others through visualizing and others through 'doing'. When I talk to educators they can usually fit the children they know, and themselves, into one of these categories.

Our system favours those who learn most effectively through the auditory mode and fails to accommodate the needs of those who learn most effectively through the visual mode. This is increasingly problematic as we move towards a culture where much information is screen-based and presented in global, diagrammatic and picture-based modes. We still have an apartheid for those who persist in a preference for learning through the kinaesthetic mode. Our education system encourages the myth that those who choose to work with their hands are of less intelligence than those who deal in abstractions. Clever children are filtered into groups where 'academic' subjects are taught. Less able children are channelled towards practical workshop curriculum choices. The concept of 'the intelligent hand' is not part of our cultural heritage. We ignore more generally the importance of the physical aspects of learning within our curriculum priorities. Yet we know that early physical, as well as emotional, health and well-being bode well for the development of both the brain and the mind (Meggitt 2001; Peter Smith in Chapter 9 of this book).

When we listen to the rhetoric of early years practitioners, we would anticipate that they at least would pay careful attention to structuring and supporting children's learning in practical work across the ability range in art and craft, technology, block play, role play, small figure play, sand and water and so on. Yet even before the introduction of the Foundation Stage and KS1, National Curriculum and the National Literacy and Numeracy Strategies, research evidence from infant classrooms (Tizard *et al.* 1988; Bennett and Kell 1989) indicated that teachers spent most of their teaching time with children engaged on seat-based literacy and numeracy tasks. For children the status activities in the classroom were marked by where their teachers, driven by pressure from the world outside schools, spent their time. Practical, play-based learning activities were generally perceived as low status and occupational, mainly for less able children; something to do when you have finished your work or have time for a bit of a laugh.

Every time teachers make a clear distinction between the 'important' aspects of learning (the 'real work' of learning the basics of literacy and numeracy) and the low status of practical activities (the 'play' or 'choosing time' activities) they are beginning the process of focusing on a narrow range of intelligences of the children for whom they are responsible. By their actions they are negating their claim to want to educate the whole child and beginning to shut down potential areas of growth. They are laying the foundations of the apartheid separating the intellectual from the practical, the academic from the applied and vocational.

To design a curriculum around a framework such as Gardner's eight intelligences would take courage, but would perhaps educate children with a truly grounded set of basic skills for life. Those would be some impressive fish to catch!

Delivering the curriculum

Theoretical models emanating from the sociocultural paradigm of research and scholarship into young children's learning (Anning *et al.* 2004) challenge the Piagetian paradigm of the child as a lone scientist learning about the world from direct experimentation. In sociocultural models learning is perceived as a social process. The child is held within the culture of the family, community or school and works towards mastery of the genres within each context. Children learn as much by observing and imitating the behaviours of those around them as they do by active engagement in tasks.

The Vygotskian model of teaching and learning implies an interventionist model of pedagogy. Instead of waiting for the child to accumulate enough experience to move on to the next stage, the adult or more experienced child supports the learner's progression. For early years educators these models of how children learn imply a much more active role for teachers than their training may have indicated. They are no longer relegated to the status of hovering, full of uncertainty, above children, waiting for them to 'move on'.

We are learning from new research into how children learn within the informal contexts of home and how this is reflected (or not) in their experience in preschool group settings (for example, Brooker 2002). For many children the switch from a domestic culture of play, based on real life problem solving, to the 'peculiar' school tasks of worksheets, sorting plastic shapes and playing in waist-high containers of sand and water, can be traumatic. Teachers are often so socialized into perceiving these school-based activities as 'the norm' that they neglect to explain to children their purposes.

There are ways of making the transition to the genres of school learning more humane, without resorting to what Egan (1988: 200) dismissed as 'the mild babysafe school', where expectations of children are low and the diet offered is patronizingly limiting. For example, the modelling of symbol systems is a significant source of empowerment for children to help them move towards increasing levels of abstraction. Research done on

emergent modes of literacy (Kress 1997), on the acquisition of understanding of mathematical symbols (Aubrey 1997), and on the use of drawing to make sense of the world (Anning and Ring 2004), give plenty of
support to the notion of modelling these tools for thinking through
play-based activities. For educators, there is real excitement in observing
children accruing knowledge and understanding of these tools. Each one
is a separate code to crack and for young children, in a well-structured,
active learning environment, cracking the codes can involve personal
adventures rather than stacks of worksheets to complete.

A second important tool for empowering children to learn is narrative.
Constructing stories in the mind – or storying as it has been called – is one
of the most fundamental means of making meaning; as such it is an activity that pervades all aspects of learning (Broadhead and English exemplify
this particularly in Chapter 5 of this book). Egan (1997) believes that we
should turn the content of the curriculum for young children topsy-turvy.
He argues that young children are not necessarily turned on by a diet of
trivial and often sentimental stories:

> . . . programmed reading schemes, and the absence of powerful
> emotional, dramatic, and intellectual content . . . typify many pri-
> mary classrooms . . . Disney-esque sentimentality is the exact emo-
> tional equivalent to intellectual contempt.
>
> (p. 199)

He argues that children should be introduced instead, through stories, to
the universal human emotions of love, hate, fear, anger and jealousy,
which are the source of their earliest understandings of the world. Such
universal concepts can often be encapsulated in bipolar opposites – good/
evil, diligent/lazy, cruel/kind – and he argues that an early years curriculum should be developed around such themes. He labels the years birth
to 7 as the Mythic Phase and believes that during this time children should
recapitulate the main features of the myths of oral cultures. Like Gardner,
Egan pleads for serious attention to be paid to sound as a way of promoting development. He argues that young children's intellectual lives are
most attuned to an oral culture – sounds rather than words – and that by
introducing 'the technologies' of writing and reading at too early a stage,
we impoverish their intellectual lives by forcing them to operate with
tools for thinking which actually depress their powers of reasoning and
slow them down.

Conclusion

I have argued that we have research evidence and scholarship available to
us providing frameworks for a radical alternative to our National Curriculum (building on the Foundation Stage) for young children. Such alternative curricula would aim to empower children with tools for reasoning

and representation, giving them the capability to explore a whole range of ideas, experiences, feelings and relationships. It would introduce children to the cultural tools – print, mathematical symbols, graphicacy, rhythms, rhymes, communication through speech, metaphors, fine and gross motor activities – which they see being used all around them in their home culture and communities, rather than constraining them within a straitjacket of 'school' learning. Much of the learning would be based on well-structured and resourced play-based activities. Our Reception and Key Stage 1 children are, by many other cultural standards, still at a kindergarten stage of education. School starting ages of 6 and 7 years are more common in other societies.

If the curriculum was genuinely designed around children's learning needs, perhaps then we would encourage a generation of children with a love of learning rather than groups of anxious and dispirited 'beginning readers' already feeling that they are failing.

Bronowski in the *Ascent of Man* (1958) quotes Newton:

> I do not know what I may appear to the world, but to myself I seem to have been only like a boy playing on the sea shore and diverting himself and then finding a smoother pebble or a prettier shell than ordinary while the greater ocean of truth lay all undiscovered before me.

It would be a real achievement to reframe a curriculum for young children at the beginnings of school in the UK to set them on a journey to becoming adults with such a sense of curiosity and playfulness.

Questions to set you thinking

1 What were the processes by which a National Curriculum and Foundation Stage were introduced into early years settings?
2 How did these central government initiatives impact on your setting or classroom?
3 What justification might we make for designing alternative models for the education of 3- to 5-year-olds and 5- to 7-year-olds in preschool settings?
4 What function would play have in such models?
5 How would our new understanding of how young children learn influence the pedagogy of play in early childhood education?

<table>
<tr><td>**2**</td><td># Learning to play, playing to learn: babies and young children birth to 3</td></tr>
</table>

Ann Langston and Lesley Abbott

Summary

This chapter considers the role of play in babies' and young children's development, highlighting its importance right from the start. It confirms the long established view that play and learning are inextricably linked and the way in which early interactions between babies and their carers become the building blocks of playfulness. It then explores how, through the components taken from each of the four aspects of the *Birth to Three Matters* Framework, adults can support children's play to ensure that they become strong, skilful at communicating, competent at learning and healthy. Examples throughout the chapter illustrate that it is often the most 'taken for granted' experiences such as nappy changing, feeding or talking to, and with, babies and children that create appropriate contexts for play.

Introduction

As this book emphasizes throughout, play is central to the healthy development of babies and young children. It is through play that children learn about themselves, explore people and things, communicate and become strong and healthy. The vast amount of development that occurs between birth and 3 years in particular is captured in the *Birth to Three*

Matters Framework (DfES 2002), developed in response to the Green Paper, *Schools Building on Success* (DfES 2001), reflecting the government's commitment to babies and young children.

Gopnik *et al.* (1999) summarize evidence from research in philosophy, psychology, neuroscience, linguistics and other disciplines to provide an account of how babies and young children learn about the world around them, about people and relationships and language, linking their discussion to what is known about brain development. They assert that 'we know from science that nature has designed adults to teach babies, just as much as it has designed babies to learn, and that it indicates we should talk, play, make funny faces and pay attention to our babies when we are with them – but that we simply need the time to do this' (Gopnik *et al.* 1999). The *Birth to Three Matters* Framework encapsulates the essence of this approach to babies' and young children's play.

The *Birth to Three Matters* Framework

Materials in the Framework are designed to support effective practice in out-of-home settings and provide guidance for practitioners working with babies and young children. The Framework characterizes children as strong, skilful at communicating, competent at learning and healthy, and describes their development in four dynamic areas, referring to young babies from birth to eight months as 'Heads up, lookers and communicators'; babies from eight to 18 months as 'Sitters, standers and explorers'; young children from 18 to 24 months as 'Movers, shakers and players' and children from 24 to 36 months as 'Walkers, talkers and pretenders'. The materials include a set of 16 cards and a video, to which we will refer throughout this chapter. Each of the 16 cards contains a section headed *Play and practical support*, which highlights the importance of play and suggests activities and things that adults and children might do and offers practical advice that can be followed in order to develop babies' and young children's play and learning.

Play

For young children play and learning are inextricably linked, the one often leading into the other. Babies and young children seem primed to learn from their earliest moments, imitating what they see and hear and responding to the special people in their lives. The play of young babies is constructed initially through interactions with others – parents, carers, siblings and the environment – as they respond to the images and sounds that surround them.

One of the most dramatic abilities of the newborn that shows she is ready for contacts with other people is her ability to imitate another person's facial expression. A baby just a few minutes old, if content and alert, will gaze intently at the face of another person, watching her seriously. If the adult clearly and slowly moves her own face, for example opening her mouth wide or protruding her tongue, the baby will watch intently and then imitate the adult expression. It is as if the baby can already sense that she and the other person are in some way the same (Murray and Andrews 2000: 19).

It is through this type of interaction that the roots of play emerge; repetition becomes important as child and adult take turns, clearly enjoying themselves, as first one, then the other, becomes the leader in the game. Babies' responses widen to encompass objects as well as people as their attention is caught by a mobile, or a toy just out of reach. With growing mobility and language skills young children's play extends to include finger plays, action rhymes, stories, songs and pretend games. Their increasing independence then allows them to engage in exploration and physical play and they represent their experiences through a range of responses.

Play in the Framework

The way in which play will be examined is through an exploration of the *Birth to Three Matters* Framework, in which play is seen as central to each child's development in each of the aspects of the Framework, visually:

- *A strong child.*
- *A skilful communicator.*
- *A competent learner.*
- *A healthy child.*

Each of these aspects comprises four components, which focus on ways that the child develops in a particular aspect. Thus, in order to become 'a strong child' s/he needs to develop a sense of self and to become confident in her own abilities and to have a secure sense of belonging.

A strong child
Visions of the baby featured in the book *Avocado Baby* (Burningham 1993) may spring to mind when we think about a strong child and the choice of title was deliberate, intended to convey an image of the child as capable, emotionally strong, self-assured and rooted firmly in community with others. The four components that make up *A strong child* are:

- *Me, myself and I.*
- *Being acknowledged and affirmed.*
- *Developing self-assurance.*
- *A sense of belonging.*

As the component *Me, myself and I* indicates, babies are being made aware of the human world outside themselves and, importantly, aware that they themselves exist, as a result of being touched, talked to and gazed at (Alvarez 1992). Play is central to this realization; even in the first month of life babies are making clear distinctions between people, objects, self and others (Stern 1985; Rosser 1994). Play episodes become quickly established between a baby and his/her carers through gentle caresses, light tickles, exaggerated facial expressions of amusement, surprise and so on. Even whilst feeding, the play behaviours that adult and child build together are important in establishing the kinds of play relationships that will develop later. As the baby becomes more able to participate and take control, the way in which a sensitive adult allows for this will influence the baby's feelings of efficacy. The adult behaving 'contingently', i.e. being responsive to the baby's signals, plays an important part in helping the baby to realize that she is able to influence her own life and the behaviour of those around her.

Mirrors reflect the self back to the observer. The provision of mirrors in different places helps babies explore what they look like. The video sequence for *Me, myself and I* shows a young baby gazing thoughtfully at a mirrored cube over which she has control and is able to change its angle and direction. Board books for young babies often have mirrors on the cover with which the child can interact whilst listening to the story, turning the pages and playing with the book. Later, mirrors can be convex or concave, providing different images of the self, as large, or small, stretched, or shrunk, offering opportunities to explore other selves.

Being acknowledged and affirmed by important people in their lives leads children to gain confidence and inner strength. Huge changes take place as young children progress through the broad areas of development described, beginning with 'Heads up, lookers and communicators'. These descriptions of children's rapid development during the first three years of life emphasize children's own active involvement in, and responsibility for, their development and learning. The range of opportunities afforded to young children to move beyond their immediate environment, to choose playmates of different ages, together with materials and resources which will stimulate their developing imaginations, are significant in widening the play environment in both physical and human terms. There will be implications for organization and planning and, in some cases, a rethinking of rooms and groupings in settings where babies are separated from older children, if this important need is to be met.

Encouraging all children to participate in making rules and helping them to understand expectations and boundaries contributes positively to their feelings of being valued and acknowledged, and affirms their sense of belonging. Older children can acknowledge the needs of younger children in their play, being gentle when using shared equipment or in leading the play by modelling how to play 'hide'.

Developing self-assurance in babies and young children requires skilful adults to observe and note how babies become confident in exploring what they can do with less dependence on adults, and to respond by providing resources and playful activities in which children can engage independently. Collaborative games and communal sharing times encourage children to take more responsibility, and talking to young children about their play and discussing the resources needed and where they might find them develops their sense of self-assurance as they move away from the adult to find what they need.

Having the confidence to move away from a trusted adult, in the knowledge that they are never far away, depends on the child having *A sense of belonging*. 'Snuggling in' with a variety of objects and people in different places, such as cosy corners with soft, inviting surfaces and interesting play materials, provides babies and young children with comfort and security and increases the sense of belonging, as does play that involves music and sensory experiences. Encouraging young children to make decisions about which toys and people to play with, helps them develop a sense of being valued members of the community and increases their independence and sense of control.

In asserting that 'play matters', Bruce (2004c), looks at examples of babies, toddlers and young children involved in free flow play. In claiming that the twelve features of free flow play (Bruce 1991) 'can be used as a tool for observing and reflecting on play at any stage of life', she highlights the *Birth to Three Matters* video sequence in which a baby and older child are sharing a book with their childminder, demonstrating the playfulness of the adult and the sense of belonging and opportunity to 'snuggle in' offered by this activity.

Photograph 2.1   Encouraging young children to make decisions increases their independence and sense of control

A skilful communicator

Communication is a complex and important skill that is fundamental to human relationships (as is clearly acknowledged particularly in Part 2 of this book). Because humans appear primed to communicate from birth we often underestimate the skills that must be developed if babies and children are to become sociable and effective communicators. The four components that make up *A skilful communicator* are:

- *Being together.*
- *Finding a voice.*
- *Listening and responding.*
- *Making meaning.*

The first component, *Being together*, involves listening as well as signing, speaking and non-verbal communication. The play experiences children need in order to become skilful communicators are those that encourage them to want to communicate with others and include not only verbal but also non-verbal responses such as the movement of their whole bodies. These experiences can be developed initially through having a warm and supportive relationship with a special or key person, both in the home with family members and out of the home, when for example babies and young children attend daycare. The intimate rituals of care often rely on the humour and inventiveness of the carer, to make even the most mundane encounter a pleasure, engaging the young baby or child in a communicative exchange.

So, for example the card *Being together* reminds practitioners that 'Mobiles above changing areas, feathers to tickle and music to share, help young babies to enjoy being together and communicating with their key person'. This same idea is explored in the video where a young child and his key person are observed during a nappy change. This routine activity is transformed by the involvement of the practitioner with the child to become a pleasurable play experience through a shared agenda of listening, imitating and responding. As the child's 'hello' is echoed, repeated and re-presented to him, he gains the courage to assert that a small toy the practitioner has handed him to play with is his, shouting 'mine' loudly several times as he enjoys the sound and power of *Finding a voice* (his own). It is noteworthy that young children's language at 18 months is related 'to differences in earlier infant–care-giver joint episodes – the frequency, quality, responsiveness and duration of such episodes' (David *et al.* 2003: 76).

At the same time as sharing interactions such as these, 'conversations' rely on the attunement of others to the baby or young child, listening to what they have to 'say' when the child uses her voice, face or body to communicate and supporting the child to listen in return when a companion is speaking. *Listening and responding* occurs in games and rhymes, such as 'I see a teddy bear, brown eyes and curly hair', where the child is involved in listening and pointing to his own or someone else's hair and eyes, or in which the child is encouraged to join in with a repeated phrase such as 'Run, run as fast as you can, you can't catch me, I'm the gingerbread man!'

As babies and young children enjoy the pleasure of stories, songs, rhymes and jingles they learn to anticipate endings and play with words and sounds. These extend and build on cooing, vocalizing and babbling to skills such as inserting missing words in a well-known rhyme. Word play rapidly follows as children introduce variations on a theme to explore strings of sounds or words that have novelty value, such as the word 'woollies', used by one grandmother to describe sweaters and cardigans, which revealed her grandchildren's delight in this new word and which prompted 'much laughter and falling about, accompanied by repetitions of "Woolly, woolly, woolly" ' (David *et al.* 2003: 81) from them. The latter illustrates clearly how through *Making meaning* children play to learn and their delight in the novel sounds becomes part of the process by which they develop an interest in rhyme and begin to make meaning when they encounter print in the environment, another example of becoming a skilful communicator.

That babies and young children enjoy the world of books and stories is no longer in doubt since studies have illustrated the pleasure as well as benefits of introducing them early to literacy. The video shows an example of a baby and young child whose pleasure is obvious as they listen to a story read aloud by their carer. When children are encouraged to engage with print they are being taken on a journey that begins with sound and pictures and leads to an awareness of its purpose and construction.

A competent learner

The contribution of play to cognitive development cannot be under-estimated since the two are closely linked and as children learn to interact with other people and the environment they also learn to think. In the *Birth to Three Matters* Framework children's learning is seen as active, dynamic and continuous, resulting in part from their own inborn capacity to learn but also from the experiences that are offered to them. The four components that make up *A competent learner* are:

* *Making connections.*
* *Being imaginative.*
* *Being creative.*
* *Representing.*

The drive a baby has to learn can be observed in the first weeks and months as babies strive to form relationships with caregivers, respond to familiar voices and fix their gaze on patterns such as strong stripes or circles on their toys.

This interest in people and the environment is part of what the Framework describes as *Making connections*, which is increased and extended when babies and young children receive positive feedback about their actions and their play becomes sustained as they become deeply involved in self-chosen activities. The distinction between play and learning is often invisible when babies begin to play, perhaps focusing on their own fingers, absorbed in the unpredictability and excitement of the physical movements they make, developing at the same time the visual acuity required to support coordination. This may later be built on when they take delight in pulling off a sock and trying to put it back on again, attempting initially to use the whole palm before acquiring the required dexterity of using the fingers, first to place it and then to pull it into position.

Associated with the ability to make connections is *Being imaginative*. Through being imaginative babies and young children begin to explore the world through imitating, mirroring, imaging and re-enacting what they have seen and heard. From observing and reflecting experience, babies become adept at body movements and facial gestures which form the basis of communication about likes, dislikes, fears and sadness. As they learn to express their ideas and feelings through experiences and activities children become capable of projecting into 'what it would be like if . . .', taking on assumed roles with few, or only the minimum of props. This allows children to explore in their play, feelings that they may not be able to express, or even those they are unaware of at a conscious level. Seeing a small child lifting a crayon to her mouth with a big intake of breath may appear peculiar to an observer unless and until a knowledge of the child leads the adult to reflect that the child is processing her experience of 'granddad's behaviour' as he imbibes his medication from an inhaler. Or the two-and-a-half-year-old who systematically bends the doll's legs one after the other, playing out the 'patterning exercises' he has seen carried out on a sibling who needs regular physiotherapy. From observation to replication to transformation, children's imagination develops continuously as they encounter books, stories, rhymes, problems, birthday parties, adults' smiles or tears, animals, TV programmes, walks in the street and shopping trips, each offering different perspectives on experience to reflect upon, to process and both to play at and to play out. One beautiful example of this was described to me by a friend whose grandsons, one aged 2 years, the other five months old, were out shopping in Lucca, their home town in Italy. As they walked around the city's walls an old lady enquired of their mother, 'What are the children called?' The mother looked at the older child, Giacomo, and said to him, 'Tell the lady your names', whereupon when asked his own name he said 'Giorgio' and asked what his brother was called replied 'Giacomo'. Delighted at his inventiveness this 2-year-old laughed heartily when his mother asked him why he had switched his own name with his baby brother's!

Being creative has many similarities to being imaginative as it is about the drive of all individuals to express themselves in their own way. This creative process is explained by Duffy (2004 and Chapter 13 of this book) as an orientation to the world in which the child is curious, exploratory and questioning. This disposition to create can be nurtured by others as they scaffold children's interests and support their need both to know and to transform, or it can be quashed by structure and too great an emphasis on outcome rather than process. For a young baby, being imaginative may simply be the experience of enjoying a lullaby, whilst later it may be about how a child expresses herself in her play through mark making, art, junk modelling, problem solving, language, music making or fantasy.

Play in which young children show resourcefulness is indicative of their inborn creativity and their desire to respond to the world through marks and symbols is fundamental to this drive. In the *Birth to Three Matters* Framework this component is described as *Representing*. So, from play that is imaginative and creative, process-based and free, emanates the desire to represent the world as it is experienced. The discovery that one thing can stand for another – like the crayon that became an inhaler – subsequently allows young children to leap from the experience of the concrete object to the system of symbols and signs they see around them. This, in turn, informed by knowledge about books and the roles of pictures, symbols, signs and words, leads to the understanding that marks represent something else, and children begin to make their own approximations of pictures, words and writing, like apprentices bent on the complex task of becoming literate.

A healthy child

There is no doubt that play and health are inextricably linked, and the relationship between the two features in much of the literature on healthy living, diet and nutrition; the importance of physical exercise, physical play, and playing sport are also considered important throughout life (see Peter Smith's discussion in Chapter 9 of this book).

The *Birth to Three Matters* Framework, however, considers being healthy as meaning much more than having nutritious food and being free from illness. For babies and young children, being special to someone and cared for are vital for their physical, social and emotional health and well-being. Health and social well-being underpin and determine children's responses to their environment, to people and to experiences. Play is a means by which babies and young children explore their environment and the people who are special to them. The four components that make up *A healthy child* are:

- *Emotional well-being.*
- *Growing and developing.*
- *Keeping safe.*
- *Healthy choices.*

Emotional well-being can be fostered in young babies through playful interactions with a special person in their setting. Baby massage sessions reduce stress and make young babies feel nurtured and valued. Songs and stories that babies and parents can share and enjoy at home encourage playful responses in which puppets, musical instruments, soft toys and everyday objects can be used to enhance the play and increase enjoyment and understanding.

Through play young children can explore emotions beyond their normal range. Even reading about 'going on a bear hunt' can benefit a timid child. Puppets, pictures and stories provide opportunities for babies and older children to be together and allow children to express and talk about feelings and experiences.

Meeting children's physical needs is fundamental to their well-being. *Growing and developing* children who are physically well will have the energy and enthusiasm to benefit from the range of activities on offer to them. Young children have a biological drive to use their bodies and develop physical skills, and for babies and very young children the provision of a range of objects to be sucked, pulled, squeezed and held encourages exploration and development of physical skills. As they grow, the provision of safe outdoor experiences, such as climbing and balancing equipment, swings and slides, pushing and pulling, riding opportunities, support the development of both large and fine motor movements.

The video sequence that supports the growing and developing child shows children playing in a well-planned outdoor environment exploring their feelings, overcoming their fears and extending their skills as, supported by a sensitive adult, they test out the climbing wall, balance on a wooden snake, explore tunnels, roll balls, negotiate pathways and hills, paddle and dig in the sand. This is similar to the pedagogic garden described by Stephanie Harding in Chapter 10 of this book.

Keeping safe not only involves the provision of play materials and experiences that challenge and extend young children's developing skills, but also the provision of opportunities for babies and children to have choice in an environment kept safe by knowledgeable adults who know there should be a balance between freedom and safe limits. Play is an ideal vehicle through which children can discover boundaries and limits, learn about rules, discover when to ask for help and learn when to say no.

For babies, the provision of different arrangements of toys and soft play materials encourages crawling, hiding and peeping. Puppets, role-play materials, songs and rhymes help young children focus on whom they can trust and the importance of sharing their fears with an adult.

Outdoor play poses challenges for those working with children in the birth to 3-age range, not only in relation to safety issues, but also in terms of appropriate equipment and materials for such young children. It is this area of provision for physical play, both in and out of doors, that challenges practitioners working with children with disabilities. When other children are climbing, exploring and running, a child with a physical disability may become frustrated and will require sensitive adult support, additional resources or adaptation to equipment. Goddard-Blythe (2000) points out the dangers of failing to appreciate what babies and toddlers learn through movement, yet children who have limited opportunities to play, particularly outdoors, may lack a sense of danger and require the support of adults who are aware of their need to move and take risks.

Being able to choose is important for both children and adults. The component *Healthy choices* focuses on discovery, demonstrating individual preferences, making decisions and becoming aware of others and their needs. Post and Hohmann (2000: 89) remind us that:

> Infants and toddlers in group care have *no* choice about being in childcare. Each part of the day, however, presents opportunities for choices and decisions they *can* make . . . what to hold, look at, or whether, how and how long to participate in an activity . . . Making these choices and decisions on a daily basis and being able to change their mind from one day to the next tends to give children a sense of control over the day.

The provision of a wide range of play materials from which young children can choose is at times important; at others it can be overwhelming. Creating time to discuss options so that children really do have choices is one of the ways that practitioners can demonstrate their respect for the choices children make about what and who to play with.

When children's play follows their own agenda it may not be what practitioners would choose. Reacting to children's choices which practitioners might consider not to be healthy, for example a child making a gun from building blocks, or always choosing the same play materials, presents the practitioner with dilemmas which require discussion and support from other team members. In such cases the context of the play should be understood, since play offers a window on a child's world that adults need to understand in order to help the child move on. Knowing a child is from a stressful environment may change the adult's view of why the play is repetitive or violent, and her responses may alter significantly in order to accommodate the child's needs rather than turning to those which suppress the processes in which the child may be engaged. The provision of non-specific play materials allows for play to move in different directions, which can often help children to find new areas to discover.

Conclusion

David *et al.* (2003), in the review of literature for *Birth to Three Matters*, conclude that research from a number of disciplines informs us that babies and young children need to play and interact with their parents and other significant people in their lives because it is in these enjoyable everyday exchanges and conversations that their brains develop – are 'redesigned' even – as a result of learning. So the role of play in young children's lives is multi-layered; it has intrinsic value, arising first through encounters with people and objects, and then becoming the vehicle through which young children begin to explore. Finally it becomes a launch pad from which children learn to get along with others, to be persistent, to cope with failure and to accept themselves for the people they are. Indeed, when babies and young children engage in play they are having fun and learning to learn and the dispositions they develop towards these things will influence both the quality of their personal lives and the choices they make in the future.

Questions to set you thinking

1 How might play episodes with a young baby in the first weeks of life be characterized?
2 This chapter shows how the *Birth to Three Matters* Framework highlights the fact that in order to play and learn children need opportunities for both dependence and independence. What is the basis of this apparent contradiction in relation to *A strong child*?
3 We are reminded, in the chapter, that a resourceful carer can 'make even the most mundane encounter a pleasure, engaging the young baby or child in a communicative exchange' – how might examples of these 'mundane encounters', for example, nappy changing, be transformed into communicative exchanges?
4 What role does imitation play in children's play and learning?
5 Exploratory play can involve risk. How can a practitioner ensure that children have opportunities to grow and develop safely whilst providing challenging play experiences for children in the first three years?
6 How might some of the dispositions developed through play in the first three years influence the quality of children's lives and/or their future choices?

3 | Play and special needs

Theodora Papatheodorou

Summary

In this chapter the term special needs and current policy requirements regarding the identification of, and intervention for, the
needs of young children are discussed briefly and an assessment
framework outlined, as the background to discussing play-based
assessment and intervention. Emphasis is placed on underlying
conceptual foundations; what early years practitioners need to
explore during play-based assessment; how to use it, if required, in
combination with developmental checklists; how to use it as the
basis for further ecological and multidimensional assessment; how
to plan play-based intervention. Finally, the chapter concludes with
a section on how play-based assessment can be used routinely to
plan the early years curriculum on the basis of children's needs
rather than the identified learning outcomes of the curriculum and
how to fuse assessment and intervention.

Introduction

The value and importance of the use of play to support and facilitate
children's development, learning and behaviour is highlighted throughout this book. This chapter will focus on the use of play to identify and
meet the needs of young children 'at risk' of experiencing difficulties in

their learning, behaviour and development. It will also show how play can be utilized in planning activities and programmes which address those intended learning outcomes that aim to meet the identified needs of individual children and/or groups of children.

Clarifying the meaning of 'special needs'

The term 'special needs' is often associated with children's needs that arise from some kind of disability and/or condition that affects their learning, development and behaviour. It is also used as a generic term to refer to any kind of need that requires support that is additional, or different, to that offered to all children in any formal and informal educational setting (DfES 2001). The Children Act 1989 (Home Office/DfEE/DoH 1989) uses the term children 'in need', offering a similar broad definition. Interestingly, development is defined as physical, intellectual, emotional, social or behavioural development.

The revised Code of Practice refers to 'children with special educational needs' (SEN), adopting the definition offered in section 312 of the Education Act 1996 (cited in DfES 2001: 6), which states that:

> Children have special educational needs if they have a learning difficulty that calls for special educational provision to be made available for them. Children have learning difficulties if they:
>
> i have a significantly greater difficulty in learning than the majority of children of the same age; or
> ii have a disability which either prevents or hinders them from making use of educational facilities of a kind provided for children of the same age in schools . . .
> iii are under compulsory school age and fall within the definition at (a) or (b) above or would do if special educational provision was not made for them.

The Education Act 1996 clarifies that special educational provision is understood as any educational provision that is additional to, or otherwise different from, the educational provision made for children in maintained schools and for the under-2s provision of any kind. It also points out that children should not be regarded as having learning difficulties because the language spoken at home is different to the one used in schools.

In this chapter the term special needs will be used to refer to a range of needs that may place children 'at risk' of not developing and learning to their full potential. Other terms will be used as they appear in the literature. The usage of these terms does not, however, imply that they can be treated as synonymous or that they can be used interchangeably.

The importance of the identification of young children's needs

In line with a number of current policies, there is a requirement that:

• children's needs should be identified early;
• support should be provided for children to achieve their potential; and
• provision should shift towards prevention (DoH/DfEE/HO 2000; DfES 2001; DfES 2003; DfES 2004; DfES/DoH 2004).

The revised Code of Practice for SEN, for example, has placed particular emphasis on the importance of the early years as a stage where young children's needs should be identified early, with the aim to provide support for individual children, adopting a 'graduated response' that 'should be firmly based within the setting' (DfES 2001: 33).

The 'graduated response' involves two forms of support: 'Early Years Action', which is primarily based on the existing expertise and resources of the early years setting, and 'Early Years Action Plus', which is characterized by the involvement of external support services for more specialist assessment, advice and resources. According to the Code of Practice: 'This approach recognizes that there is a continuum of special educational needs and, where necessary, brings increasing specialist expertise to bear on the difficulties a child may be experiencing' (DfES 2001: 33).

The National Services Framework for Children (DfES/DoH 2004: 23) has also highlighted the importance of early intervention by pointing out that:

Delaying early intervention can result in irretrievable loss of function or ability (e.g. postural management) or the intervention being less effective (e.g. speech and language therapy). Early intervention has a positive effect both in terms of promoting development and minimising decline or regression among children with developmental disabilities.

However, although such policies have promoted the inclusion agenda by broadening the boundaries of education to reflect the diversity of today's societies (Odom *et al.* 2004) and have increased awareness of its benefits, in a recent Ofsted report (2004) it was noted that educational settings have not done enough to use the potential of making appropriate adaptations to the curriculum and teaching methods to support pupils' learning. In addition, although embedding individual objectives and instructional approaches into curricular planning and routines seems to be a simple concept, the evidence shows that this has not been successfully implemented (Pretti-Frontczack and Bricker 2001).

Photograph 3.1   Practitioners need to consider adaptations to the curriculum and teaching methods to support SEN pupils' learning

Issues surrounding the early identification of young children's needs

Whilst some children's needs may be identified early through developmental, paediatric, physical, audiological and visual assessments (this applies especially to children with identified disabilities and conditions), a number of children may enter early years settings without identified special needs, but nonetheless may potentially be 'at risk' of experiencing difficulties which, if not met, may hinder their development and learning. The requirement of current policy to support children to achieve their potential and for provision to move towards prevention places particular emphasis on the identification of children 'at risk' of showing or developing special needs.

According to the Early Years Transition and Special Educational Needs (EYTSEN) study the term 'at risk' is difficult to define but in general it is taken to indicate cognitive, social and behavioural risk covering a spectrum of abilities such as intellectual and conceptual ability, verbal and non-verbal ability, phonological and pre-reading ability, spatial and number awareness, and ability to socialize and get on with others (Sammons *et al.* 2003). Some signs which may indicate that a preschooler is potentially 'at risk' include: speaking later than most children; problems with pronunciation; slow vocabulary growth and often inability to find the right word; difficulty in rhyming words; trouble in learning numbers, alphabet, days of the week, colours, shapes; extreme restlessness and distractibility; trouble in interacting with peers; difficulty in following directions or routines; slow development of fine motor skills.

It is acknowledged that the cognitive and social/behavioural domains are interrelated and affect each other (Sammons *et al.* 2003) in a complex and dynamic way determined by the opportunities and experiences offered to children over the course of their lives (Bronfenbrenner 1979; Bronfenbrenner and Morris 1998). Therefore, young children's measures in these domains remain relative with no single sign alone taken as evidence that a child is 'at risk'.

Developmental and contextual issues

In this context, the identification of young children's needs is far from an easy task. Considering existing knowledge about children's development and the complexity of factors that affect such development, it is hard both to make predictions about the course of children's development on the basis of existing and often limited information about them, and to judge whether identified needs are of a temporary and/or transient nature or signs of potentially serious future problems. There is a consensus in opinion now that not all children develop according to identified normative patterns, nor is their development continuous following predictable stages. Instead, development can be idiographic and discontinuous, consisting of periods of rapid changes and periods where little change is observed. In the same way, not all children develop at the same rate in all areas; some children may show higher levels of physical and motor development, while others may have better personal or social outcomes (Vasta *et al.* 1999). Shortcuts, diversion, alternative routes and fast tracks are possible on the journey to adulthood. In addition, at some stages individual children may be identified as showing particular 'needs' or causing concern, but not at others (Sammons *et al.* 2003). At these stages, children's lives may present particular challenges for both the children themselves and the adults looking after them. For instance, physical development and, at some stages, a rapidly growing body require children constantly to make adjustments and change the cognitive schema of their body, to acquire spatial awareness and function appropriately in a given space. During this period, clumsiness and awkward movement may be witnessed, especially when the environment provided does not offer children opportunities to experiment with their bodies and the space available. In the same way, demands made upon children as a rite of passage (e.g. transition from home to nursery school) may require from them personal and emotional maturity which they may not have yet gained.

Developmental discrepancies in young children are less obvious between children with disabilities and their same-age peers than is the case with older children (Odom *et al.* 2004). Other factors may also affect a child's performance such as cultural differences, language barriers, availability of learning resources and experiences at home (Vacc and Ritter 1995).

Early years professionals' attitudes and values

Whether or not children's development, learning and behaviour will be of concern depends on individual early years professionals' knowledge, experience and values. Sammons *et al.* (2003) argue that the concept of special needs should be viewed as a 'social construct' that is placed on 'particular points along a developmental continuum' (p. 1). Therefore, whether identified needs will be considered as 'special' and where they will be placed along the developmental continuum depends much on individual early years professionals' personal and professional judgement.

Assessment tools and procedures

The identification of young children's needs is further clouded by the lack of appropriate tools, instruments and procedures. It is now acknowledged that the tools, instruments and procedures used with older children to identify their needs are not suitable for use with young children (Vacc and Ritter 1995; Odom *et al.* 2004), for example, normative and performance-oriented assessment tests undertaken in a formal way and in 'controlled' environments may not give the full picture of young children's development, learning and behaviour, as these are demonstrated in the naturalistic environment of the early years setting.

The identification of young children's needs: an assessment framework

Initial attempts (e.g. the Bayley Scales of Infant Development) to assess young children's needs were influenced by psychometric and normative models of assessment which sought to determine whether individual growth, compared with the norm for a group of same-age children, would predict later development and performance (Meisels and Atkins-Burnett 2000). Currently, the rejection of such formal psychometric and normative assessment has led to new developments in the field which require a model of assessment that understands and interprets children's needs at different levels of functioning and informs appropriate intervention accordingly (Papatheodorou 2005).

Assessment is required to be both ecological and multidimensional. Ecological assessment aims to examine the dynamic interrelationships within and between systems (e.g. early years setting, family) and over time and the way they affect the development and learning of individual children. Multidimensional assessment requires the collection of information from multiple sources by using multiple methods (e.g. interviews with parents/ the child/professionals, observations, documentary evidence such as samples of children's work and reports) for multiple domains – that is, social, emotional, cognitive and motor development, language and communication, academic performance (Neisworth and Bagnato 1988, Meisels and Atkins-Burnett 2000). The ultimate goal of such assessment is to acquire information and understanding that will guide the planning of activities and programmes aiming to facilitate the child's development, learning and behaviour.

Play-based assessment

The issues outlined above clearly have implications for the knowledge, skills and competencies which early years professionals should have in order, within the 'graduated response', to be able to identify early the needs of young children who are potentially 'at risk' of experiencing learning difficulties and to adapt and modify the learning environment and curricular activities to prevent such difficulties. The Code of Practice clearly mandates that: 'Where a child appears not to be making progress either generally or in a specific aspect of learning, then it may be necessary to present different opportunities or use alternative approaches to learning (DfES 2001: 33).

Indeed, early years professionals are often the first to carry out an initial assessment to identify individual children's needs and now, according to the recommendations in the Code of Practice (DfES 2001), it is a requirement to do so. Such initial assessment usually takes place informally and indirectly in the naturalistic environment of the early years setting where children are engaged in play. Through procedures and play activities that are familiar and meaningful, the children can perform to the best of their abilities and unfold their potential (Sheridan *et al.* 1995; Wilson 1998; Meisels and Atkins-Burnett 2000; Sayeed and Guerin 2000).

Play-based assessment may involve several phases that provide different information about the child's functioning, strengths and areas needing support. Such phases include unstructured facilitation where the early years practitioner follows the child's lead and expands on its play, and structured facilitation where activities are organized to elicit behaviours which the child has not demonstrated spontaneously in the first phase (Meisels and Atkins-Burnett 2000). In both unstructured and structured facilitation, play activities are organized in a way that allows children to interact and engage with play materials (familiar and unfamiliar), peers and adults (Sayeed and Guerin 2000; Odom *et al.* 2004).

In line with the notion of Vygotky's Zone of Proximal Development (ZPD), play-based assessment offers the opportunity to identify:

• the children's current level of learning and development;
• their potential for learning and development;
• the skills the child needs;

- the strategies required to be adopted by adults for children to achieve their potential.

As Feurstein *et al.* (1979: 49) would argue, play-based assessment involves 'an active, involved, and involving process . . .' which aims to reveal the 'hidden potential lying buried beneath the surface of the manifest behaviour . . .' (pp. 55–6).

Play-based assessment: what to look at

Research evidence has demonstrated that children's level of involvement and engagement in play activities is an important indicator of their current level of development and learning and potential needs. Involvement and engagement being understood as 'active participation' (Odom *et al.* 2004: 22) that is 'intrinsically motivated' and 'exhibited . . . in the absence of external coercion, threat or reward . . .' (Leavers *et al.* undated) are important concepts, as their definitions reflect fundamental elements of play (Bruce 1994). Odom *et al.* (2004: 23), in an extensive systematic review of literature, report that the overall engagement of children with or without special needs does not differ but 'the complexity of engagement does differ'. For example, children with special needs tend to interact more with adults and less with other peers and play materials. When social toys are available, cooperative play and peer interaction increases, but in general children with special needs display low-level play activity when they use play materials and objects.

The following case study illustrates a complex engagement in unstructured and structured play activities that involve the use of play materials and interaction between children and adults. These have been used by the teacher to form an initial picture of George's current level of functioning and potential, areas of difficulty and the support required for George to overcome these difficulties.

Case study: George – Reception class

George joined the Reception class in September. His teacher's initial impression of him was that he was a shy and timid boy. Now, almost mid-term, his teacher Mrs Nabbs, is concerned that George has gradually become more withdrawn. Actually Mrs Nabbs thinks that she knows very little about George's overall performance and learning. He responds to direct requests, but his responses are either monosyllabic or non-verbal.

In response to her concerns, Mrs Nabbs decided to conduct some systematic observations during unstructured (free play) and structured activities. During free play it was observed that George was always directed to play activities by staff or followed their suggestions on what to do next. He played alongside other children, but he hardly ever initiated play activities or made choices of play materials. His responses to children's requests and comments were usually non-verbal (e.g. nodding for agreement, passing toys on to them, looking at children when he was addressed without responding). Often, however, he would stop playing and watch other children showing interest and enthusiasm.

Mrs Nabbs started to wonder whether George's behaviour was a sign of lack of confidence and/or social skills and/or poor language and communication skills. She also considered whether George had any undiagnosed hearing impairment that affected his language and communication and overall response. Further observations, which involved interaction with other children, partly reinforced Mrs Nabbs's initial hypothesis.

George is asked to join two children in the activity area which at this time represents a restaurant called 'Healthy Food'. George and another child are sitting at a table: Annie is the waitress taking the orders.

Annie: Here is today's menu. (She passes a menu catalogue on to each child.) We have vegetable soup with croutons, fish and chips and, for afters, fresh fruits.
John: I'll have fish and chips and ice cream, please.
Annie: Sorry sir, we have only fresh fruits. It's healthy . . . you know . . . (Turning to George) What would you like, George?

George does not reply.

Annie: Would you like some soup?

George nods, yes. Annie insists on a verbal response.

Annie: George, say: I would like to have some soup and, for afters, fresh fruits, please.

George repeats this after Annie.

Annie leaves the two children, pretending she is going into the kitchen to fetch the orders. It takes some time before she returns. Meanwhile, John is distracted and leaves the table and the restaurant. Annie returns with a tray. She asks clearly disappointed: 'Where is John?' Then, turning to George says: 'Oh, well, now it is me and you . . . It's your turn to be the waiter.'

Annie sits at the table. She instructs George what to say. He responds and clearly repeats what Annie says. He pretends he is bringing some food for Annie. He seems to be relaxed, enjoying the play. They both now sit at the table. They pretend to eat.

This incident reinforced further the teacher's hypothesis about George's lack of confidence, which in turn might have inhibited his interaction and communication with other children. But the initial hypothesis about language difficulties and hearing impairment was not supported well. Once confident, George would open up, interact well in a one-to-one situation and enjoy playing.

Mrs Nabbs complemented these observations by planning a structured small-group activity with involved interaction between children and interaction with the teacher. The story of the three little pigs was the focus of the structured activity, followed by circle time and role play. The circle time aimed to discuss issues arising from the story and it was organized so that children could explore alternative scenarios, provide solutions to problematic situations that the three little pigs encountered, and negotiate roles for each child for the role play. The teacher discreetly facilitated role negotiations so that George would take the central role in the role play.

Once all children were dressed up and took up their roles, there was an impressive transformation of George who confidently followed the scenario, adding new dimensions to the role play. This activity provided a deep insight into George's potential and how this potential would be unfolded with appropriate support.

This observation seemed to confirm further the initial hypothesis about George's lack of confidence. Once confident to participate, George would demonstrate good language skills and communicate well with children. This was especially evident during role play where he participated in a non-personalized activity. There was no evidence that George might have had any hearing problems.

The case study outlined shows that play-based assessment provides an opportunity for initial concerns to be either supported or refuted on the basis of evidence that is systematically gathered. To a large extent, the child takes the lead while the adult is observing or participating without affecting the pace or flow of the play, but adults intervene in situations and instances that offer the opportunity for the child to unfold his/her potential. In George's case, if the teacher had not intervened to place him in the central role in the role play activity, his transformation and potential might not have been made known. In addition, being embedded within the particular context and culture of the early years setting, play-based assessment becomes an easily accessible and spontaneous activity that leads to rewarding and self-reinforcing outcomes.

Play-based assessment and the use of developmental checklists

Play-based assessment can be used in combination with a number of other assessment tools such as developmental checklists (e.g. the 'Play-based assessment prompt sheet' suggested by Sayeed and Guerin (2000) and the 'Checklist of pragmatic skills' suggested by Wilson 1998) that have been specifically designed to look at young children's development and learning. Using these checklists as points of reference, play-based assessment should identify the difficulties which children experience that often go unnoticed and should inform the interventions of early years professionals based on the implementation of developmentally appropriate practice.

Play-based assessment: some reservations

Initial play-based assessment may not always provide a clear picture of the child and sometimes the evidence collected from the observations may be proved to be contradictory. Therefore, information from different sources by using multiple methods may be necessary before any judgements are made about the child's current development and learning, potential special needs and support required. For example, in George's case, a hearing test would be required if the evidence continued to suspect potential hearing impairment. In this way, play-based assessment becomes the starting point for further ecological and multidimensional assessment.

Play-based individualized intervention

The easy accessibility, spontaneity and informality of play-based assessment does not make it a casual activity. Play-based assessment requires careful planning and has a clear purpose to inform intervention that is tailored to address the needs of individual children. On the basis of the evidence of play-based assessment, teachers should draw up an Individual Educational Plan (IEP) or, in the case of young children, an Individual Play Plan (IPP) (Figure 3.1) to embed and keep track of intended learning outcomes and objectives for individual children. Raver (2003) points out that without this structure many opportunities for intervention may be overlooked.

Individual Play Plan (IPP)
An IPP should summarize:

1 the intended learning outcomes in the form of short-term objectives and the long-term goal aimed for the child;
2 environmental support, that is, play materials, resources and changes required in the learning environment;

Name: George S...   **Date: 25 October 2004**

Duration: From: 1 November 2004	to: December 2004		
Long-term goal: Increase George's confidence			
Short-term objectives: initiate interactions; make requests; make choices of play materials; increase social interaction with other children and adults in whole-class situations;			
Intended learning outcomes	**Environmental modifications**	**Teacher/staff support**	**Support and resources required**
Curriculum modifications			
Structured play activities to (i) require the engagement of all children in the group, (ii) lead to achievable and rewarding outcomes to boost confidence and (iii) practise and expand learnt skills	Provide play materials that require social interaction; Organize group membership which promotes peer tutoring and support; Include Annie in the group membership	To guide and facilitate George to make choices for play materials and activities, initiate requests, be involved in conversations; Offer opportunities for engagement with social play materials; Acknowledge George's achievements; Offer praise/rewards	All staff to be aware of (i) the intended learning outcomes for George, (ii) how play materials and activities have been chosen and (iii) how to support George; To provide play materials that require social interaction **Family involvement** Discuss with parents the strategies; Involve parents and siblings to follow similar strategies at home
Monitoring/recording	George's progress to be observed once a fortnight, by Mrs Nabbs during structured and unstructured play activities		
Evaluation criteria	Initiation of conversation and interaction, sustaining conversation and interactions, interaction with more than one child in group situation, volunteering to participate in group activities.		

Source: adapted from Papatheodorou 2005

Figure 3.1   Individual play plan

3 modification and/or simplification of curriculum play activities to incorporate the identified intended learning outcomes;
4 selection of play activities and routines that are likely to promote the learning, use and expansion of the identified skills and learning outcomes;
5 support required by other children, the teacher and other members of staff and, if relevant, from specialists;
6 how the child may be supported at home, if required;
7 information about the monitoring and the evaluation of the progress made;
8 review dates. (ECRII 1999; Odom *et al.* 2004)

Ongoing difficulties may indicate the need for a level of help above that which is normally available for children in the particular early education setting (DfES 2001).

Identifying individualized intended learning outcomes

In identifying the intended learning outcomes it is important, as Feurstein *et al.* 1979: 56) argue, to replace 'the static goal . . . with a dynamic goal, which . . . seeks to measure the degree of the individual's modifiability by providing him with a focused learning experience'. For example, taking George's case, the teacher identified short-term objectives (the child to initiate interactions, make requests, make choices of play materials, increase social interaction with other children and adults in whole-class situations) in the domains of social interaction and communication, where his difficulties were mainly witnessed, and the long-term goal (building up confidence) in the personal development domain (Figure 3.1).

For the teacher, building up George's confidence was the dynamic and transformative goal that was to be achieved through a series of carefully planned short-term objectives. The teacher was not just interested in recording how often George interacted with others or initiated inter-actions in a given period of time. Instead, she was interested to see how such behaviours contributed to George's confidence and transformation during the time of intervention. This example illustrates that the identification of intended learning outcomes (in the form of short-term objectives and the long-term goal) requires a coherent hypothesis that is supported by sound knowledge and understanding of children's development and the implementation of the early years curriculum.

Embedding learning outcomes in the overall short-term and long-term planning

For short-term objectives and the long-term goal to be achieved, the IPP should be embedded in the planning of the overall programme as it is implemented in the natural context of the early years setting (Odom *et al.* 2004). Such 'naturalistic' intervention enables access to a coherent and meaningful programme of support rather than having partial and unrelated input offered by individual IPPs implemented out of context (Gimpel and Holland 2003). In addition, incorporating and implementing IPPs through the existing curriculum minimizes disruption to existing structures (Curtiss *et al.* 2002). This is not to underestimate the difficulty of the professional task of planning and preparing activities that address the IPPs of all children in the early years setting.

Planning play activities, changes in the learning environment and support required

Depending on the hypotheses about the difficulties which individual children experience, often modifications in the content and mode of delivery of curriculum play activities and in the learning environment may be proved enough to eliminate or prevent some of the difficulties which children may experience (Quinn *et al.* 1998). Research evidence has shown that the seriousness of children's needs affects how they respond to different teaching approaches (Odom *et al.* 2004). In general, adult-directed intervention is more effective for young children with less serious difficulties, while the more 'naturalistic' child-directed intervention is more effective for young children who experience more serious difficulties. However, research evidence has also shown that direct instruction produces better results for the acquisition of skills but that children show greater generalization of skills when intervention is activity-based. In this context, meaningful and developmentally appropriate practice typified by a balance of child-led and adult-directed activities should inform the planning of an IPP (Pascal and Bertram 2001; Raver 2003).

Similarly, the introduction of planned activities, the place and time where they are offered and the suggestions provided to the child during the activity need careful attention. In addition, environmental changes such as the grouping of children and the membership of such groupings are significant decisions, especially when social interaction and communication are pursued (Odom *et al.* 2004). In George's case, Mrs Nabbs identified particular activities in which George should participate and how he should be introduced to these activities. She also deliberately included Annie, with whom George developed a rapport, in small-group activities and situations (Figure 3.1).

Monitoring and evaluation the individual play plan

An IPP is incomplete without the identification of a monitoring system which states when, how, by whom and how often information will be collected to make judgements about:

1 the way the IPP is implemented (e.g. its consistent and regular employment, demands made on time and staff that cannot be met, skills and competencies not available, disruption in the programme, any unforeseen circumstances etc.);
2 the child's response to the IPP (e.g. acquisition of new behaviours and skills and how these affect the child's outlook) (Horner *et al.* 2001; Curtiss *et al.* 2002).

Finally, for evaluation purposes, it is important to identify the criteria that will be taken into account in making judgements about the effectiveness and successful implementation of an IPP (Curtiss *et al.* 2002). The short-term objectives of the IPP broken down into small observable and measurable elements may form the criteria for ongoing evaluation. For example, in George's case, such criteria include: initiation of conversation and interaction; sustaining conversation and interactions; interaction with more than one child in group situation; volunteering to participate in group activities. The long-term goal set out in the IPP is the focus of summative evaluation. Whether this goal has been achieved or not will be decided by the data collected at the end of the programme by using the same instruments and methods used in the initial play-based assessment.

Play-based assessment for early years curriculum planning

Finally, play-based assessment can be routinely used to identify the individual needs of all children (and not only the needs of children raising concerns) and, consequently, to plan curriculum play-based activities and programmes to address the needs and/or prevent further future difficulties of *all* children in an early years setting. The *Foundation Stage Profile*, for example, instead of being used as an instrument for summative assessment only, can be used on a regular basis to form a clear picture of each individual child's needs and to build a profile of the needs of groups of children and/or the whole class (Figure 3.2).

Although the *Foundation Stage Profile* (DfES/QCA 2003) has not been designed to assess young children's special needs, it may be used as a point of reference (instead of any other developmental checklists) for play-based assessment to identify children's current level of development, their potential for future development and the support needed to achieve such potential.

To facilitate the embedding of individual objectives into planning, Raver (2003) proposes a 'group objective matrix' (Figure 3.2) to help track each child's objectives. In each developmental domain specific objectives may

Developmental domain	George	Annie	Jo	John	Jack	Andrea	Zoe	Mo
Personal, social and emotional development • • •								
Communication, language and literacy • • •								
Physical development. • • •								
Creative development • • •								
Mathematical development • • •								
Knowledge and understanding of the world • • •								

Source: adapted from Raver 2004

Figure 3.2   Group objective matrix

be identified which are ticked against the name of each child, as required. The IPPs drawn up for individual children may be used to develop the group objectives matrix. In this way, the starting point for planning play activities and programmes is not the intended learning outcomes suggested in early years curricula (in this case the Foundation Stage Curriculum) but the children's needs, as these are identified through play-based assessment, using the *Foundation Stage Profile* as a point of reference.

The fusion of play-based assessment and play-based intervention

In this context, assessment becomes an ongoing process and it is fused with intervention in a virtuous spiral. According to Meisels and Atkins-Burnett (2000: 249–50):

> Through intervention – by putting into practice the ideas or hypotheses raised by the initial assessment procedures – more information will be acquired that can serve the dual purpose of refining the assessment and enhancing the intervention.

For Meisels and Atkins-Burnett (2000: 250) 'assessment is of limited value in the absence of intervention. The meaning of assessment is closely tied to its utility, which is its contribution to decision making about practice or intervention or its confirmation of a child's continuing progress.'

Questions to set you thinking

With another member of staff, or all members of staff in your setting, consider:

1 What is your current practice regarding the identification of young children's needs?
2 How can play-based assessment and intervention be incorporated into your current practice?
3 Can you identify changes that need to be made in your current play practices?
4 What demands will be made upon, for example, staff time, training, play resources and materials?
5 What changes can be incorporated into short- and long-term planning for play and SEN in your setting?

Part 2
Play, language and literacy development

4 Play, storytelling and creative writing

David Whitebread and Helen Jameson

Summary

In this chapter we illustrate the power of playful approaches and activities in stimulating children's storytelling and creative writing. Despite the recent support for playful approaches in the Foundation Stage, other current developments in primary education have increased the downward pressure to use exclusively formal teaching methods, particularly in the area of literacy, to ever younger children. By contrast, the evidence from research indicates the clear and considerable benefits of playful approaches being pursued with older and more able children. In the second half of the chapter we present examples of work using *Storysacks* and other props which can be highly effective in stimulating imaginative oral storytelling and high-quality creative writing with a variety of older children of all ability levels. The particular examples we discuss involve able Year 2 children and Year 4 children with emotional and behavioural difficulties (EBD).

Introduction: age, ability and learning through play

Without doubt, the introduction of the *Curriculum Guidance for the Foundation Stage* gave 'official' recognition and status to something that early years practitioners have recognized for many years, namely that 'Well planned play is the key way in which children learn with enjoyment and challenge during the foundation stage' (QCA/DfEE 2000: 25). The importance of play in the Foundation Stage now seems to be accepted and indeed encouraged for children up to the age of 5 years. In contrast, however, play is being squeezed out of the curriculum from the beginning of Year 1 onwards, as Angela Anning emphasizes in Chapter 1. The emphasis on formal learning in Key Stage 1 denies the fact that these children are still in the early years of their development. Indeed, the term 'early years' seems to have been hijacked in schools to mean 'under-5s' and has become synonymous with the Foundation Stage, rather than under-8s as was previously assumed. The change in language following the introduction of the National Curriculum regarding the group of children in school aged between 5 and 7 from 'infants' (with its connotations of babyhood) to 'Key Stage 1' (a much more formal title) again emphasizes the move away from regarding these children as still relatively young and in need of a less formal, play-based curriculum.

The only areas where slightly older children are still encouraged to play are those where there is evidence of special educational need or early deprivation (for more information on SEN and play see Chapter 3). In 2001 the government announced it would be giving £6m to set up and run 150 toy libraries in deprived areas. This followed research (commissioned by the Department for Education) by London University's Institute of Education, tracking nearly 3000 children between the ages of 3 and 7, which concluded that children who have high-quality play equipment at home outperform those who don't and that these educational advantages stay with children at least through primary school. The then Education and Employment Minister, Margaret Hodge, was quoted as saying:

> Every parent knows that toys and play equipment can be expensive. As a result many young children from deprived areas are going without essential early play that is crucial to child development.
>
> (*Daily Mail*, 20 February 2001)

Anyone visiting a special school, be it one for severe learning difficulties (SLD) or emotional and behavioural difficulties (EBD), cannot fail to notice all the extra play equipment available to the children and the extra time and emphasis placed upon play. This is despite the fact that many of the children in these schools are still required to follow (or at least pay lip service to) the National Curriculum. The assumption seems to be that able children from Year 1 onwards, who are doing well in school, do not 'need' to play as much as their less able or educationally less 'successful' peers.

This appears to be a dominant view even amongst many in the teaching profession. As Eyles (1993) reported, when considering the importance of play, it was clear that most of the teachers she interviewed believed that:

> . . . time spent on play activities should decrease with the increased age of the children . . . and many children in Year 2 classes did not

seem to be involved in any identified play experiences in the classroom . . . By Year 2 the overwhelming opinion (of the children) was
that they did not play! Where 'play' did take place with the older
age-group it was always referred to as 'not work' and therefore
learning was not taking place during the activity.

(Eyles 1993: 45)

Within the teaching profession the idea of 'readiness' for certain skills
and concepts is often assumed; young children who have not reached the
position of being 'ready' for a new skill/concept are often encouraged to
play in order to develop the necessary pre-skills/concepts. As Moyles
(1989) has emphasized, 'Immature children are prime candidates for
carefully conceived play activities, through which basic conceptual
understandings can be achieved' (p. 59).

In contrast, able and successful children are often encouraged to go
straight to formal learning and it may be deemed 'unnecessary' to give
them the same amount of play opportunities. This is even more apparent
as children get slightly older. By the time they are in Year 1 or Year 2, if
they have no learning difficulties, developmental delays or other problems, the emphasis on formal, sitting-down, pencil and paper learning
increases to the point of complete exclusion of play, particularly for able,
high-achieving children.

Given the opportunity, all children, regardless of age, often choose to
play and indeed even adults still like to play (as can be demonstrated in
our culture by the phenomenal sales of adult computer games, board
games and puzzles, along with the large number of adults taking part in
sports, historical re-enactments and activities such as paintballing and ten
pin bowling). Despite this, the assumption remains, following Piaget (see
Sutton-Smith 1966), that play is indicative of immature functioning, a
developmental 'stage' that children go through, and that if this is successfully transcended they will then be ready for formal schooling, with little
need for any more play in order to learn. How wrong the contributors to
this book prove that to be!

A number of related pressures are currently reinforcing this trend
towards squeezing playfulness out of the school curriculum beyond the
Foundation Stage, and making it difficult for teachers of children of 5 and
older to justify the inclusion of playful opportunities and approaches in
their classrooms. The requirements of the National Curriculum, with
national tests for 7-year-olds, backed up by the publication of school
league tables, have clearly increased the downward pressure to use
exclusively formal teaching methods with children in Key Stage 1, as
Angela Anning emphasizes in Chapter 1. Furthermore, there is a general
perception that parents prefer more formal approaches. This is backed up,
for example, by research commissioned by the American Toy Institute in
the USA (ATI 2000) which found that 72 per cent of parents thought it
very important for their children to start (academic) learning early, whilst

54 per cent believed there was already enough play time in schools. The emphasis on 'delivering' the curriculum in teacher training in recent years has also tended powerfully to reinforce the view among student teachers that children are only learning when they, the students, are teaching (Moyles 1989).

In the present climate, the concern is that our young teachers are not being given the opportunity to test out the validity of this view. This is all exacerbated in the UK, of course, by the extraordinarily young age at which children start formal schooling. Our formal approach in Year 1 is in stark contrast to most other industrialized countries around the world, where children are commonly 6 or even 7 years old before they start formal school (Woodhead 1989; Tricia David and Sacha Powell's commentary in Chapter 16 of this book).

There is still a paucity of research to give us firm evidence as to whether this debate over formal versus playful education and/or the appropriate age for formal schooling to start really matters in the long term. However, one important longitudinal study by Schweinhart and Weikart (1998) followed a group of disadvantaged children who were randomly allocated to attend one of three preschool programmes. The programmes in question were High/Scope (where children are encouraged to follow a pattern of plan–do–review), Direct Instruction (teacher-led, with academic lessons) and Nursery School (teachers used themes and children had free choice of activity for much of the time). Initially, all three groups showed an increase in IQ, followed by a decline to the age of 10. However, the most startling difference was in the long term. At age 23, both the nursery and High/Scope groups were doing better on a range of 'real-life' measures (e.g. rates of arrest, emotional problems and suspension from work). Schweinhart and Weikart (1998) hypothesized that an emphasis on child-initiated and playful activities in these two preschool programmes developed the children's sense of social responsibility and their interpersonal skills, and that this had a positive impact in later life.

Play and creativity

With this apparent paradox between the emphasis on play-based learning for the Foundation Stage and for educationally disadvantaged children and the sudden introduction of a more formal approach for Year 1 onwards, we have been keen to investigate whether, in fact, for older (Year 1 and above) and more able children, playful approaches to learning may be beneficial. This possibility seemed to be worth investigating given the powerful range of evidence and theory from psychological research supporting the developmental significance of play, particularly in relation to problem solving and creativity (see also Howe and Davies, Duffy, and Pound, respectively Chapters 11, 13 and 14 in this book).

Psychologists have been researching and developing theories about the nature and purposes of children's play since the middle of the nineteenth century. It has been suggested as a mechanism for letting off steam, for providing relaxation, for relieving boredom, for practising for adult life, for living out our fantasies and many more (see Introduction). That it is important in children's development, however, has never been in doubt. As Moyles (1989) demonstrated, for every aspect of human development and functioning there is a form of play.

It is only in the last twenty to thirty years, however, that its significance for thinking, problem solving and creativity has been fully recognized. Bruner (1972b), in a famous article entitled 'The nature and uses of immaturity', is generally credited with first pointing out to psychologists and educationalists the relationship across different animal species between the capacity for learning and the length of immaturity, or dependence upon adults. He also pointed out that as the period of immaturity lengthens so does the extent to which the young are playful. He argued that play is one of the key experiences through which young animals learn, and also the means by which their intellectual abilities are developed. The human being, of course, has a much greater length of immaturity than any other animal, plays more and for longer, and is supreme, of course, in flexibility of thought. The more recent neuroscientific evidence has very much supported Bruner's position.

Play, in Bruner's view, is all about developing flexibility of thought. It provides opportunities to try out possibilities, to put different elements of a situation together in various ways and to look at problems from different

Photograph 4.1   That play is important in children's development has never been in doubt

viewpoints. This is very close to Craft's (2000) more recent definition of creativity as 'possibility thinking'. Bruner demonstrated this in a series of experiments (see Sylva *et al.* 1976) where children were asked to solve practical problems. Typically in these experiments, one group of children was given the opportunity to play with the objects involved, while the other group was 'taught' how to use the objects in ways that would help solve the problem. Consistently, the two groups subsequently performed at a similar level, in terms of numbers of children completing the task with total success, when they were individually asked to tackle the problem. However, in the 'taught' group there tended to be an 'all or nothing' pattern of responses, with the children either succeeding immediately by accurately recalling and following their instructions, or giving up following an initial failure. By contrast, the children who had the experience of playing with the materials were more inventive in devising strategies to solve the problem and persevered longer if their initial attempts did not work. The same proportion of children as in the 'taught' group solved the problem almost immediately, but many of those who didn't solved the problem at a second or third attempt, or came close to solving the problem, by trying out different possibilities.

Observation of children gives some indication of why play might be such a powerful learning medium. During play children are usually totally engrossed in what they are doing. It is quite often repetitive and contains a strong element of practice. Two further elements that have been high-lighted by psychological research and theory also contribute to an under-standing of its vital significance in learning and creativity. These relate to its role in children's developing sense of control and self-regulation of their own learning and to their developing powers of symbolic representation. Both emerge from the influential theoretical writing of the Russian psychologist Vygotsky (1978).

According to Vygotsky's position, during play children create what he has famously referred to as their own 'zone of proximal development', that is, they set their own level of challenge, and so what they are doing is always developmentally appropriate (to a degree which tasks set by adults will never be). This also involves the notion that play is spontaneous and initiated by the children themselves; in other words, during play children are in control of their own learning.

Guha (1988) has argued that this element of control or 'self-regulation' is particularly significant. There are many examples in psychological research of tasks where being in control has turned out to be crucial for effective learning. Guha cites, for example, experiments concerned with visual learning in which subjects are required to wear 'goggles' that make everything look upside down. They are then required to sit in a wheel-chair and learn to move safely through an environment. The results of such experiments show that subjects moving themselves around the environment (and having a lot of initial 'crashes') learn to do this much more quickly than those who are wheeled safely about by an adult helper.

The parallels here with Bruner's 'play' and 'taught' groups is striking. There are also clear implications for how we can most effectively help young children to learn. Whenever a new material, task or process is introduced, it is clear that children's learning will be enhanced if they are first allowed to play with them in a relatively unstructured manner. When new information is being introduced, children need to be offered opportunities to incorporate this into their play also.

The other important implication of Vygotsky's notion of the 'zone of proximal development' for teachers, however, is that there is an important role for the teacher in participating and intervening in children's play. Smith (1990), in an extensive review, examines the evidence relating to the issue of structured and unstructured play. He concludes that there is a role in learning for both kinds of play; sensitive adult intervention can usefully enhance the intellectual challenge, mainly by opening up new possibilities and opportunities (see also Neil Kitson's comments in Chapter 8 of this book). Manning and Sharp (1977) have provided a very thorough and practical analysis of ways in which teachers can usefully structure and extend children's play in the classroom.

In relation to its role in the development of creativity, the other element in Vygotsky's analysis of the cognitive processes in children's play relates to its pivotal contribution to the development of symbolic representation. Human thought, culture and communication, Vygotsky (1978) argues, is all founded on the unique human aptitude for using various forms of symbolic representation, which would include drawing and other forms of visual art, visual imagination, language in all its various forms, mathematical symbol systems, musical notation, dance and drama and so on. Play, crucially, is recognized in this analysis as the first medium through which children explore the use of symbol systems, most obviously through pretence. Play becomes, in this view, a 'transition' from the 'purely situational constraints of early childhood' to the adult capability for abstract thought (Vygotsky 1978). So, as an adult, when you have had an interesting experience upon which you wish to reflect, or a problem to solve, or a story to write, you have the intellectual tools to do this in your mind. Lacking these tools, the argument follows, children require the support of real situations and objects with which the ideas are worked out through play.

The precise ways in which play, thinking, learning, development and creativity influence one another have been the subject of extensive research (see Craft 2000; Whitebread 2000; Lillard 2002 for useful reviews). Lieberman (1977), for example, revealed a general relationship between playfulness traits and various measures of divergent thinking over twenty years ago. Of particular relevance to our own research, which we report in the final part of this chapter, Pellegrini (1985) showed that the verbal narratives of preschoolers who especially enjoyed pretending were more elaborate and cohesive than those of age-mates who preferred other forms of play. One of the chief areas of contention in the research

literature, however, has been the direction of causality. Is more sophisticated play responsible for stimulating, or just the product of, particular
aspects of cognitive development? This is clearly a crucial issue pedagogic-
ally. The study reported in the following section attempted to unravel this
kind of issue.

A study of pretend play and imaginative storytelling

We have previously replicated, in a variety of content areas, the study
by Sylva *et al.* (1976) in which the impact of play on practical problem
solving in young children was investigated. As in the original study,
on each occasion, children given the opportunity to engage with the
material to be learnt in playful contexts performed as well as 'taught'
groups in situation-specific aspects of the task. They also demonstrated
more creative approaches and more positive dispositions that seemed
likely to have long-term benefits in relation to their development as
learners.

Construction, both by its nature and within the framework of a primary
school curriculum, is a practical activity, easily developed through play.
Given the more formal prominence placed upon developing reading and
writing skills, we were interested to see if the same kind of pattern
observed between play and taught conditions would emerge in relation
to the rather different area of children's oral and written storytelling.
The first sample chosen for this research (Whitebread and Jameson
2003) consisted of Year 1 and Year 2 children (aged 5 to 7) in an
independent school. We were particularly interested to be able to study a
very specific sample group of children who were all (with the exception
of two intellectually average children) of at least 'above average' intellectual ability (as measured by Ravens Progressive Standard Matrices IQ
Test). In fact, the average IQ of the group was 131, which is within the
top two per cent of the population as a whole. Every child in the group
had a reading age at least six months above his/her chronological age.
Given that this was an independent, fee-paying school all of the children
come from reasonably affluent backgrounds. All of the children in the
sample were of a white British ethnic origin with English as their first
language. All of the children had had experience of nursery/preschool
education and many opportunities to play during school time up until
the end of their Foundation year. However, none of them had had
experience of playing with *Storysacks* or story props prior to the start of
the research. All of the children had a great deal of experience of stories
being read to them at school and also of being asked to write stories of
their own.

This sample would normally be expected, according to the generally
held views discussed earlier, to have the least need for play; consequently
we were intrigued to have the opportunity to discover whether play

would actually have any beneficial effect upon their storytelling and writing.

Following the general structure of the original study by Sylva *et al.* (1976), 35 of this group of able 5- to 7-year olds in an English independent school were asked to produce oral and written stories after they had been read a story and had experience of story props under 'play', 'taught' and 'control' conditions. In order to engage in the play condition, *Storysacks* were used. In English schools, there has been an increasing use in recent years of *Storysacks* as originally devised by Griffiths (1997). These consist of sets of toys and artefacts relating to items and characters in a story. (For an example of a *Storysack*, see Photograph 4.1). In a letter from Neil Griffiths to the first author of this chapter (2004) he made the following observations:

> *Storysacks* are a tried and tested practical approach for strengthening literacy, involving parent and families in their children's learning. They are highly flexible and versatile in their use and by their nature offer a tactile, participatory approach to learning. Above all, they are a resource that motivates, raises confidence, extends concentration and listening skills and helps to gain a greater insight and understanding of a storyline for children and adults alike. A *Storysack* allows a child to enter the three-dimensional world of a story.

Within our study, sets of *Storysack* materials were used for three stories appropriate to the age range. The children were read each of the stories, and then had follow-up activities which varied according to a 'play', 'taught' or 'control' condition. The order of stories and conditions was varied for different sub-groups within the sample in order to control for

Photograph 4.2   An example of the contents of a Storysack

the differential effects of the three stories, and for ordering effects between the three conditions.

The children were read the stories in groups of 10–15, using a picture book version. In the 'play' condition, the group was then allowed ten minutes to play with the story props in groups of five without any intervention from the teacher. In the 'taught' condition, the teacher then worked with the group for ten minutes, discussing and modelling with the story props other possible stories, but did not allow the children to handle the props. In the 'control' condition, the children were shown photocopied sheets of the story characters with their names, but no further help or guidance was offered. All the groups were then asked to write their own stories containing one or more of the characters in the story they had just heard. It was emphasized that this should be different from the original story.

These written stories were analysed according to the time taken to write them, the number of words they contained, their National Curriculum level, using national government guidelines (QCA 2001), and the number of points of information, beginnings, conflicts and resolutions which were the same or different from that in the original story.

Later in the day, after each condition, the children were also given the opportunity to record an oral story using the same story characters. They were assessed for the time taken to tell them, the number of prompts needed and the confidence with which they were told. The children were also assigned a 'General Confidence' score (outside the experimental conditions) by one teacher who had taught all of the children.

The results of the analysis of the children's written stories arising from the three conditions showed that in the taught condition, although the children included more conflicts and resolutions in their written stories than the control group, they spent less time writing their stories than in the other two conditions, and they included more 'same' points in relation to the original story than the play condition and fewer 'different' points than either of the other two conditions. They also included more 'same' resolutions than either of the other two conditions. In the play condition the children also included more conflicts and resolutions than the control group. However, more of these conflicts and resolutions were different from those in the original story than in either of the other two conditions and their stories were of higher quality (as measured by NC levels) than in the taught condition (see Figure 4.1 for one example).

The analysis of the children's oral storytelling showed that in the play condition the children showed more confidence than in either of the other two conditions. This difference appears to have been mostly attributable to a greater number of children lacking confidence after the 'taught' condition. After the play condition, the children also showed more confidence in this oral storytelling than in their regular classroom activities.

It was extremely interesting to observe that, despite investigating a

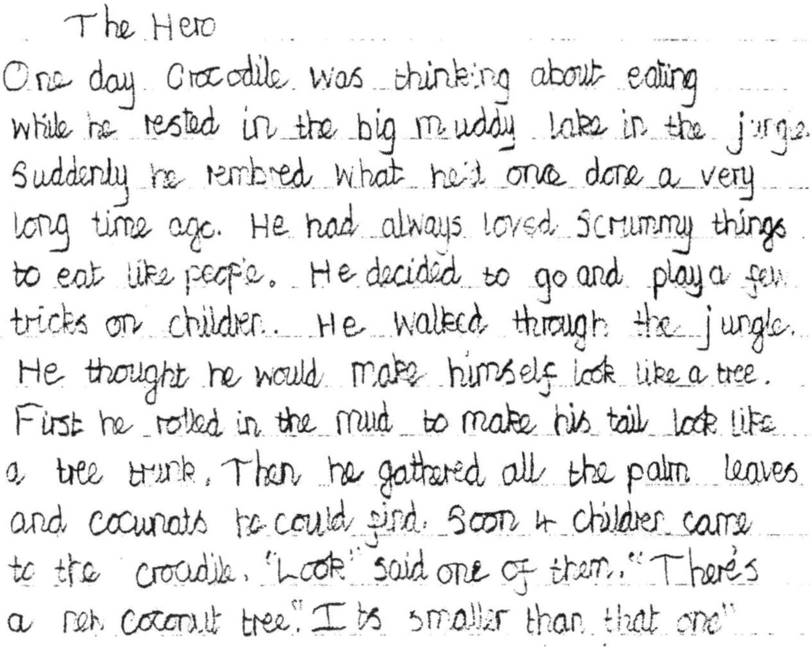

The Hero
One day Crocodile was thinking about eating
while he rested in the big muddy lake in the jungle.
Suddenly he rembred what he'd once done a very
long time ago. He had always loved scrummy things
to eat like people. He decided to go and play a few
tricks on children. He walked through the jungle.
He thought he would make himself look like a tree.
First he rolled in the mud to make his tail look like
a tree trunk. Then he gathered all the palm leaves
and coconats he could find. Soon 4 children came
to the croudile. "Look" said one of them. "There's
a new coconut tree". It is smaller than that one"

Figure 4.1 A child's written story

completely different area of learning to Sylva *et al.* (1976), our findings, like theirs, clearly showed the value and importance of play in enabling children to be confident and creative. Similarly, children who were part of the taught group show heightened anxiety when faced with a task and responded with an all-or-nothing approach as defined by Sylva *et al.* (1976).

The results of our analysis of various aspects of the stories showed a high level of congruence with each other and supported the theory that children who were not given an opportunity to play, and had only the experience of watching the teacher (control and taught groups), felt that they had to model the teacher as closely as possible in order to be able to complete the task. This inhibited these children's creativity and, for many of them, also appeared to increase their anxiety and fear of failure.

Considering that the only difference between the independent variables was an isolated ten-minute opportunity to play or be taught, it was impressive just how significant these results were. In a curriculum that is increasingly pressed for time to fit everything in, it is reassuring to note that just ten minutes spent playing has such a significant effect on both confidence and creativity (among other things). That these results were obtained with a deliberately able group of children suggests that the idea that such children in the 5- to 7-year age range do not 'need' to play to learn may be seriously misguided.

Our research confirms that play is indeed vital in enabling young children such as these to be confident, persevering and creative learners in more than one area of the curriculum. It is also crucial to note that, far from detracting from children's learning, the standard of writing actually rose after play. Given that the sample were all slightly older and very able children (who are often assumed not to need or benefit from play in the same way as younger and/or less able children) this is especially important. This should enable us to feel less 'that children are only learning if they are being taught' and more secure about making play the basis for learning in the early years and beyond.

However, the fact that children in the taught group did appear to have higher confidence scores than the control group, as well as a higher total number of conflicts and/or resolutions present, would also seem to be important, and it is of some little consolation to teachers that teaching does appear to have at least some positive benefits. Our education system currently relies upon children being able to learn, remember and regurgitate facts, details and information at increasingly high levels as they progress through it. The National Literacy Strategy requires children to be able to read and write well at a young age (certainly much earlier than in many other countries as already discussed). It would appear that a combination of play (to encourage confidence and creativity) alongside teaching/modelling (to introduce and develop new concepts and skills) might provide the best possible pedagogical environment to foster young children's learning.

The success of this combination of learning through play and teaching/modelling has also been observed when working in a special school for boys with emotional and behavioural difficulties. Year 4 boys (aged 8 to 9) became engaged with story writing in a way previously unknown, when allowed to play with story props/toys first. These boys, who had a history of violent and/or disruptive behaviour, became highly animated during play (in groups of three or four) with a selection of soft toys (an owl, a snowman, a boy and a girl). They then used these characters to write stories, sustaining concentration and application that far exceeded anything previously observed. Whilst this group was not the subject of a formal research project, it certainly appeared that this type of play was able to engage their interest and foster confidence in a way that encouraged them to write extended stories.

Conclusion

We have seen the benefits of pretend or fantasy play upon storytelling and writing for children from the Foundation Stage up to at least Year 4, both in schools where children were highly advantaged and in schools where children had special needs based upon their emotional and behavioural difficulties. Observations on such a wide range of ages and backgrounds, showing that all children benefit from having opportunities for this kind of structured imaginative play, should encourage practitioners to incorporate more of this kind of opportunity into their curriculum planning. It seems likely that this will enhance their children's confidence and creativity as learners.

Questions to set you thinking

1 Is learning through play only important for young children and those with special needs or does play continue to be an important approach to learning throughout life?
2 Is play of any benefit to able and/or advantaged children or is it only useful for children who are disadvantaged in some way?
3 Do you believe children are only learning when you are teaching using a formal approach?
4 What are the benefits of giving children opportunities to explore through play without any fear of failure or pressure to achieve?
5 How can you use your knowledge of research to justify your approach to play?
6 What research might you conduct to verify the findings of the research outlined here?

5 | Open-ended role play: supporting creativity and developing identity

Pat Broadhead and Carey English

Summary

In this chapter the authors describe how their partnership between education and theatre is bringing new insights in relation to open-ended role play. Coming from different starting points – research and performance – the two authors have each come to recognize the value of open-ended play resources in relation to both social and cognitive development for young children. The chapter considers the links between creativity and social and cognitive development and identifies observation as a central tool in understanding learning processes and in creating and sustaining a stimulating learning environment. The authors argue that a stimulating environment is one in which children's interests, knowledge and experience can find voice alongside the planned curriculum delivered with particular learning outcomes in mind. Open-ended role play has the potential to liberate the child's voice and to provide assessment opportunities in relation to the early learning goals.

Introduction

Children learn to play within a cultural context; their intellectual development and personal identities are shaped by prevailing cultural norms. But, as we will also see in Chapters 17 and 18 of this book, children are not just adapting to adult culture when they play. If the learning environment is facilitative, they will *add* to the prevailing culture through their interactions with peers and adults (Lobman 2003). Carlina Rinaldi, Director of Schools implementing the Reggio Emilia approach, explains:

> It is our belief that all knowledge emerges in the process of self and social construction. Therefore the teacher must establish a personal relationship with each child and ground the relationship in the social system of the school. Children, in turn, do not passively endure their experience but also become active agents in their own socialisation and knowledge building with peers. Their actions can be understood as more than responses to the social environment; they can also be considered as mental constructions developed by the child through social interaction. Obviously there is a strong cause and effect relationship between social and cognitive development . . . Conflicts transform the relationship a child has with peers – opposition, negotiation, listening to others' points of view and deciding whether or not to adopt it, and reformulating an initial premise – are part of the process of assimilation and accommodation into the group.   (Edwards *et al.* 1998: 115).

Rinaldi emphasizes the links between the social and the intellectual and the growth of a strong self through resolution of peer conflict. This chapter considers how open-ended role play in early years settings can create a space for young children to be creative, to build identity and to be cooperative, and what this means for educators in facilitating learning through open-ended role play.

Creativity and culture: current early years contexts

Creativity is an intellectual activity rooted in personal interests and current preoccupations: it is a search for personal meaning (Csikszentmihalya 1996). Creative acts may have a physical manifestation or outcome but creativity also operates through thought and insight, a point also made by Duffy in Chapter 13 of this book. Craft (2000, 2002) recognizes 'little c' creativity where everyone has potential to be creative by being imaginative, by solving problems, by achieving outcomes of distinction and by using resources in unusual and innovative ways. Vygotsky (1978) talks of resources as the 'tools' with which children transform themselves and their knowledge and understanding of the world.

The creative process is rooted in intuition, 'chance connections that bear fruit' (Fisher 1990: 31). Intuitive intelligence is recognized as an integral and necessary contributor to the intellectual repertoire (Gardner 1983, 1993a; Handy 1997). Fisher identifies the damaging change in the learning process that can occur 'around the age of three and four and last a lifetime. The child learns to stop guessing and inventing answers when his efforts are rejected' (1990: 30). Guessing and invention are rooted in intuition and are the foundations of creativity just as they are the foundations of learning through play; to suppress these qualities early in the child's life is to have a potentially damaging effect on their capacity to perceive themselves as problem solvers capable of functioning as equals in the company of like-minded peers.

Since 1990, it might also be claimed that the chance for young learners to make meaning personal has diminished further in early years settings as formal, teacher-directed learning experiences have gained ascendancy. In formal settings, learning is valued when what is demonstrated by the child as 'learned' connects with the teacher's plan for teaching. Whilst this is by no means unreasonable, it is potentially limiting in terms of making meaning personal for the learner and for becoming and being creative. Outcomes-based learning has dominated educator planning and this approach inevitably limits the children's opportunities for redirecting the learning goals towards their own interests and preoccupations, as Angela Anning compellingly acknowledges in Chapter 1 of this book.

Since the introduction of the Literacy and Numeracy Strategies in the late 1990s and their close associations with raising standards, with test scores and with public league tables, the emphasis in Reception and Year 1/2 classes has come to rest more substantially on the formal delivery of teacher-initiated tasks and activities (Pollard and Filer 1996). Play has diminished in status in many Reception and Key Stage 1 settings and there remains a fundamental lack of understanding of what the priorities and principles of the Reception class should be (Adams *et al.* 2004). Practitioners speak of pressures from primary colleagues to prepare children for school, from parents anxious that their offspring perform well in tests and a pervading sense of adult-initiated activities being of greater importance within the learning process than child-initiated activities. Relentless change and hierarchical curricula have buffeted early years teachers and left them uncertain (Anning 1997). The stress that early years teachers have felt has been considerable as they have sought to match a linear curriculum with the unpredictability of young children's learning and development (Wood 2004a).

It is recognized that an effective early years learning environment is created from a well-informed and purposely conceived balance between adult- and child-initiated activities (Siraj-Blatchford *et al.* 2002: Siraj-Blatchford and Sylva 2004). The *Curriculum Guidance for the Foundation Stage* (QCA/DfES 2000) reiterates this view and more recently it has been further articulated (see, for example, QCA undated). However, it remains an underdeveloped concept, making it difficult for practitioners to put into practice. Whilst it may be child-initiated activities that hold the greatest potential for creativity, this will only be possible in learning environments where adults are sufficiently well trained and aware of how their structuring and intervention scaffolds the learning that comes to the child through creative endeavour.

In this chapter the authors share their experiences of an innovative and challenging partnership they have developed between education and theatre in the classroom; a partnership which required the authors to think laterally and creatively. To be creative, we have had to learn to inhabit each other's world and to trust one another – just as educators and pupils must do in an early years learning environment.

Becoming sociable and cooperative: an intellectual endeavour

One of us (Pat Broadhead) has been researching into the development of social and cooperative play for many years (1997, 2001a, 2004). Focusing on observations of children playing with peers in traditional and more open-ended areas of provision (sand, water, role play, large and small construction and small world) she has developed the Social Play Continuum (SPC). The SPC describes action, language and interaction in four domains – the associative domain, the social domain, the highly social domain and the cooperative domain (Broadhead 2004). The characteristics of the SPC have been distilled from many observations in Nursery, Reception and Year 1 settings.

The SPC was tested and refined with Reception teachers (Broadhead 2004: http://www.routledgefalmer.com/companion/0415303397). The SPC can be used to observe and record the play of interacting peers, as an assessment tool for individual children or as a means of reviewing and developing provision for learning. It illustrates how children's play in the cooperative domain is characterized by 'high cognitive challenge' (Sylva *et al.* 1980; Siraj-Blatchford and Sylva 2004) through problem setting and problem solving, through a shared understanding of goals, through a highly imaginative use of ideas and resources as play themes are established and through high levels of absorption and concentration. In the cooperative domain, children are likely to resolve their own altercations as part of their play and seldom seek adult intervention until the play is finished and their goals are achieved.

The SPC allows play to be identified as domain-specific, across the four domains described above. On completion of 65 joint observations with Reception teachers, it was possible to quantify how much cooperative play each area of provision had generated. Both Pat and the teachers were somewhat surprised to find that role play (home area in two classrooms, a shop, a party and a café in remaining classrooms) had stimulated the least amount of cooperative play – only one out of 12 observations across the five classrooms. Conversely, 5/11 observations of sand play were cooperative, 3/12 of large construction were cooperative, 3/16 of small construction and small world were cooperative and 2/12 in the water play were cooperative. What surprised the project members about the role play was that they felt that it was provided to stimulate cooperative play but according to the characteristics of the SPC it was stimulating social play with its lower levels of cognitive challenge. Ten of the 12 observations of the role play had been in the social domain and one observation was in the highly social domain.

In reflecting with teachers and heads in a project meeting on why this might be, one teacher suggested that the other areas of provision, because they were not pre-themed, were open to much greater possibilities for thematic development linked to the children's interests, current experiences and preoccupations. This had some resonance for all the teachers. They had seen bricks and small world become houses flooding (this was happening in the children's city); they had seen the sand tray become a place for genies and monsters (featuring in literacy work); they had seen the water tray become a 'blood shop' (origins unknown); they had seen small construction and small world become outer space (cinema experiences). This led us to extend our joint research and to develop what we called at the time an open-ended role play area, resourced with large and small cardboard boxes, pieces of fabric, wooden clothes-horses, tubes, and such like.

Each of our joint observations of this new area of provision, using the SPC and across the five Reception classes, showed the open-ended role play to be in the cooperative domain with high levels of cognitive challenge through joint problem solving and through the emergence of highly creative play themes (12/12). The flooding stories were re-enacted in cardboard boxes with fabric; the clothes horse in one class became a tent, a cave, a party and then a roller-coaster. We observed one girl, an elective mute, in 'dead chicken' play with a peer using large pieces of fabric – the Reception teacher remarked that this was the elective mute child's first observed interaction with another child (Broadhead 2004). Our observations began to identify new characteristics for the SPC. We saw much of what Page (2000: 34) describes as:

> . . . imagination and creativity, inventiveness, independent critical thinking, foresight and projection, decision-making, the ability to grasp connections between seemingly disparate phenomena and ability to deal with surprise, conflict and irresolution.

In one Reception class, at circle time discussions, the teacher remarked that she was tired of calling it the open-ended role play area and asked what it should be called. One little girl remarked: 'It's the *whatever you want it to be place* because it can be whatever you want.' The name has stayed. An article was written (Broadhead 2001b) and it was this that prompted the initial link between Carey and Pat.

Theatre in the classroom linked with play-based learning

Carey English specializes in theatre for 3- to 5-year-olds. In observations of 3- and 4-year-olds, she had seen a strong connection between theatre and

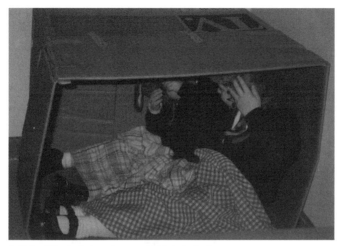

Photograph 5.1   The 'whatever you want it to be' place

the children's open-ended play with a few props. She saw real potential for a performance in the classroom with props that could be left behind to support children's self-initiated, open-ended play. From this standpoint she developed *Upstairs in the Sky*, a multi-layered play illustrating how trust and acceptance becomes collaboration, which in turn generates creativity, pleasure and emotional well-being.

The first theme of the play is how conflict can lead to collaboration. Two delivery people, Him and Her, enter the classroom with a large box, comically debating whether this is the right place. The teacher confirms it is, reassuring the children that these two people are welcome. The box is the *Make-it-Yourself* story kit for all the children; their names are on a list that is read out. The note instructs the delivery people to 'instal' the kit: 'use anything in the box in any way you like to make a story'. Music on a CD (also left behind after the performance) accompanies the performance. This is their first challenge. 'He' doesn't do stories – in thirty years, his main mission has been to deliver. 'She', however, is on her first day at work and likes nothing better than to make stories and have fun. They tentatively reveal the box's contents – beautiful pieces of fabric in a range of colours and textures, several cardboard boxes nesting inside each other, cardboard tubes, cotton wool, silver foil, recycled and natural materials twigs, cones, and so on.

They use the materials to tell separate stories – one tells Little Red Riding Hood, the other, Snow White – they fail to collaborate. They try to ignore each other and then begin to take each other's props. It ends in a loud argument. Audiences sometimes shout out and tell them to play together, be kind, share and tell the same story. Other audiences quietly wait for the characters to sort themselves out, responding to their disagreement with smiles and sometimes with brief looks of concern – theatre should tap into the whole emotional experience for the audience. The conflict is resolved by 'Her' who begins to weave the stories of Snow White and Little Red Riding Hood together. By accepting his story she accepts 'Him' and he contributes to and concludes their joint story. A sense of trust is established and, after apologizing, they agree to try again.

With generosity towards each other, they create the story of Princess Veronica and her grandfather King Jim, much loved but very old. At the end of a long life, King Jim disappears 'upstairs in the sky' into a beautiful cloudscape. His granddaughter Princess Veronica is worried about him and goes to find him. He tells her that he is safe and happy and he won't be coming home . . . some things change. But some things remain the same; his love for her will always be strong and she can revisit him in her memory. Reassured she returns to everyday life.

This second theme of loss is sensitively presented so that any child (or adult) who has experienced bereavement can empathize; the themes are discussed in preparatory in-service education sessions. For those children who have not experienced bereavement, they will recognize a sense of loss and respond to it in their own way. Bereavement and loss are real issues in children's lives (National Children's Bureau 2004).

The third theme of the play is being brave and trying something new. Princess Veronica has to climb a dark staircase to reach her grandfather's room at the top of a tall tower. Her eyes adjust to the dark and she becomes more confident. When confronted with an invitation to cross a silver bridge into the cloudscape where she might discover what has happened to her beloved grandfather she realizes that if she doesn't try she'll never know. With the confidence she has gained by the meeting with her grandfather she strides out to meet another day in a life without him.

To conclude the play, the delivery people get a call on their mobile phone and leave, amidst smiles and goodbyes, to make their next delivery. They leave a tableau of cloudscape and sunrise with a host of high-quality resources beautifully displayed and an invitation to come and explore. The children always want to explore the set and props after a performance.

Being classroom-based has particular impact: 'The children talk about it and think about it more than if they had had it in the school hall. In the classroom, they have a sense of ownership. They are more relaxed and tuned in' (Reception teacher). This chimed with observations as children watched *Upstairs in the Sky* in their nursery as this extract shows:

> There were clearly alternating periods of laughter, calm and excite-
> ment along with some sadness. Not every child responded in the
> same way at the same time but there was a general consensus of
> different emotional responses. There was a deep emotional engage-
> ment throughout from a majority of children and a whole range of
> accompanying facial expressions. The 'sad' moments were just long

Photograph 5.2   Players from Upstairs in the Sky

enough. Any longer and one or two children may have become distressed but the changing expressions suggested that they could cope with the depth of feeling that they were experiencing.

(Broadhead 2003)

The children's sense of play has been validated by the experience – theatre is play; they have seen adult role models playing and their teachers and carers watch and enjoy the performance, giving it status. They are hungry to have their turn. What happens next is informed by how creatively their educators respond to the children and to their play with these open-ended materials.

The two authors have developed preparatory inset for the educators. With a supporting video, this helps educators to:

- prepare for the performance and recognize and consider the underlying themes of *Upstairs in the Sky*; themes designed to evoke an emotional response from the audience;
- understand that observing the children's play is the key to recognizing their interests and preoccupations and to the ongoing development of the *Make-it-Yourself* story kit;
- become familiar with the Social Play Continuum as a tool for observing and understanding learning through play;

- consider the relationship between child-initiated and teacher-directed learning in their classrooms/settings;
- plan for the integration of the new resources into the curriculum.

The in-service sessions have been well received: 'Fantastic, very inspiring. Very good and practical but with a theoretical underpinning; the importance of play and observations. Great to see a bit of the play and know we will get a good performance' (Infant teacher).

In the final part of the chapter we offer some practical insights and raise some questions to support the development of open-ended role play in the classroom.

Why provide open-ended role play?

Whether it's the 'whatever you want it to be place' that emerged from Broadhead's research or the *Make-it-Yourself* story kit that emerged from English's work, the claims are the same. Detailed observations of children's play in each context showed how the flexibility of the resources allows children to collaborate and cooperate in cognitively challenging and emotionally satisfying play. If identity is socially constructed (Pollard and Filer 1996; Filer and Pollard 2000) and if identity is linked to effective learning, then these open-ended resources offer a social context that allows children to build reciprocal play ideas, to challenge and respond to the ideas of others, to resolve altercations without asking adults to intervene, to re-create their own interests and experiences and to set and solve problems together – in effect, to be creative.

In both contexts it has been observed how children love to explore the insides and outsides of boxes, their 'enclosure' schemas then leading on to many related play themes (Athey 1990; Nutbrown 1994). Some of these were drawn from the performance of *Upstairs in the Sky*, showing the impact of a good quality initial stimulus. Some were drawn from other interests and preoccupations – often related to the media and superheroes (Marsh 2000), or to experiences closer to home – playing at school, counting together, reading together. In one classroom, Broadhead observed a girl and boy playing at teacher and pupil with flash cards that the teacher had located close to the 'whatever you want it to be place'. She was a competent reader; he had learning difficulties. They played together in role for several minutes, each of them surprising the observing teacher, the girl with her facilitative and encouraging skills, the boy with previously undisclosed levels of reading competence. Open-ended resources allow children with a wide range of differing social skills, language skills and personal knowledge and understanding to share experiences at their own level of competence and ability.

In a post-performance questionnaire, practitioner respondents were asked to circle 'Yes' or 'No' in response to the statement: 'The children use the *Make-it-Yourself* story kit creatively'. Fourteen circled 'Yes', three created the statement 'mostly', two circled 'No' and one had not received the sheet in the questionnaire. Interestingly, the two who circled 'No' were planning to continue with the provision into the following school year: 'to make it an integrated rather than introduced feature' and saw other benefits from the play for the children – 'play is developing with practice'.

How do children respond to open-ended role play?

Post-performance observations of *Upstairs in the Sky* showed that the materials quickly generated a lot of imaginative play and the children could initially be boisterous. The questionnaire asked respondents to select two statements from nine to 'describe children's responses to the *Make-it-Yourself* story kit'. One class teacher selected: 'They often get noisy when playing' and also: 'They prefer this to the home corner/traditional role play area'. In the section where respondents were asked to pick statements 'that are closest to how you feel about the *Make-it-Yourself* story kit', this respondent selected: 'Open-ended role-play materials support the children's learning very effectively.' Thirteen other respondents also selected this statement as one of their two choices from a possible nine choices. Noise may not necessarily mean 'not learning' it seems.

The preparatory inset raised this issue with some associated practical strategies applicable to all forms of open-ended role play. Some educators felt that a resource of this kind, if not introduced with a specific stimulus like the performance, might be better introduced when children had become familiar with one another and with the classroom, rather than being a 'term one' activity.

Ongoing circle time discussions about the resource can serve several purposes:

- To alert children to its intended introduction to the classroom and consider with them what it might contain – a basic set of resources could be expanded and extended over time based on children's ideas or on what they might bring from home (with permission).
- To reassure children that the resource will be available for a good period of time and everyone will get chances to play with it. If something suddenly appears in the classroom, children may worry that it will just as quickly disappear and this will discourage thoughtful and engaged play.
- To talk about what the children played at, to give their play high status, to share ideas about new and ongoing play themes and how they have developed.

Ongoing questioning can help the children to establish ground rules:

- Is there enough for everyone to play at once?

- How can we share it?
- Where are we going to put it?
- How often will we be able to play with it?
- How do we decide who can play with it?
- How should we take care of it?

Joint ownership brings joint responsibility. Children develop thoughtful responses. In response to 'Can everyone play with it at once?' one boy said 'Green group can play with it on Wednesday afternoons.' This was a creative suggestion as it was Wednesday afternoon and he was in green group!

Our research suggests that children benefit from extended play periods to develop their play themes and their reciprocity between interacting peers (see also Jane Hislam's discussion in Chapter 7 of this book). This is what takes the play into the cooperative domain with its higher levels of cognitive challenge. Five or ten minutes are seldom sufficient. Children need regular access to become expert players. In the questionnaire responses, one early years coordinator when asked to pick two statements that described the children's responses to the *Make-it-Yourself* story kit had ticked both: 'It sometimes creates behaviour management problems' and 'They often cooperate when playing with these materials.' In a brief additional comment, the respondent had noted: 'These [the two points] turn into teaching points and over time it becomes better.' This respondent had also commented elsewhere on the questionnaire: 'We now observe the child for half an hour. It used to be shorter, 10 minutes, but your course has made us reflect on our practice and the need to observe for longer.' More detailed observations seemed to be informing adult–child interactions that in turn can help the play to develop.

How can educators develop open-ended role play?

The in-service sessions encourage practitioners to observe the children's play for as long as possible to see play themes emerge and develop and to see the momentum of the play build, leading it into the cooperative domain. The Social Play Continuum is designed to support practitioners to recognize prevailing play themes as a source of children's interests and preoccupations; research has shown that it may take time for play themes to develop and for reciprocity and cooperation between peers to develop, hence the recommendation for extended play periods (Broadhead 2004). It is difficult for adults to take meaning from children's play unless they focus on language, action and interaction. The SPC is designed to encourage such a focus and although somewhat complex-looking on first sight, it supports observers in concentrating on the nuances of behaviour and interaction rather than undertaking a fairly superficial glance in search of minimal evidence for a particular learning outcome. Its aim is to develop an enhanced understanding for educators of learning through play, which is why it combines the social and intellectual aspects of play. In response to the questionnaire statement: 'Observing gets easier with practice', 15/20 respondents circled 'Yes'. Only one circled 'No' (but in other ways was very positive about the *Make-it-Yourself* story kit, perhaps suggesting that she still saw observing as an ongoing personal challenge).

Observations reveal that 4- and 5-year-olds can develop story themes quite quickly whilst younger children might spend more time exploring the resources. For older children, their play can become drama and this was especially the case with the *Make-it-Yourself* story kit where drama, characters, storyline and improvisation had been so powerfully modelled by the actors. In response to the questionnaire statement: 'Children become absorbed in their play for long periods', 16 questionnaire respondents ticked 'Yes' and only three ticked 'No'.

The flexibility of the materials has allowed home cultural experiences to find 'voice' in ways that were inclusive rather than singular. In an early years centre in Southwark, London, the teacher observed children using the fabrics as African wraps to bind their babies (teddies) on their backs, as their own mothers or neighbours might have done. The questionnaire asked respondents 'What has been most surprising about the *Make-it-Yourself* story kit?' The replies focused around:

- the extent of the children's imagination both in their play themes and in using the resources: 'the depth and variation of children's knowledge and roles';
- children's high levels of concentration;
- the range of children who chose to use it: 'individuals who have never role played now join in';
- the replaying of *Upstairs in the Sky*;
- high levels of enjoyment: 'the children seem to enjoy it more than other role play which they got bored with quickly';
- the gender balance: 'the boys and girls enjoy it equally', and 'the boys enjoy the boxes and the girls the fabrics';
- levels of cooperation: 'the children are far more willing to share'.

There are some challenges for practitioners. The *Make-it-Yourself* story kit, like the open-ended role-play materials that Broadhead's teachers developed, take up quite a bit of space when children are fully engaged with them. Some educators resolve this by packing away their home areas for a while; some move the resources into a corridor or adjoining room or into an outside area. If the designated space is too large, then the individual resources can be widely dispersed. When this happens, the play often deteriorates. It seems that it is in bringing the resources together that children gain the most in terms of cognitive and social challenges. One Foundation Stage leader in a London primary school sent a letter home to parents after the performance of *Upstairs in the Sky*. Parents had not been told about the performance beforehand because it works better as a surprise for children but the teacher concluded the letter: 'Don't be surprised if they begin to search out old tubes, boxes and fabric to tell stories in your homes', bringing the world of school and home a little closer. The questionnaire asked if parents had been supportive of the play. Thirteen of the 20 respondents circled 'Yes'.

Conclusion

With regular access to open-ended play, including other areas of provision – such as sand, water and large and small construction – teachers noted concentration extending in some children and leadership skills emerging (Broadhead 2004). The children then brought these skills into their more formal teacher-directed activities and committed themselves more readily perhaps because the children came to accept that play would not disappear. Making the space for these activities and providing resources that are stimulating and attractive gives a clear message to children that the chance to play to their own agendas will stay.

In addition to increasing the levels of sociability and cooperation, and developing the imagination, open-ended play can have an impact in relation to the *Curriculum Guidance for the Foundation Stage*. Language is developed through running commentaries and reporting back at circle time. Through exploring materials and their properties (building towers, making drums, and using tubes as ball runs) the children develop their knowledge and understanding of the world. The physical may come through climbing or through manipulating fabrics and tools (resources), the mathematical though shape and space. Regular observations of children's play in these areas shows a deepening engagement with the early learning goals; observations also assist the educators in reflecting on ways of improving the provision. When children are provided with simple, open-ended play materials in a sympathetic environment and their play and interaction is observed comprehensively, we would argue that the child-initiated activities can fulfil the adult-initiated objectives of the *Curriculum Guidance for the Foundation Stage* – and more.

Questions to set you thinking

1 What areas of provision do you make available that allow children's interests, experiences and preoccupations to find voice in their play?
2 Do playing children get sufficient periods of time in the day/week to develop their play themes and interests and to set and solve problems with peers that arise from their own agendas?
3 When observing children's play, can you recognize the intellectual challenge involved in cooperation between peers?

4 Is the chance to play a reward for pleasing the adult or an entitlement for everyone?
5 Do you talk to parents and other colleagues about the benefits of play for supporting children's learning?
6 Do you talk at circle time about cooperation and conflict resolution?

Note

This paper is an expanded version of an article by Carey English and Pat Broadhead that first appeared in *Topic* (2004) Autumn, Issue 32: 13–18: Theatre and open-ended play in the early years – combining to promote opportunities for creativity.

6 | Play, literacy and situated learning

Nigel Hall

Summary

This chapter considers the relationship between play and literacy and explores how both provide opportunities for situated learning. Through a case study of 5-year-old children working in association with a socio-dramatic play area themed as a garage, the chapter demonstrates how the situated nature of the experience takes them into areas of world knowledge that are highly unusual in the education of young children.

Introduction

Associating socio-dramatic play with literacy is a relatively recent innovation. Before the mid-1980s I had never seen a classroom with intentionally and systematically incorporated explicit literacy experiences within socio-dramatic play settings. Indeed, around that time I was told by many people working with nursery children that they did not have print in their classrooms because it would confuse the children. One wonders how any child survived a walk down a British high street! After the mid-1980s this began to change and for a while linking play with literacy became highly popular, even getting serious attention in the National Curriculum English documentation. The Programme of Study (DES 1990) claimed that:

Activities should ensure that pupils . . . read in the context of role play and dramatic play, e.g. in the home corner, class shop, or other dramatic play setting such as a café, hospital or post office. Such reading might include a menu, a sign on a door, a label on a packet, or a sign above the counter.

(p. 29)

Any joy was premature, for just after this the 'Three Wise Men' were invited to rewrite the documentation and anything with the word 'play' in it disappeared (Alexander *et al.* 1992). The pressure of the National Curriculum resulted in play and literacy becoming distant memories in most classrooms, a process that was even (if possible) exacerbated by the appearance of the *Framework for Teaching* documentation of the *National Literacy Strategy* (DfEE 1999). All learning now was to be directed by teachers who stood at the front of their classrooms delivering some pretty formal instruction. However, as this was happening, so there was beginning a resurgence of interest in play and literacy, something that was given a huge boost by the appearance of the *Curriculum Guidance for the Foundation Stage* (QCA/DfEE 2000), which reasserted the importance of play and in places explicitly linked play to literacy.

The arguments for the association of literacy and play are very clear.

- *It enables children to experience a wide range of different situations within which literacy is appropriately embedded*
  There are very few episodes in life that have no print associated with them. By providing relevant and associated print within play settings, children are able to experience literacy in meaningful and purposeful ways. Such provision allows children to work with literacy in contextually appropriate settings.
- *It enables children to have holistic experiences of literacy*
  Within realistic play settings, literacy is not fragmented by artificial instructional processes. Literacy is used for whatever is appropriate in the play: going shopping, having a meal in a restaurant, going on a train journey, visiting a hospital and so on. The literacy occurs because it is needed in the context of the play, not because instruction demands it.
- *It enables children to control the ways in which literacy is used and experienced*
  Within play, it is the children who determine how literacy is used. It is inevitable that they will often use it in ways which are unconventional. However, equally often they will reveal that they have a wide understanding of the different uses of literacy, where certain forms of literacy are appropriate and when they are needed. When the children make the choices, learning becomes a much more powerful activity (see also Jane Hislam's comments about children's voices in Chapter 7 and the notion of *Storysacks* in Jameson, Whitebread, and Chapter 4 of this book).
- *It enables children to demonstrate what they know rather than what they copy*
  When literacy is used for real, people switch between the modes of

reading and writing or use them together. We do not always set out in advance to use either reading or writing. It is our perception of the situation that structures our response. Equally, in literacy-related play it is the pretend event that determines the nature of the literate response rather then a page in a workbook.

- *It enables children to cooperate in learning about literacy*
  In play, children interact closely in order to achieve more satisfying play. When children do this it opens up so many opportunities for cooperative learning. Children can often be more successful in helping other children learn than can professionals. Children at play use different experiences and knowledge and in the course of play these are shared (as Bruce highlights in Chapter 18 of this book). When one child demonstrates a novel aspect of literacy, it is instantly available to the others in the play. In this way the meanings of literacy are negotiated and shared by the members of the group at play.

The above reasons are embedded in a critical understanding of literacy. If literacy is to be seen simply as the mechanical acquisition of a relatively small number of skills associated with some narrowly defined technical skills, then any relationship with play is slight. However, across the last forty years there have been some major re-evaluations of the nature of literacy, and particularly literacy in early childhood (for a detailed review see Gillen and Hall 2004). This reconceptualization sees literacy as a social enterprise, and this creates a very close relationship between play and literacy.

The critical link is the notion of 'event'. Literacy is almost always situated in an event. We read and write for purposes that are linked to events, even if it is an event of writing and reading for pleasure. There is always a meaningful purpose that gives any literacy activities within the event direction and focus. The event situates any literacy within it. An example will make this clear. If we need to buy food we might make a list, follow directions to a shop, and read the labels and instructions on the packaging. We will probably read the prices, read about special offers and even look at the calories in the food we want to buy. We may tick things off our list as we go round the shop and will almost certainly check the receipt once we have paid. In this shopping event there is a huge amount of literacy and it all occurs for a purpose – filling our stomachs. It is the purpose that creates the event, and it is the event that creates the need and purpose for literacy. Literacy is experienced – a situated activity, situated within a complex social event.

A case study

In this case study I want to explore not simply how the situations experienced by the children can involve literacy events and play, but to probe

Photograph 6.1   Literacy is a social enterprise and this creates a very close relationship between play and literacy

rather deeper and consider some of the unusual social knowledge that can emerge from situated learning experiences.

In the school concerned a cross-school theme on transport was in existence and the teacher decided that for one term her socio-dramatic play area would become a garage. Despite the small area of the classroom, this was considered sufficiently important that it would occupy a substantial space. The intention was that the children would visit a real garage and then, using various materials (for craft, design and technology experience), would build equipment, and furnish the garage area, which was to have a workshop space and an office. Once the area was built, the children would then be free (subject to normal management procedures relating to noise and numbers) to play as they wished in that area without adult interference. Described in that way, the garage was not significantly different to most other play experiences for these young children. It has become common practice within such play for a range of literacy resources to be available in play areas, and for relevant signs, notices and labels to be developed within such areas (Hall and Robinson 2003), the expectation being that children will make use of these by incorporating them into their play.

What was to be different about this experience was that most of the literacy was associated with the play, but outside it. Inside the play area the children could play as they wished, but that play provided the social context and motivation for external engagement in a range of relevant, complex literacy events.

A couple of important principles were to guide this 'external' experience. The first was that it was to be 'event-based'. Most of the literacy
experiences associated with the garage were intended to be situated
within events in which literacy was a means to an end rather than the end
in itself. They were to be life events within which literacy had a role. The
second was that the children's experience with the garage was to be made
slightly problematic. The problematicity would help the children be
personally engaged with responding to situations (see Neil Kitson's observations in Chapter 8 of this book). The events/problems were introduced
in a variety of ways. Some were simply announced by the teacher,
some came by way of letters arriving in the classroom, and some were
introduced by other individuals.

The children experienced an extensive range of events but three will be
examined briefly in the rest of this chapter.

Planning permission

As the children were enthusiastically discussing the erection and fitting
out of the garage area, the teacher initiated the first event by suddenly
stopping them and introducing a problem. She explained how she had
forgotten that people cannot simply build something anywhere; one has
to have permission. This clearly had to be discussed by the children who
wanted to know why, and from where they got permission. Their initial
notion that was that the headteacher could give permission but the
teacher explained that one had to apply to the Town Hall. Some of the
children wrote to the Town Hall asking for permission:

> Please can we build a garage at Hazel Grove Infant School. We want
> to knock the house down and can we have some ladders [*sic*].

> To the Town Hall,
> Please can we build a garage and we want to build a ladder and we
> want to have some spanners and please can we start knocking the
> house down can we have some planning permission [*sic*].

Clearly the children have some confusion about what kinds of things
require permission from the planning department, and the very notion of
'planning permission' seemed in many of the letters to be treated as a
physical rather than a social object. It appears to have the same status as
spanners or ladders. This did not deter the teacher; as long as most things
were within the children's understanding she felt that some new and
difficult concepts could be tolerated. Indeed, such experiences were one
of the ways in which they would learn that life was rather more complex
than they had previously thought.

The Planning Department at the Town Hall, suitably forewarned, sent
the children some planning application forms. Rather surprisingly,
although the form introduced the children to rather novel requirements

in relation to their previous experience of playing, most of them were well within the comprehension of the children. They were able to answer questions about size by pacing out their area (it went on to the form as '12 fusteps long and 9 wad'), about whether the proposal was for a temporary period and if so for how long, and they were able to describe the previous uses ('a house') and with what the garage was going to be made ('kara-gated card'). They became aware of some environmental considerations by answering questions about the removal of surface water ('in the sink') and foul sewage ('down the pipe'), and after being warned about the dangers of touching any oil on their initial visit, were able to document on the form some hazardous substances. They were able to say how many people were going to work in the garage, indicate the opening hours and whether there would be any plant or machinery ('car lift mshin'). Several of the children filled in the forms and all the children drew plans of their garage. These were sent back to the Planning Department who quickly gave their permission.

This event already involves a considerable amount of literacy but this knowledge is also integrated into some pretty fundamental social concepts.

Probably for the first time in their lives these 5-year-olds became aware of a notion of authority and regulation that lay outside the family and the school. They began to see that a bureaucracy is involved and that work-places do not have freedom to exist and do whatever they want. However, at the same time they could see the point of many of the questions they were answering. Even a 5-year-old these days can appreciate the need for workplaces, especially industrial ones, to have concern for drainage, haz-ardous substances, and such like. In an embryonic way, these very young children were beginning to see how work cannot be decontextualized from the wider world in which it is situated. Even in this relatively simple procedural event the children have explored a range of texts which, as authentic literacy texts, moved them away from the autonomous nature of school literacy practices.

The letter of complaint
The children had commenced building things for their garage, and the excitement was mounting when the teacher introduced the second event. It was a rather dark January afternoon when she produced a letter that had arrived in the class earlier that day. The children were all sitting around her as she opened it and read it out.

> I have heard that you are going to build a garage. I wish to complain about it. Garages are very noisy, very dirty, and very dangerous. Someone may get hurt with all the cars. I do not think you should be allowed to build a garage.

The letter was opened in front of the whole class – in the following transcript, *T* is the teacher and *C*, the children:

C: I know what she's trying . . . I know what she's trying to say . . . We can't build the garage.

T: She's trying to say we can't? I wonder what we should do about this letter?

C: I know, we'd better say we want to build the garage 'cos . . .

C: I know, rip it up and put it in the bin!

C: No.

T: Well, you know I'm a bit worried because . . .

C: Or write a horrible letter.

T: Write a letter to her . . . a horrible letter?

C: Yeah.

C: Mrs Booth, we're not going to build a real garage but a pretend one.

T: Tell her it's only pretend you mean?

C: Yeah.

C: Say we're going to knock her garage down if she doesn't let us build one.

The teacher tried very hard at this point to bring the children round to a more reasonable point of view. She constantly got the children to think of the consequences of what they suggested, but it was almost as if there was a competition to think of the most awful thing to do to the neighbour. This took over, and it was only when they started to think they might be sent to prison if they hanged the letter writer that they decided that it might be better to send a less hostile letter. Even as the conversation moved towards this, individual children still persisted with alternative or devious solutions to the problem. The children, shocked at the letter, needed to contest the writer's position in order to preserve their garage:

We won't make a garage. We'll make something else.

We won't have a radio. I will not make the car fall on me. I won't let the oil go on me. Please do not worry.

The children did not respond with cloned letters; they voiced their personal responses. As can be seen from these two examples, not all the responses were in agreement. The teacher used this as a further opportunity to explore audience reaction. If the letters were sent to Mrs Robinson, then she would get conflicting information. This was presented to the children as a problem.

C: She'll have to choose. She'll have to choose which one.

T: Choose which one to . . .

C: Read.

T: No, she might read both of them. No, which one to be . . .

C: Believed.

In spite of what seems like a breakthrough in understanding at this point, other children still continued to talk about taking signs down if she came to visit and of trying to trick her into believing that there was no garage. All the children's letters were sent off to the neighbour.

It was some time before the neighbour replied and in the meantime an episode had occurred during another event, the grand opening of the garage. At the opening, the local garage owner, Mr Pipe, visited the children's garage and while trying to insert his large frame into their small cardboard garage area had knocked over their model car lift. The teacher showed the children the accident book the school had to keep and they decided their garage should have one. Mysteriously, the neighbour got to hear about the accident:

> I am glad you have replied to my letter. One or two of you wrote that you will not be having a garage but I do not believe you because some of the other children said you had made one. Are you trying to kid me? I am pleased to hear that you will try to make it quiet and clean. I am still not sure about it being safe. I have heard that there was an accident on the opening day. Is that true?

So the problem returns with complications, and they now had to deal with being found out, which produced another set of highly individual responses. In the first example the child takes a somewhat holier-than-thou attitude – it was the others, not her! In the second example the child is keen to negotiate, while in the third example the child is still not prepared to come clean. Admitting to forgetfulness was as near as he would come to conceding guilt.

> I am sorry that the children are making a garage. The other children were lying.

> Promise you won't tell me off if I tell you the truth, will you?

> I forgot. We have got a garage.

To reassure Mrs Robinson further, the children had to come up with an account of the accident to show it was not serious. As often happens when an accident is witnessed by a number of people, the children offered differing accounts. But they now understood that it was important to make their stories tally. So from a selection of possibilities such as the car fell over, Mr Pipe fell over, Mr Pipe tripped over, the car lift fell on Mr Pipe, some agreement was reached. Thus, the children who wrote about the accident gave roughly the same information:

> The car lift was made of plastic and the garage is made of card and Mr Pipe laughed and we will be careful and I will be kind and I will be nice and there was an accident and we have written it in our book and we have an accident book.

The neighbour was reassured, and the children's persuasive letters had been successful.

This event helped the children understand another way in which literacy was embedded in social structures. In this case literacy was mediating the relationships between the garage and someone who lived in the neighbourhood. They now realized that workplaces had to have regard to the views and feelings of people in the local community. More importantly, the children realized that there is negotiation involved in the process; they were able to engage with the neighbour, either to reassure her or in some cases blatantly lie to her. The liars, though, were ultimately caught out and had to engage in some retrospective justification. This event also continued to raise the children's sense of health and safety issues, in relation to which Mr Pipe's accident proved providential. The development of their own accident book, the need to document accidents, and the requirement to be able to explain them and offer reassurances about future conduct, all added to the sense of work and workplaces needing a sense of social responsibility. The children understood that they had obligations to other people and, perhaps more importantly, realized that other people were observing what went on (and for the duration of the project any mention of the neighbour's name brought hostile looks and comments from some of the children).

Repairing the nursery bike

Knowledge of the garage being built in the Reception class had spread throughout the school, and the teacher of the nursery class (the 3- and 4-year-olds) told the Reception class teacher about there being a broken bicycle in the nursery. It was decided that the nursery class would discuss the broken bike and then write to the garage to see whether it could be repaired. The children in the nursery were encouraged to write on their own in their invented script, and then some of them visited the class with the garage and were asked to read their letters to the older children.

The next phase of this event was for the Reception class mechanics to discuss the problem. They talked about going to have a look at the bike and what they would do when they got there. They considered having to test the bike, having to do the repair when they got there or having to prepare an estimate as a result of listing the faults (a notion introduced to them by the teacher). The discussion offered the opportunity for the children to explore their own ideas but it was also a time for intervention as the adult helped the group to consider possible ways forward and reminded them of previous experience when they had looked at broken objects and considered what was wrong with them. They were reminded about note-taking and provided with clipboards to take to the nursery. After this, groups of children, dressed in their mechanics' uniforms, took their clipboards to the nursery. They made notes and diagrams, returned to the classroom and set about writing to the nursery children with their analysis.

They began to draft estimates and, while they had little problem identifying the problems, they had less idea about the costs involved. The children had little understanding of the difference between pennies and pounds and had not yet got a clear grasp of the larger numbers, but they were aware that the nursery did not have much money to pay for the repair.

T: Now you be thinking, don't write it down yet, how much do you think it's going to cost?

C: 20p.

T: Does it cost just pennies in the garage? I know whenever I go to the garage it's pounds and pounds and pounds. It costs pounds to have a car repaired; you've got all the little parts that cost quite a lot of money.

C: How much was it?

T: I think mine might have been about £60.

C: It might be 44p.

C: It's going to cost £100.

T: You think it would be £100, do you?

C: No, they haven't got that much.

T: Perhaps we ought to pretend we are a real garage. We could pretend and think what it's going to cost if it was for real.

In the end the children decided on a cost of £44 and each sent a copy of their estimate to the nursery. It should be stressed here that while things like estimates had been discussed as a whole class, each child wrote his or her own text. Writing in this class was always an individual activity. One child wrote:

Mr Pipe garage
the handle bars twist they is safe
is need new oil
is wobbly seat
the paint came off
is squeaking
44 pounds to fix the bike [*sic*]

The next part of the plan was to render the children's world a little more problematic and consequently the nursery teacher wrote back to say that the price was far too high and could they make it any cheaper. At this point the teacher decided to explore this issue by taking the children back to the garage they had visited right at the beginning. When they arrived they discussed why things cost so much to be mended. The conversation covered elementary economics of running a business, including the cost of materials, having to pay for labour and electricity and needing to make a profit. Later in the classroom each child then responded to the nursery teacher's letter with his or her own justifications for the costs.

We are sorry that we can't cost any less and we have to pay our costs and we had to put screws on and off and Mr Pipe turned the lights on in the morning Mr Pipe has to pay the mechanics and the secretary

> We can't make the money much cheaper. It is expensive because Mr
> Pipe has got to pay for the things for the garage. He has to pay for the
> tools and the screws and nuts and turns the electricity on.

What might have been a rather simple procedural activity of playing at
mending a bike has been transformed into a much more complex operation. The customer (the nursery) initiated the action; the mechanics had
to respond by inspecting, analysing and estimating. The children's understanding of the financial and economic aspects of the operation of a
garage, and of engaging in a transaction, were considerably extended by
the discussion with Mr Pipe, after which point they were able to respond
and justify their prices. It is perhaps worth reminding the reader that these
were 5-year-olds and it can seem extraordinary that such young children
could engage in and handle competently the intricacies of this extended
process. However, they did so comfortably. They seemed to have no problem at all in understanding why the different elements in the process were
needed.

Experiencing a wide range of complex events (and there were more
than identified in this article – for instance, they advertised their garage,
and they discussed job specifications, advertised for posts and had to apply
for jobs in the garage) meant that playing in the garage was no longer
simply a question of being a mechanic and mending things. They did (and
'they' means both boys and girls) pretend to change wheels, weld metal,
lift cars on the hoist, type in the office, and do all the practical things done
by people who work in garages. But alongside these rather physical mani-
festations, their experience was also about rights and permissions, about
social responsibilities and freedoms, about relationships with other
people, about the nature of employment practices, and about the economics of work. Alongside and embedded in all of these was literacy. Reading
and writing were the tools through which events were introduced, com-
plaints mediated, permissions granted and costs defended. Work was no
longer a set of discrete skills performed in a special space. Being a player in
the garage was to do with having fun but it was also learning about safety,
permissions, and having regard for the consequences of building places. It
was about relationships with neighbours, about employee specifications
and about payments and costs. It was about experiencing complexity, living
with tension and taking on the world. It was a situated learning experience.

Was all this deeper level knowledge water off a duck's back for these
children? When the garage area was getting to the end of its useful life a
letter arrived in the classroom from Manchester Airport telling the children that another terminal was needed and it had to be built in their classroom. The letter asked for the children's responses. The children were
divided. There were those who pointed out that the garage was starting to
fall down anyway, and there were those who were adamant that they did
not want an airport because they liked the garage. However, both sets of
children were quick to point out that if a new terminal was built:

It is not OK if it is too noisy

Be very quiet

You have to do permission to the Town.

The aeroplanes have to be made out of cardboard.

Conclusion

Clearly, while inexperience may limit the children's understanding, something gets through and is remembered. The event-based nature of children's play, its real-world associations and clever interventions from a teacher made for a powerful, extended and broad learning experience. It involved the children using authentic literacy, making choices related to a range of purposes, relating to different audiences, handling complex webs of knowledge and orchestrating equally complex responses. The play setting of the garage provided the overall context within which literacy was situated in ways that were close to being truly authentic and the learning that took place operated at many different levels.

Questions to set you thinking

1 When you watch children in your classroom or setting engage in socio-dramatic play, how would you identify the features of the events that occur in their play?
2 Why is it helpful to build problematic elements into children's play?
3 Given the example of the garage in this chapter, how would you design another theme so that it incorporated situated literacy experiences for children?
4 How might the age of a child make a difference to the literacy-related behaviours you could expect to see in a socio-dramatic play setting?
5 If an 'event' in play is not a literacy event, but an event that simply incorporates literacy, how could you have built into the garage play elements from curriculum areas other than literacy?
6 How could you justify to a parent the use of socio-dramatic play to teach knowledge about literacy?

7 | Story-making, play and gender

Jane Hislam

Summary

Young children of both sexes act out roles, often as narratives, with great intensity and seriousness of purpose. As they do so, they develop language skills, try out behaviours and ways of being girls and boys and become more confident communicators and story-makers. This chapter emphasizes that, although adults cannot fully participate in this imagined world, they are crucial in supporting and encouraging it for all children. Adults are agents in raising the status of play and can do so through different kinds of provision, close observation and recording of what happens. Research shows that there is a need to rebuild practitioners' confidence in play and story-making and to provide more freedom in early years settings for adults and children to create story-worlds together. The role of play in ensuring that both boys and girls have sufficient opportunities for story-making through role play is also discussed.

Introduction

As adults, we are 'always on the periphery of the child's world' (Paley 2004: 24). Those who are sometimes able to enter into and support this delicate web of imaginary activities are likely to be the people who know, respect and listen to the child the most, significantly the children's parents, friends and siblings, and occasionally their teachers. The children's world is peopled by characters from real life – from their own families and communities – but also by an imaginary set of people from an inner world, as we can see in the case of Chloe who acts out the Chloe she hopes, perhaps, to become. Adults may refer to this as fantasy, but to children it can appear more real than the real world itself.

Case study: Chloe

Three-year-old Chloe is in the swimming pool. She is already confident and assured in the water, dipping, diving and twirling beneath the surface. Her mother, meantime, desperately tries to hold a conversation with a friend. Chloe keeps up a constant stream of 'pretend play' language each time she surfaces. At one point she says to her mum, 'Pretend I'm Chloe.' 'But you *are* Chloe,' says her mum. 'Yes, but *pretend* I'm her and we're dancing.' It takes the minimum of mum's attention for the 'action' to unfold and develop and Chloe happily plays on in her assumed role of 'Chloe the dancer/ swimmer'. Some minutes later, an elderly man attempts to engage Chloe in a conversation about her 'dancing–swimming'. The play is disrupted and although Chloe listens politely, she is obviously eager to return to her 'game'. The spontaneous flow of talk that accompanies the child's absorption in her play has been interrupted.

Smilansky and Shefatya (1990: 112) describe how young children act out roles within which they can 'make choices, formulate and carry out a plan of action, be spontaneously creative, compose something new . . . in a continuous cycle'. In these play scenarios, it is the child who controls and orders the world, rehearsing roles and trying out possibilities.

Children's play does not necessarily require an adult audience. Indeed, as we have seen, an adult audience may unceremoniously disrupt or bring the play to a close. But despite the fact that adults are unable to join in with the intensity of children's play, they can be, and often are, important facilitators and even 'agents of change' as children develop confidence, language and literacy skills and self-knowledge through play (Kent Schools Advisory Service 2003 – see also Neil Kitson's discussion in Chapter 8 of this book).

It requires a certain mix of conditions for this kind of play to flourish. Exposure to stories and songs is an active ingredient in this mixture (Wells 1985; Rosenquest 2002). Play derives elements of its content and structure from the stories of both life and fiction. But children also need to have a sense of ownership and control over the characters, settings and problems of their story-making, both boys and girls. This is what makes the activity of *oral* storytelling closer in kind to children's spontaneous play than reading from books. Storytelling is 'the most natural way for (them) to make sense of their world. We all have a story to tell – we're a community of storytellers.' This quote is taken from a headteacher in Lewisham (reported in *Nursery World*, March 2003) whose nursery children had been listening to oral stories told by Year 6 children. In turn, the older pupils listened to the young children tell their own stories and carefully recorded them. Paley (2004), on whose work the project has partly been based, talks about 'the flow of ideas' that moves from story into children's play and back again. As a nursery practitioner, she has made this flow of ideas a central feature of her teaching and an important means of listening intently to her pupils. She comments on children's play, autonomy and story-making, and expresses her very real concerns about how play is being undermined. She urges a strong stand be taken to retain the central place of play in children's learning. Paley describes how the activity of story-making allows children to 'enter the culture of the community' (2004: 5). She offers powerful examples of how girls and boys are able to give voice to the things that are of most importance to them through the stories that they tell and play out.

The status of play in the teaching of literacy

In the first edition of this book, I wrote a chapter which focused on the fantasy play experiences of a class of 6-year-olds as they acted out roles in the 'home corner' and also extended their play – literally making it flow into the classroom as a whole (Hislam 1994). In the sequences (reported again briefly below) the teacher and researchers paid close attention to what children said and did, video-recording these in order to reflect upon the children's play, the roles they adopted and the stories that emerged. This gave a picture of the social patterns of the classroom, and in particular revealed fascinating insights into gender roles and language development.

Since the first edition, the status of play and its profound significance for young learners has remained a central focus for many educators. But sadly, there have been pressures of many kinds on teachers and other practitioners that may actually have impaired play provision for young learners (Adams *et al.* 2004). That same class of 6-year-olds no longer has a home area and many practitioners express concerns that opportunities for play have been eroded and at times removed completely from early years settings. I have heard teachers claim that they have had to 'hide away' play equipment, or label children's activities as something other than 'play', especially at times of school inspection. Not only is the word 'play' seemingly frowned upon in some quarters, but also there are severe pressures of time on teachers. There is literally no time to play (Moyles and Adams 2001). For children beyond the age of 5, a new

Photograph 7.1   Observing children can reveal fascinating insights into gender roles and language development

orthodoxy about the teaching of literacy requires children to construct and deconstruct text types and become competent readers and writers in a predominantly teacher-led and prescribed manner.

This approach to the teaching and learning of literacy appears to have filtered downwards into some early years settings (see e.g. Moyles *et al.* 2003). The excessive demands on teachers to evaluate and assess learning in order to demonstrate measurable achievement may mean that it is difficult to convince others of the value of something as ephemeral as fantasy play, however important it appears to be to children (see Angela Anning's comments in Chapter 1 of this book). It can seem that mere lip-service is paid to the idea of 'children being children' and that the aim of formal education is to make them into something else as quickly as possible. There are many examples, of course, of how play can be introduced into the Literacy Hour (Bromley 2003) and there are some moves towards greater creativity throughout the Key Stages (DfES 2003). In the meantime, there has almost certainly been a threat to what has been called 'mankind's oldest and best-used learning tool' (Paley 2004: 8).

Play – imaginative, verbal and physical – is closely linked with the activity of storytelling (see also Chapters 4 and 5 in this book). Storytelling and story-making are widely acknowledged as important to the growth of young learners, not only in English but also in children's home languages where that applies. The richest play environments can simultaneously offer the richest language and literacy experiences. In these settings, story and play live alongside each other, a recurrent theme in all chapters within this book.

Supporting children's language and story-making through play

It is clear that children's access to, and development in, language will depend in large measure on the opportunities they are given for shared experiences and talk (Kent Schools Advisory Service 2003). It is essential for children's voices to be heard, and for teachers to listen and seek to understand what they are saying. Both play and story-making (which are themselves often one and the same activity) are the means of children finding their voices and also a platform for being heard, as Nigel Hall demonstrates in Chapter 6 of this book. There are many problems to be overcome in providing opportunities for young learners to develop oral and literacy skills. The children themselves may be facing great personal or social challenges. Parents sometimes 'lack the confidence and knowledge to implement powerful parenting practices, such as attentive listening, singing songs, playing rhyming games and sharing books' (Attenborough 2003). Additionally, the formal learning environment may not be conducive to interactions with adults and peers that are likely to promote learning or practitioners may deny their own instincts in relation to children's play.

Such is the case in some current research being conducted by the present author with a number of key under-5s practitioners representing a range of roles and professions – Sure Start workers, playgroup leaders, speech therapists, librarians, teachers and others. These practitioners were asked to talk about their own levels of confidence in telling stories. After participating in a number of development sessions, they were also asked to reflect on the value of these activities for their young learners, many of whom are children for whom English is an additional language. These adults wanted particularly to develop their own use of oral storytelling in the context of play. All of them felt that working with parents was a key part of their role and all wished to promote play and language activities for young children whatever the under-5s setting. When they described the many contexts in which story was used, they frequently made explicit links with play, often involving children in physical play or enabling them to tell stories in a play setting, e.g. a home area. They had clear ideas about the value of storytelling with the youngest of children (age 1 to 2). Storytelling was linked to the health and well-being of the whole child through physical play, a sense of fun, closeness of relationships with significant adults and the child's real experiences. However, the practitioners expressed concern that these opportunities were sometimes limited and not always given high status by others. They nonetheless believe that children's confidence in oral communication is most likely to develop in situations where they have a genuine audience and, as already emphasized, their 'voices' will be heard.

Literacy-rich environments

Storytelling helps children (and adults) to 'discover the worth of their own voices and those of others' (Medlicott 1996). The urge to make stories is a fundamental human characteristic. The fact that young children, given the right conditions (see below and Nigel Hall's comments in Chapter 6 of this book), will quite naturally invent stories often goes unremarked by teachers, even those dedicated to creating a 'literacy-rich' environment. Indeed, in recent years, since the introduction of the National Literacy Strategy in 1999, that environment can focus very narrowly on printed texts and how they provide a model for children in their developing skills as readers and writers. Important though this is, the most powerful model for learning about literature in its widest sense is established through oral storytelling. Stories can be shared most powerfully through oral means, such as those earlier referred to as part of the Peer Group Education project set up in Lewisham (Pappas 2003).

As already reported, early findings from my current research with a group of under-5s practitioners suggest that whilst all are committed to the idea of oral storytelling in principle, there are significantly different levels of confidence in practice. Some had never told – as opposed to read – a story. In creating an environment which is structured and safe for children to engage in role play, make stories and invent songs and rhymes, it is probably essential to increase the teacher's own sense of ownership, creativity and play (Broadhead and English, Chapter 5 of this book). For adults to allow their young learners to play and develop a strong 'voice', they themselves may need to experience at first hand the deep satisfaction of being heard – and of playing with language and storytelling themselves.

The language of play, as well as the many non-verbal interactions that take place in the context of play, can help teach children to learn what is expected of them in a new social setting. Paley describes this process in closely observed detail (1984: 2004), giving insights into what happens when the very young child moves into a complex group setting where the needs of many different children must be recognized and acknowledged. These conditions can 'both enhance and limit a child's experiences' (Rosenquest 2002: 241). Early years workers need constantly to think of how to create a structured learning environment which extends possibilities for young children, empowering them to make choices and to grow in confidence. Rosenquest describes how careful planning in the choice and use of stories can allow for sustained attention and personal responses from even the youngest child.

In longitudinal effective practice research, the best practitioners attempt to extend 'child-initiated' interactions (Siraj-Blatchford *et al.* 2002), recognizing the fact that children are social and active agents in their own play but need encouragement and scaffolding. In being left to their own devices in play, children will often act out the preoccupations of the moment – for example, something lost, a broken limb, or something not being 'fair'. Children do not need to be persuaded that 'make believe' is an important part of living in the real world. Adults, however, may need convincing: Paley (2004) argues strongly for teachers and others to give due status to these worlds of make-believe by recording episodes and then taking the time to analyse and reflect on what they see happening (as Siân Adams recommends in Chapter 15 of this book). This evidence is important, not only to inform teaching, but also to provide a tangible means of convincing others.

By becoming more aware of the many facets of children's play in domestic areas and other contexts, practitioners can learn a great deal about children's thinking, motivations and desires. For example, it is important to recognize that when children act out roles, or create their own narratives, they are in a very real sense acting out a whole range of possibilities and attempting to make sense of their world, including their place within it as a girl or as a boy. It is to gender differences in play and story-making that I now turn for the remainder of this chapter.

Gender in play and language

Dealing with 'difference' of any kind is challenging for practitioners who work with young children (as Theodora Papatheodorou emphasizes in Chapter 3). Practitioners' concerns about how gender impacts upon children's progress in language and literacy and about aspects of children's play and popular culture have arguably deepened over the last few years (Marsh and Millard 2000; Connolly 2004).

In 1984, Paley observed that children were 'working hard at the business of being different'. Around the same time, Wells (1985) reported differences between the kinds of things girls and boys talked about in their play at age 5 years. Preschool recordings also showed up a greater likelihood of parents having 'conversations with boys whilst engaging in exploratory play' (p. 102).

Children in the first decade of the twenty-first century seem equally absorbed in the business of 'being different'. A study on 'what boys had to say' whilst engaged in block-building and oral storying (included in 'Writing in the Air', Kent Schools Advisory Service 1999) revealed many fascinating differences between boys and girls as evidenced through their play and spontaneous narratives. For example, a young boy, Robbie, approaches some girls washing dolls' clothes in the water tray and says:

I like doing this, my mum doesn't wash her clothes like this. I'm going to build a washing machine.

(Schools Advisory Service 1999: 15)

He then proceeds to give a running narrative commentary as he 'builds' a washing machine out of blocks.

My own experiences also reveal similar responses from children:

I'm going to put him in his party dress (dressing bear) . . . (pause) . . . her I mean.

(Six-year-old in midst of a game)

When I grow up I'm going to be a boy and marry Daisy.

(Three-year-old boy)

Young children will act out 'mini-stories' such as these as they engage in block play or adopt roles in the home and dressing-up areas. Although these may be in very fragmented form, such spontaneous oral events can teach adults who are prepared to listen carefully much about the way their young learners think and feel and their life experiences.

The social worlds of children

Children inhabit a social world that is organized, to a large degree, according to gender. The expectations and responses of significant adults exert a subtle but powerful pressure on boys and girls to behave in sex-appropriate ways. It is likely, and perhaps inevitable, that children will explore gender boundaries and identity in socio-dramatic play as they seek to come to terms with who they are as individuals. Their play will render valuable information and offer insights to educators who wish to understand children better in order to enrich their development and to meet their needs as individuals within a social context. The home area in early years settings offers an especially interesting situation for adult observation since, in this setting, children in school and preschool contexts will be most likely to practise and explore gender roles as part of spontaneous play.

The view that children are active participants in the construction of their own gendered and social worlds has increasingly gained ground (Marsh 2000). In the 1970s and early 1980s, social learning theories tended to concentrate on the acquisition of sex roles and the learning of sex-appropriate behaviours through children imitating and modelling adult and peer behaviour. Included in many studies and research reports were accounts of the supposed influence of toys, games and television and how these influences might be manifested in children's play. Many parents and teachers continue to feel troubled about the ways in which the media, particularly television and, in more recent years, video games, manipulate children's views of gender appropriacy (including their choices of play things) through constant bombardment from advertisers to consume images of gender alongside products. Advertisements for children's toys and games contain direct messages about sex-appropriateness not just in content but also in their construction, for example in the use of colour, soundtrack or even camera shot.

However, a view of children as passive consumers has been seen as an inadequate explanation of the ways in which they actively engage in the construction of their own reality through their play and other experiences (see for example Steedman 1985; Barrs 1988; Davies and Banks 1992). We need to look beyond the idea that children soak up ready-made stereotypes to a view of children as busily working out for themselves what is appropriate and acceptable. This is often evident in the role play context.

Talking to children about their play can reveal interesting dimensions to the play observations themselves (Hislam 1994: 39). A 6-year-old boy was asked if he liked playing in the 'Wendy house'. He shook his head vigorously and grimacing replied, 'Girlish!' 'Why is it girlish?' he was asked. 'It's dumb. Only *girls* play in there.' Later, with the minimum of change in play provision, the same child said that the newly created police station was 'Great: you can arrest anyone you like!' 'Is it girlish?' he was asked. 'No, it's boys', was the response. Peter was not alone in expressing the view that such a context was only for girls and could therefore be dismissed as a boys' play area. Teachers are often surprised by the discovery that only a small minority of the boys enters the role play area. In this instance the area was almost entirely inhabited by girls, and yet the extent of the sex separation had not struck the teacher before systematic observation revealed it to be the case. If teachers are working from the premise that socio-dramatic play is a valuable part of the children's experience, it is alarming to discover that only around half the children appear to be engaging in it at any one time. D'Arcy (1990: 83) comments:

> The play area or play house is a largely female domain and children often assume stereotypical roles on entering it. Girls are pleased to act out stories and situations. However, boys seem unhappy in deferring to the girls in this context and I have often observed boys changing roles to become animals, introducing elements of aggression, noise and disruption to the situation.

During observations in a class of 6-year-olds it was possible, by recording who went into the play area, to confirm that girls greatly outnumbered boys. On several occasions boys went into the area, but the girls, who could be heard complaining to the teacher, usually chased them out, saying that the boys were 'messing things up'. In other domestic areas observed boys were recruited as 'animals' and occasionally as 'babies'.

Initial observations indicated that boys were rarely involved in socio-dramatic play, thus inhibiting the boys' opportunities for story-making and language play. But further examination revealed that play was not necessarily confined to the home corner itself. There appeared to be a high level of general awareness of domestic scenarios by children in other parts of the classroom. For example, if the play involved the 'baby' having to be taken to hospital, this was soon common knowledge throughout the classroom. On several occasions children who were sitting doing mathematics or making models were temporarily engaged in discussions concerning the play. At this level, play frequently involved many of the boys. Later, when the play area became a police station, this 'corridor' of play across the room extended. Sometimes it involved actual movement of the play action itself, as in a story of a chase for the 'jewel thief'. In a subtler form, children outside the area became part of the action as 'bystanders' and commentators.

These insights on the use of play space both in and outside the home area challenged an assumption that boys were not involved in socio-dramatic or fantasy play or that there were few interactions between the boys and the girls. It appeared that there were several layers of play in operation but because the domestic area was specifically marked out as a 'girls', area, boys, who tend to 'care more about boundary lines than do the girls' (Paley 1984: 54) would not go into it. Significantly, these discoveries highlighted the value of focused observation. Admittedly, this is not easy, but much domestic play passes without remark, partly because less value is usually attached to it than other classroom activities. But the context is rich in language and story-making, as we have seen.

Observing and interpreting play

A voluntary or assigned division by sex will be familiar to teachers in a range of play situations. In the use of construction materials, for example, there have been numerous accounts of differentiated and segregated play. Home and school expectations and attitudes will affect the range of play observed; the account above perhaps represents an unusually exaggerated sex distinction. Dunn and Morgan (1987: 280) report that 'both sexes used things in the home corner equally'. However, they were differentiated in the *ways* in which they used it. Many educators have observed that boys, in particular, are less likely to use opposite-gendered toys. Adults often exert subtle pressure on boys to conform to narrow expectations: disapproval or even hostility may be expressed towards boys who dress up in 'female' clothes or play with dolls. Differences before schooling in peer and adult attitudes, for example where boys are punished for playing with 'girls'' toys (Langlois and Downs 1980), are assumed to play an important part here. It is unlikely that teachers themselves feel completely neutral about these issues, much as they might wish to, because censorship in this area is so strong. Much that is written about the importance of educators giving 'free choice' to children fails to address these problems or the inner conflicts which can arise for the responsible adult. It is not always easy for adults to make counter-stereotypical interventions in real-life situations.

In the classroom described, different uses of the area and the playthings within it became most obvious after a change of status. Following visits of police personnel to the school during police week, the home area became a police station. In addition to the existing telephone and other resources, helmets, a typewriter and a pot plant were installed. The effect was dramatic. Boys flooded into the area immediately and became equally adept at storytelling related to police chases and other incidents. All the previously heavy users of the area remained, although some of the girls were clearly rather bewildered at first. Very quickly different patterns of use became established. The typewriter and the telephone were immediately appropriated by a few boys together with some makeshift handcuffs that were a central prop in several different stories.

After a brief period of exploration and orientation, an elaborate game began to develop whereby each person had a role, or even several roles to play. From time to time the play action spread into the main area of the classroom and the excitement level was noticeable. The range of roles was extended although many domestic roles were retained. A number of girls continued to make tea and put people to bed, just as before. The improvized 'cells' gave an added dimension to this and the cushions became beds as several 'robbers' were brought in and summarily stretched out. The boys certainly became involved in aspects of the play previously owned by the girls and, although not called fathers or children, they assumed roles within a loosely domestic framework. At first glance, the girls appeared to be almost literally 'swamped' by the boys. There was an

Photograph 7.2   Changing the home area to a police station made dramatic differences to the play

increase in noise level and much broader language and movement involved in the play.

Later, and on reflection, it was felt that the boys had been subsumed into the girls' patterns of play more than previously supposed: together they had established a territory where oral negotiations could take place. One girl appeared to take a general managerial role in relation to the play, and was often heard in director role, telling other children to be 'so-and-so' or not to go out until they had had their tea.

Significantly, the language altered and became adjusted to the situation. One child was overheard on the toy telephone, saying, 'Hello. Is PC Parker there?' and then holding the telephone casually away from his ear, he added in an aside to another child, 'He's a nice guy.' In many of these exchanges there was an unself-conscious but quite deliberate adoption of adult roles in which children were exploring things that people say, their intonation, the way they interact and their body movements, all in the context of the police station 'story'.

Children playing in the police station were literally acting out the experiences of their own lives as well as their vicarious knowledge of the world (Moyles 1989). They also drew on images from television and books: the police station gave a different scope for this. In the home corner the boys may have felt that they had nothing to play out or develop as storylines which related to recognizable elements of their own life experience now or to come. However, Paley (1984) came to the conclusion that children are not necessarily as caught up with the surface features of play as we might imagine, and that we must be careful to differentiate between their desire to conform to gendered roles and their involvement in an inner and personal world of exploration. Not only do children explore social roles but they also 'play' with states of mind or feeling states in which they are able to experiment with situations they are not actually feeling or experiencing. Caution must always be exercised before imputing that children are 'playing things out' in either a conditioned or a therapeutic sense. It is always likely that at some level children's play acts as a kind of personal mirror and that through play children are coming to grips with their own realities. Through play they may be getting to know themselves a little better and finding out how to negotiate relationships with their peers and with adults in the here and now, rather than rehearsing for an uncertain future. Or they may just be enjoying the new opportunities for storying.

It was clear that the development of the police station had an effect on the children's play. Most significantly, the boys entered the play area and acted out a range of roles within it using appropriate language and engaging with a range of storylines.

Conclusion

As we have seen, educational settings (including the home) can offer adults interesting insights into language, play and story-making as well as throwing light on how children think and behave in terms of gender. There is evidence that teachers and other adults may sometimes limit play opportunities, and with it opportunities for extending language experiences. This may be because they lack the confidence themselves to enter into 'imaginary worlds' such as those created through oral story, song and drama. It may be because they feel constrained by outside agencies to give 'hard evidence' of learning, particularly in language and literacy that is not seen to be compatible with 'play'. Yet, as we have seen, many opportunities exist if practitioners listen to children's voices and ensure that they are really heard.

Questions to set you thinking

1 How far are you able to relax and enjoy watching and listening to children during language play?
2 Do you make time to note down and record what you hear children say and do?
3 Do you vary the context for play and story-making in your setting? (See Moyles 1989 for an extended list of stimulus area ideas.)
4 Are both boys and girls involved in choosing, discussing and planning for the play?
5 Do you build into your programme 'real-life' experiences for both boys and girls and encourage socio-dramatic play in home areas and other contexts for spontaneous play and language, including the outdoors?
6 How far do you respect the seriousness of children's play (as well as its light-heartedness)?
7 Can you justify to others the role of play in children's language and literacy development?
8 How often do you tell, as well as read, stories to children and encourage them to retell stories and tell their own?

8 Fantasy play and the case for adult intervention

Neil Kitson

Summary

This chapter emphasizes the importance of fantasy play and socio-dramatic play in the cognitive, social and emotional development of young children. Socio-dramatic play offers great learning potential for those working with young children. Structuring the play enables practitioners to extend and enhance children's learning through creating situations and generating motivation to encourage the children to behave and function at a cognitive level beyond their norm. This is most effective when done through sympathetic and interactive interventions. Educators within the socio-dramatic play situation can stimulate, motivate and facilitate the play, encouraging the children to work at a deeper level than they would if left to their own devices. Not only does the adult in role provide the children with a model of behaviour but the role can be altered to bring a galaxy of 'people', problems, challenges and so on, into the play. Only when educators acknowledge and recognize the importance of their role in children's fantasy play will they feel able to intervene and begin to develop its true potential.

Introduction

Over recent years there has been a growing interest in the way that young children use fantasy play within their basic strategies for learning (Smilansky and Shefatya 1990; Wood 2004b; Edgington 2004). It is seen as a powerful and dynamic tool to engage children in the learning process (Kitson and Spiby 1997). Moreover, it is instinctive and a basic activity which doesn't need to be taught. Children would appear to develop the ability to engage in fantasy play by themselves and independently of educational environments. Whilst there is nodding acceptance that these activities are a 'good thing' and situations are provided to allow children the opportunity to involve themselves in such play, what is less widespread is the adults involved becoming part of that learning process. It is very common for adults who are working with children to view children's play as being for children only and feel that fantasy play, even more than other forms of play, allows children to operate without adults almost as a form of therapy. Whilst engaging in such activities allows children a sense of intellectual freedom – it is their story played out to their evolving rules – children will frequently repeat the same forms of play, engage in the same role activity, model the same type of behaviours, and resolve similar problems. This then is the case for adult intervention. Effective intervention can channel this learning, helping children to construct new dilemmas and challenges, encouraging and supporting individuals and extending and motivating language performance and competence (see Manning-Morton and Thorp 2003, and Chapters 4, 5, 6 and 7 of this book). As such, by intervening in the learning we are structuring the learning, not by telling children what to do but rather offering them a structure, a scaffold, around which intellectually to explore (Parker-Rees 2004).

So what is fantasy play?

Children engage in a wide variety of play activities, as is evidenced throughout the chapters of this book. Elements of fantasy will occur at differing levels within individual children's play and games and at different levels of maturity. In order to discuss the relationship between fantasy and socio-dramatic play it is useful to put it in context and to view it as something separate from other forms of play (Smilansky and Shefatya 1990). Socio-dramatic play is, for the most part, concerned with the nature of role and of social interaction, while other types of play involve bodily activity (see Peter Smith, Chapter 9 of this book) or the use and exploration of objects (see Howe and Davies, Chapter 11 of this book). There are four main types of play: functional play, constructive play, rule-governed play and socio-dramatic play. In socio-dramatic play children demonstrate a growing awareness of their social surroundings, consciously acting out social interactions and, in so doing, experiencing human relationships actively by means of symbolic representation. The significant difference between socio-dramatic play and dramatic play is that in the latter children can pretend on their own. They can act out a situation to the exclusion of others, while the more mature socio-dramatic play, as Smilansky and Shefatya (1990) define it, requires inter-action, communication and cooperation. Dramatic play is imitative and draws upon first- or second-hand experiences and uses real or imaginary objects. This play becomes socio-dramatic play if the theme is elaborated in cooperation with at least one other person and the participants interact with each other in both *action* and *speech*.

Smilansky and Shefatya (1990: 22) propose six elements necessary for fantasy play:

1 Imitative role play: the child undertakes a make-believe role and expresses it in imitative action and/or verbalization.
2 Make-believe with regard to toys: movements or verbal declarations and/or materials or toys that are not replicas of the object itself are substituted for real objects.
3 Verbal make-believe with regard to actions and situations: verbal descriptions or declarations are substituted for actions or situations.
4 Persistence in role play: the child continues within a role or play theme for a period of at least ten minutes.
5 Interaction: at least two players interact within the context of the play episode.

Photograph 8.1   In socio-dramatic play children demonstrate a growing awareness of their social surroundings

6 Verbal communication: there is some verbal interaction related to the play episode.

The first four of these apply to dramatic play but the last two define only socio-dramatic play. This difference can be illustrated with two examples. In the first, 3-year-old Joseph put a cape on his shoulders and ran around the nursery saying, 'I'm Batman. I'm flying and getting the baddies.' This behaviour has elements of 1 and 3 present, so it can be defined as dramatic play. In the second example two girls are playing 'hospital' in the doctor's surgery. They are wearing white coats and are giving each other instructions such as, 'You go and use the phone.' Questions like, 'Can I have the listening thing now?' and statements such as, 'I've got the medicine spoon' suggest elements of imitative role play are present but they are not *interacting*: merely informing each other what is going on. They are engaging at the very basic level of socio-dramatic play. Contrast these with two children pretending to build a house for a pigeon with make-believe tools, talking as if they are doing the job: this would be an example of higher level socio-dramatic as elements 2, 3, 4, 5 and 6 are present.

Why is socio-dramatic play important?

Although it is a crude distinction, one can look at the research in terms of psychoanalytic theory as exemplified by Freud (1961) and of cognitive processing theory as suggested by Piaget, to which can be added the more functionalist views postulated by Bruner. Irrespective of their differing views on the contribution to child development, all stress the importance of fantasy play and advocate its inclusion in the ongoing education of individuals (Edgington 2004).

Freud saw fantasy as a way to gain access to the psyche. Emphasizing the function of the child's instincts in fantasy play, he suggested that through play children will show their 'inner selves'. Play becomes like a mirror to the child's subconscious and as such this play can be used as a diagnostic and therapeutic tool. The child constructs a role by projecting on to it an imaginative and emotional component. Acting out roles through fantasy play helps the child by weakening the effect of the emotional pressure and, by so doing, helps the child assimilate the traumatic experience. This process Freud refers to as 'sublimation'.

While one can appreciate the implications behind this theory, as a practitioner working with young children I have found that the situations where children have presented behaviours that could be identified as therapeutic are, thankfully, few and best left to experts.

Piaget examined fantasy play in terms of assimilation and accommodation. He set up the theoretical notion of 'schema' (a collection of associated ideas) to which new ideas and new relationships of existing ideas are conjoined through experiences. This process he calls assimilation. He suggests that in fantasy play the fantasy elements within the play can be assimilated into a particular schema. Even though it is fantasy the assimilation process occurs as if it were happening in real life. If children make up a story about going on a journey, they draw upon existing knowledge of journeys (their existing schema) and add to it any new information obtained through the play. If the new information is completely novel and there is no existing schema into which it can be incorporated (or if it actually contradicts the existing schema), the existing schema must be accommodated in order for the new information to 'fit'. As a result, new interconnections will be made. Fantasy play can help children test out ideas and concepts and help them make sense mainly through assimilation (Bruce 2001a and Chapter 18 of this book).

This appears to be far more useful as a way of explaining what occurs in the fantasy play of young children. Through their fantasy play, they create new pretend situations. These can contain within them a wide range of seemingly unconnected elements all drawn from the child's previous experiences. Fantasy acts as a way of unifying experiences, knowledge and understanding, helping the child to discover the links between the individual components, as Jane Hislam emphasizes in Chapter 7 of this book. Moreover, as children are able to control the fantasy play, they are also able to control its components. Young children engaged in a fantasy about a space journey will selectively combine a wide range of components about 'space' and 'journeys'. They will consider what it is like to go on a journey, how to get ready, how time does not stand still during absence, how good it feels to arrive, and consider aspects of space, such as darkness, distance and the need for oxygen and special clothes.

The manifestation of the fantasy element (the play) develops as the child grows older. According to Piaget, children progress through stages of functional play, through dramatic play and on to socio-dramatic play (Cole-Hamilton and Gill 2002). Throughout, children bring to the fantasy play existing knowledge, skills and understanding of the world, which they then assimilate within existing schema or create new and novel interconnections (Wood 2004b). If insufficiently valued, this natural facility for developing children's understanding changes the way in which it is manifested from the processes of accommodation.

Bruner *et al.* (1972a) see fantasy play as being a precursor for social rules. What we learn through fantasy play then forms the basis of rule-governed behaviour. They illustrate this through simple peek-a-boo games played by young children, showing how these lead to the development of structured interactions with turn-taking. In a professional capacity, I have noticed that the fantasy element developed up until about the age of 7 becomes submerged if not sustained and actively encouraged.

These observations are supported by Singer and Singer (1990) who suggest that fantasy play goes underground at around 7 years of age, to manifest itself later either as day-dreaming or outward expressions of internal thought such as poetry, art or theatre. What is needed in the early years is the development and extension of fantasy play, the legitimizing of it, so that children themselves can come to understand the value of it: through this activity considerable learning about people's lives, human interactions, the workings of society and the individual's role within it can take place. Through play, children can begin to learn to cope with life and with a range of complex social issues such as failure, loneliness and disappointment. Bolton (1979) argues that all socio-dramatic play and drama is a metaphor for the children's lives and that it is the function of the teacher to enable the children to reflect on the significance of their play in order to learn from it. Singer and Singer (1990: 152) suggest, 'Imaginative play is fun, but in the midst of the joys of making believe, children may also be preparing for the reality of more effective lives.'

We can see that there is a value in fantasy play and that it has therapeutic, diagnostic and cognitive developmental functions. This is something of a paradox for educators: while cognitive growth is enhanced by fantasy/socio-dramatic play, the very fact of this cognitive development will mean that children have less need of the fantasy in order to explore simple behaviour patterns and motives through observation of those immediately around them. Peters and Sherratt (2002) support the idea that the increasing influence the child actually has on the world, coupled with the decreased need to test out and explore family roles and the development of reading enabling the child to open up and explore new horizons, means they have less cause to explore these elements through fantasy play. Educators need to move children beyond these immediate horizons so that they can begin to look at the deeper level of 'role' and the greater complexity of life. For this to happen, they need to be challenged.

Socio-dramatic play in action

There is a rationale in both psychodynamic and cognitive developmental theories for the specific benefits to the child engaging in fantasy play. The theoretical advantages of assimilation and role-learning are clear, but how might these be developed in an early years context?

The first point to make is that the potential benefits to be gained from fantasy play are very difficult to quantify and we are forced to discuss them in general terms. Singer and Singer (1990) identify three areas where the benefits of fantasy play can be seen:

1 actual spontaneous verbal output (around 50 per cent) in socio-dramatic play;
2 a corresponding increase in social interaction;
3 a significant improvement across a range of cognitive skills after 'training' in imaginative play.

Singer and Singer (1990: 151) provide clear evidence to show the increase but are still reluctant to identify more specific factors:

We cannot avoid the belief that imaginative (fantasy) play serves important purposes in the emergence of the psychologically complex and adaptable person. Individual differences in the frequency and variety of such play seem to be associated not only with richer and more complex language but also with a greater potential for cognitive differentiation, divergent thought, impulse control, self-entertainment, emotional expressiveness and, perhaps, self-awareness.

Smilansky (1968) proposes a range of generalizations relating to the value of socio-dramatic play that, although questioned by Singer (1973), show how socio-dramatic play can influence the creativity, intellectual growth and social skills of the child. These generalized statements do, however, provide a useful basis for what might otherwise be seen as abstract constructs. Among Smilansky's generalized notions of the benefits of socio-dramatic play are the following points relating to children's potential learning:

1 Creating new combinations out of experiences.
2 Selectivity and intellectual discipline.
3 Discrimination of the central features of a role sequence.
4 Heightened concentration.
5 Enhanced self-awareness and self-control.
6 Self-discipline within the role context (e.g. a child who is playing a special role within a game might inhibit crying because the character in the game would not cry).
7 The acquisition of flexibility and empathy towards others.
8 The development of an intrinsic set of standards.
9 Acquisition of a sense of creativity and capacity to control personal responses.
10 Development of cooperative skills since make-believe games in groups require effective give and take.
11 Awareness of the potential use of the environment for planning and other play situations.
12 Increased sensitivity to alternative role possibilities so that the notion of father need not be one's own father but may include many kinds of behaviour associated with the broader concept of fathering.
13 Increased capacity for the development of abstract thought by learning first to substitute the image for the overt action and then later a verbal coding for both the action and the image.
14 Heightened capacity for generalization.
15 A set towards vicarious learning and a greater use of modelling (Smilansky in Singer 1973: 224).

It would be wrong to argue that every child engaged in fantasy play will automatically take on these functions: nor will the child *not* engaged in fantasy play fail to have these areas of learning available to them. Rather, fantasy play provides an opportunity for the child to gain access to opportunities for these identified elements.

It is important to acknowledge the role that fantasy play has in the development of morality (Peters 1981). Children test out their ideas and attitudes in a number of different situations and practise what will happen in real life but within the safety of the enactment. This safety and the feeling of success that can be engendered supports the child's learning. The success that results contributes towards building self-confidence and self-esteem. Furthermore, socio-dramatic play aids the development of the social dimension within the child. Such social contact is important to young children and, as Blank-Grief (1976) indicates, role play serves to imitate and facilitate the contact: children develop the social skills they will need later in life.

Why should adults intervene?

If children use fantasy role play so naturally why should adults become involved? So far we have talked in general terms about how young children engage in fantasy play but, to return to the title, one of the most valuable contributions that adults can make to such fantasy play is their own involvement. All too often adults do not take part in socio-dramatic play activities: those who do tend to restrict their involvement to a very superficial engagement (Hutt *et al.* 1989). By becoming part of the socio-dramatic play, the adult can capitalize upon the great learning potential offered by this as a way of working. Skilful interaction can stimulate and act as a catalyst (Moyles 1989), help focus the children's attention and set up challenges (Heathcote 1984), all of which enhance and deepen the child's experiences through intervention in fantasy. Adults are able to enhance the benefits of fantasy play and create learning areas appropriate to the needs of the children. Adults need to consider Vygotsky's concept of a 'zone of proximal development' in order that the child's greatest achievements are possible, achievements that tomorrow will become their basic level of real action and moral reasoning. What is argued here is that selective interventions on the part of the adults can make the zone of proximal development and the corresponding learning more precise. For as Hutt *et al.* (1989) indicate, it is not engagement in fantasy play that is significant to the children's development but the active intervention of the adults in that fantasy play. Children need to be encouraged to struggle with ideas, concepts and morality. In such activities failure is unknown since both adults and children are working with fantasy: nothing of the real world has been altered; nothing has changed.

What do we mean by intervention?

Interventions allow for the development of structure within the children's socio-dramatic play. As with most forms of play, socio-dramatic play has a structure and rules but, as Garvey (1976) points out, these are often subsumed as part of the action. At first glance this structure is not apparent, but it is there nevertheless. Social play needs rules that we all understand in order for the interaction to take place. The adult becoming part of the play can facilitate the implementation of the rules as well as act as a behavioural model for the children to copy. Garvey (1976) further points out that in order to play we must understand what is *not* play. Part of this is helping the children differentiate between fantasy and reality. It is useful to identify clearly for the children when socio-dramatic play is taking place. This can be done very effectively by the adult working with the children saying, 'We are going to make up a story', or 'We are going to make up a play.' In this way the children are clear about the expectations of the activity and also have a much clearer idea of when they are, and are not, involved in the fantasy. It is equally important for the adult to make it really clear when the socio-dramatic play is over. This is merely the formalization of what children do for themselves. Their play will begin with, 'Let's pretend . . .' and will terminate when either the rules are broken or the children move away from the activity with, 'I'm not playing any more!' (Garvey 1976: 176).

Any episode of socio-dramatic play entails the exercises of shared imagination and the shared development of the theme of that particular episode. Young children are naturally egocentric and find it difficult to share. By selective interventions, able adults can monitor the negotiation of the children's ideas and act as facilitators. They can help the children remain consistent within their role and so aid the development of the story. One of the great strengths of this way of working is that through the fiction a great many learning areas can be explored. Problems can be set up which children can resolve within the story. The adult working within the fiction is able to set the problems and then keep the children on task, so making them confront the challenges. For example, in a children's story they have to get past the queen who guards the gate and into the castle. By having to persuade the queen to let them into the castle the children are employing and extending social skills. Their preferred solution may well have been to employ magic but such a solution would have merely avoided the social learning potential generated.

Intervention in socio-dramatic play enables the participating adult to keep the activity going by motivating the children to persist. While some children engage in such play readily, others need to be guided and encouraged to play a full part. The adult can help to refocus the story in order to bring the group together and generate excitement by introducing tension into the story. These are both essential to the development of socio-dramatic play but difficult for young children to attain for themselves. Working in a nursery school with a group of 18 children, I was asked to make up a drama on the theme of building. The children wanted to make up a story about building a house for the people in a book that had been read to them. After sorting out what had to be done, the work started. It was not long before the children began to lose concentration in the 'building' as there was little to hold their interest. In dramatic terms there was little or no *tension*. It was at this point that intervention was needed. I then pretended to receive a phone call from the boss who was going to come round and check up on our work. We would have to make sure that the house had been put together properly. Immediately the children were drawn back into the fantasy play and found a renewed vigour and purpose, created by the injection of tension and the pressure of evaluation. Equally effective could have been completing a given task in a set time (for example, 'We've got to build the hut before night comes'), meeting a challenge ('Do you think you could help me put out this fire?'), solving a problem ('What food should we give the animals now the snow's here?') or posing a dilemma for the children to work out ('But if we take the curing crystal how will the people who own it feel?'). These inputs into socio-dramatic play become the subtle tools of the adult working with children. Within the play, the adult is able to enrich and deepen the play and open up new learning areas for the children. S/he is able to intervene and structure the learning from within, without significantly reducing the children's ownership, a strategy Neelands (1984) defines as the 'subtle tongue' of the teacher.

It is important to remember that, although the adult can guide and to some extent shape the socio-dramatic play, essentially the play and action must be that of the children. Their ideas must be used. The words spoken must be their words expressing their thoughts. It may perhaps be that the adult simply joins in an existing 'game' with the children without the intention of simply being in the group but rather of moving the children's learning on, placing obstacles in the way of their story so that, by overcoming these obstacles, learning opportunities are created. A development of this is to construct the story with the children. 'What shall we make up a story about today?' Feeding from the children's ideas, both children and adult construct the fantasy. The adult's role is again that of facilitator, stretching and extending the children while maintaining interest and excitement. This adult participation legitimizes the play and encourages the children to see what they are doing as something valuable.

Such adult participation or intervention also allows for the structuring of learning areas for the children through the selection of themes or stimulus areas (Moyles 1989). By setting up post offices and fantasy realms, the children are involved with maths, language, social skills, manipulative skills and so on. If such pretend areas become a garage or a desert island, then a new set of learning potentials is created. By selecting appropriate pretend areas for the children's needs, the adults can then give access to appropriate areas of learning (as Jane Hislam points out in

Chapter 7 of this book). If they then also interact with the children, they can enrich, deepen and refocus the socio-dramatic play from within the story, setting up challenges and obstacles to be overcome.

Adults need also to interact with children. Left to themselves, children may operate within the socio-dramatic play at a superficial level. Enriched learning comes about when the adult is working in the story alongside the children (Smilansky and Shefatya 1990, see also Nigel Hall's suggestions in Chapter 6 of this book).

Fantasy play and developing an awareness of literacy

In order to teach literacy effectively to young children we need to ensure that it engages with their own experiences. It needs to inspire and motivate and above all it needs to be meaningful (see both Nigel Hall's and Jane Hislam's chapters – 6 and 7 of this book). All too often children are presented with tasks and activities which they then struggle to relate to and make sense of. Young children need to experience the concept of a story before they can begin to talk about it (Roskos and Christie 2001). They need to feel the words in their mouths in order to feel their power. They are encouraged to interact with each other and the teacher but will often find difficulty in doing so as they are unable to see the relevance (Roskos and Christie 2001). Drawing on the notions of structure that have been mentioned previously, real meaning can be given to language so that it can become a tool. Young children whilst engaged in fantasy play derive their motivation not from the activity but from the story that they are creating. This then can be valued in its own right with the adults supporting and challenging the spoken contributions that the children have made. It can also become the catalyst for other activities that the child might become involved in. A recent example might prove helpful in illustrating this point.

Whilst working with a group of 3- and 4-year-olds we were engaged in a fantasy role play about going on a trip. As a participant in the activity I was part of a group who were making up a story about going on an adventure (albeit a very small one). I hoped that we could discover links between our story and Michael Rosen's *We're Going on a Bear Hunt* (Rosen and Oxenbury 1993) – I wanted to encourage the children to see that stories that we were a part of were linked to those in books. Now clearly one activity alone would not do this, but this was contributing to their general experience of text and narrative. As a teacher I looked for the links between the role play and their developing literacy skills, just as Helen Jameson and David Whitebread describe in Chapter 4 of this book. The language used became more complex and more technical as we set off on our imaginary trip. The children had to create pictures in their own heads of what they had seen and then relate these to the rest of the group. As part of the narrative they had to draw 'maps', leave a trail and write notes. These were done at their level so the maps and note were very primitive but the trail was good! The spoken language was challenging and was extended as the story developed. Having 'come home' after our adventures we used pictures to aid the retelling and practised the notation. We looked at key words and key sounds but all of this was still within the context of the story. The children used play and experimented with language. Their motivation and interaction couldn't have been higher. There was collaboration and cooperative working and having done all of this we then read the book *We're Going on a Bear Hunt* together. The language had meaning and the children were happy to engage with the content. After all they were not learning – they were just playing!

Is fantasy role play for all children?

Fantasy play and socio-dramatic play transcend normal barriers of learning as perceived in traditional learning settings. The ability to participate in the activity is not governed by other abilities (Peters and Sherratt 2002); it is governed by a willingness to participate. Although this idea has been widely expounded (Sayeed and Guerin 2000; Peters and Sherratt 2002), it took me a long time working with skilled practitioners to understand it. Being part of a group who were working with a number of children with severe learning difficulties showed me that these children still got a great deal out of being part of the role play even if their participation was restricted. With children in mainstream education who find accessing aspects of the curriculum difficult, fantasy role play is often very liberating. Coming from a position of not succeeding, role play can enable them to achieve. There have been several occasions when I have worked with children who had recognized conditions yet operated within the drama at the same level as the other children in the group. They were not significantly different from the rest of the group and their feelings of success contributed to a growing sense of self-esteem. A further strength of this way of working is that it provides a significant motivation for young children. Their contribution may be less but their sense of achievement can be high. Practitioners have often commented on the way that children with perceived blocks to their learning have engaged in the activity associated with role play (Van Hoorn *et al.* 2003), pointing out that the children exhibit very few of the frustrations and tensions shown when they engage with other subjects. Fantasy role play must never be seen as a panacea for learners. Rather it offers a different way of learning, focusing on different sets of skills that allow young children to develop a different kind of world around them.

Conclusion

In this chapter, the case for intervention by adults in children's fantasy role play has been made. Looking first at the development of fantasy play, the evidence supporting the need for adult intervention in such activities has been assessed and opportunities for development discussed. Links have been made to literacy development and accessibility for all children. The opportunity for children to engage in 'free-flow' fantasy play extended through direct adult intervention with minimal qualitative changes to the activity has been shown to make very significant differences to the learning potential for children. It must be remembered that the adult intervention has to be sympathetic to the needs of the children and operate within their fantasy. The adult's role is to provide a structure within which the children can interact – to challenge, to set up problems to be solved, to encourage children to test out ideas and, perhaps more importantly, to open up personal learning strategies to children.

Questions to set you thinking

1 How easy or difficult do you find it to engage in children's fantasy and socio-dramatic play?
2 What fantasy/socio-dramatic play experiences would offer meaningful and relevant contexts for children in your setting?
3 Do you have particular children in your setting who might be able to 'shine' through involvement in role-play contexts?
4 What is the potential within your setting for using aspects of the environment to develop socio-dramatic/fantasy play areas?
5 Do children in your setting engage in all six elements of socio-dramatic play as defined by Smilansky and Shefatya?

Part 3
Play and the curriculum

9 | # Physical activity and rough-and-tumble play

Peter K. Smith

Summary

Physical activity play refers to playful activity that involves large body activity – particularly exercise play which includes running, climbing and other large body or large muscle activity; and rough-and-tumble play, which includes play fighting and play chasing. This chapter describes these kinds of play. It documents age and sex differences, and discusses the ways in which play fighting and real fighting can be distinguished. The possible functions or benefits of each kind of play are considered. Implications for teachers, practitioners, playground supervisors and playworkers are discussed.

Introduction

A lot of children's play written about in books and thought about by teachers and other practitioners is play with objects, pretend play, and socio-dramatic play. Indeed, the two major classificatory schemes of play, by Piaget and Smilansky, basically focus on these. Piaget (1951) distinguished sensorimotor play, symbolic play and games with rules. Sensorimotor play would be in the first year or so (Piaget's sensorimotor stage period) and, while including repetitive muscle movements, also includes simple object play – banging, dropping, and so on. Symbolic play focuses on pretend, usually with objects (or imaginary objects). Games with rules in older children take us beyond the realm of pure 'play', and even then the archetypal games usually discussed involve objects – such as the game of marbles considered by Piaget (1951), or football. Smilansky's (1968) scheme included an extra stage of constructive play, explicitly defined in terms of object play; while she used the term socio-dramatic play in specific ways as outlined by Neil Kitson in Chapter 8 of this book.

Object play, pretend and socio-dramatic play also capture the interest of teachers because they appear to have important benefits and functions for learning skills which teachers and educator believe to be useful. Various theorists and researchers have argued that such forms of play foster problem-solving skills, creativity, language use, social skills such as role playing, and cognitive skills such as conservation ability (see for example, Bruner 1972a; Dansky and Silverman 1975; and Janet Moyles's Introduction to this book). While these claims may have been over-enthusiastically embraced once the research evidence is considered carefully (Smith 1988), it is certainly plausible that object and pretend play give useful and enjoyable experiences in which many skills can be acquired.

Perhaps as a result of these factors, physical activity play has been relatively neglected. But we know that children actually spend much time running around, jumping, climbing, skipping, play fighting and such like – often just for fun. This chapter will review these kinds of play, including play fighting and rough and tumble. What kinds of play are involved? What age and sex differences do we find? What do children gain from these kinds of play? What function might they have in development? And finally, what are the implications for practitioners?

Physical activity play

Pellegrini and Smith (1998) have provided an extensive review of the research evidence regarding physical activity play. They argued that physical activity play (defined as involving large muscle activity) has three main types following overlapping but sequential time courses.

First are 'rhythmic stereotypies', bodily movements characteristic of babies such as kicking legs, waving arms. Second, during the preschool years there is a lot of 'exercise play' – running around, jumping, climbing – whole-body movements which may be done alone or with others; this increases in frequency from toddlers to preschool and peaks at early primary school (childhood) ages, then declines in frequency. This is epitomized in the kinds of outdoor activity in the pedagogic garden described by Stephanie Harding in Chapter 10 of this book. Thirdly, and overlapping with and succeeding this, is 'rough-and-tumble play' (play fighting and play chasing); this increases in frequency from toddlers through the preschool and primary school ages, to peak at late primary or middle school ages, and then declines.

Photograph 9.1   What do children gain from physical activity play?

Rhythmic stereotypies

Rhythmic stereotypies, discussed in detail by Thelen (1979), can be defined as gross motor movements without any apparent function occurring in the first year of life, such as body rocking and foot kicking. These were also described by Piaget in his writings on sensorimotor play. The onset of rhythmic stereotypies is probably controlled by neuro-muscular maturation: they are first observed at birth and peak around six months of age. Rhythmic stereotypies can also occur in the context of adult–child interaction, for example parents bouncing children on their knees and throwing them in the air (Thelen 1980; Roopnarine *et al.* 1993).

Exercise play

Exercise play is gross locomotor movement, such as running and climbing, in the context of play. It is physically vigorous and may or may not be social. Exercise play can start at the end of the first year, as infants become mobile, and initially much of it (like later aspects of rhythmic stereotypies) can take place in the context of adult–child interaction; this peaks at around the age of 4 (MacDonald and Parkes 1986).

Exercise play is common during the preschool period, though many studies do not differentiate exercise play from rough-and-tumble or pretend play, with which it co-occurs. Thus, it may be under-reported in the literature. Like other forms of play it follows an inverted-U developmental curve, peaking at around 4 to 5 years (Routh *et al.* 1974; Eaton and Yu 1989). As children move into primary school the rates of exercise play decline, although opportunities for such play are also less, being restricted mainly to break times in school playgrounds (Blatchford and Sharp 1994). Young children seem to need opportunities for physical exercise more than older children, and are more likely to get restless after long sedentary periods and to run around when released from them (Smith and Hagan 1980).

A number of factors affect exercise play. One is simply the amount of space available: more exercise play is observed in spatially less dense environments (Smith and Connolly 1980); it is obviously easier to move around quickly in a place with lots of space than in one that is restricted (see Stephanie Harding's comments in Chapter 10 of this book). Another is prior deprivation. When children are deprived of an opportunity to exercise and then given an opportunity, the intensity and duration of exercise increases (Smith and Hagan 1980; Pellegrini *et al.* 1995). It may be the case that during the period of childhood, when skeletal and muscular systems are maturing quite rapidly, the body over-compensates for lost opportunities to exercise these rapidly developing systems. Malnourishment is another factor that inhibits exercise play (Pellegrini and Smith 1998). Finally, low levels of exercise play are observed in tropical climates (Cullumbine 1950), and in playgrounds, low levels of exercise play are observed during warm periods compared with cool periods (Pellegrini and Smith 1998), perhaps because exercise has a thermo-regulative role (Barber 1991).

Boys do more of this kind of play than girls (Pellegrini and Smith 1998). This is probably related to a more general sex difference commonly found in physical activity, where differences between boys and girls increase from infancy to mid-adolescence (Eaton and Enns 1986).

Exercise play in childhood is hypothesized to enhance physical training of muscles, for strength and endurance, and skill and economy of movement. This is consistent with the nature of exercise play, and with the results of deprivation studies showing that children engage in longer and more intense bouts of exercise play after being confined in smaller spaces and/or prevented from vigorous exercise (that is, in classroom settings). Such rebound effects appear more important in the childhood and juvenile periods, when children are more likely to get restless after long sedentary periods, than with adults (Pellegrini 1995).

Another hypothesis is that exercise play encourages younger children to take breaks from being overloaded on cognitive tasks – the 'cognitive immaturity hypothesis' (Bjorklund and Green 1992). This argues that younger children have less mature cognitive capacities, so that the benefits of concentrating at a cognitively demanding task decrease after a shorter time than for older children.

This hypothesis is of course consistent with the deprivation studies, and also with some findings that exercise play in break time results in improved attention to school tasks (Pellegrini and Davis 1993). However, school tasks are a relatively recent cultural invention, so while this may be

Photograph 9.2   Exercise play may encourage young children to take breaks from being overloaded on cognitive tasks

a benefit of exercise play, it would be difficult to argue that it is a function in the sense of being selected for in our evolutionary history.

Rough-and-tumble play

Play fighting – or rough-and-tumble play – is a common form of peer interaction throughout the school years. It involves wrestling, grappling, kicking, tumbling and rolling on the ground, and chasing. Although rough-and-tumble play (often shortened to R&T) was neglected for a long time by psychologists, there is now a reasonable body of literature on this very common form of play in children (and indeed in many mammals). It takes up some 10 per cent of children's recess time in school playgrounds (compared to about one per cent of time in real fighting: Humphreys and Smith 1987) – though this does depend on factors such as how soft or hard the play surface is! It tends to increase through the preschool and early school years, peak in middle childhood, and decrease again in adolescence (Smith 1997; Pellegrini and Smith 1998). Children enjoy play fighting, especially boys; it is more frequent in boys, but present also in girls.

Telling play fighting and real fighting apart

Play fighting looks like real fighting; in fact, they sometimes are mistaken by practitioners, who may intervene to break up a 'fight' only to be told, 'We were only playing!' Even some psychologists have confused and conflated play fighting with aggression, despite the evidence from several studies showing that the two can be distinguished by many criteria, widely accessible to children.

Unlike real fighting, play fighting is characterized by facial expression (positive affect as shown by a 'play face', laughter or smile), self-handicapping (a stronger child does not necessarily 'win'), restraint (in play, kicks and blows are not hard or do not make contact at all), role reversal (children may voluntarily take it in turns to be 'on top' or be 'chased'), and how the encounter starts and finishes (in play, starting by an invitation and ending with continued play or activity together; in real fights, starting with a challenge and ending in separation: Fry 1987; Pellegrini 1988, 2002; Boulton 1991; Smith 1997).

Most children can distinguish play fighting and real fighting, and (from age 8) can give similar cues to those described above. Even at age 4, some cues are recognized and can be explained by many children (Smith and Lewis 1985). Smith *et al.* (2004) used videotaped episodes of play fighting in a primary school playground, with children aged 5 to 8. Edited episodes were then played back on the same day to both participants and non-participants. They found that participants had insights into what is going on in an episode, which outside observers, whether adult or child, often did not have. They were able to give more criteria to explain their judgements as to why an episode was playful or not. For example, in an episode between Jahred and Jonathan, both described it as playful when watching it on the videotape. Jahred (a participant) said, 'It's a game, we're trying to learn karate', and Jonathan (a participant) said, 'It's a game about fighting and pretending kicking, but only soft.' It was more difficult for non-participants. Tomas said, 'They real fight in karate, but I think it's just playing – it's real fighting when you lie down and cry, but they didn't so it's not real fighting.'

In judging whether it was playful or not, non-participants made more use of general statements about emotion or intention, for example, 'It was a real fight because they were both angry', or 'That was a play fight because it probably didn't hurt him.' They also relied more on facial expressions, for example 'It were a mess about [playful] because he were smiling.' These criteria use the kind of information that can more readily be seen or inferred from the video clips. For example, in one episode, Duane (participant) said it was playful as, 'They are taking him to prison, and I'm the jailor', and David (participant) said, 'We are getting Mark to put him in prison.' However Stephen (non-participant) judged it as playful because, 'They are all smiling' and Awil (non-participant) because, 'They were not fighting, he was smiling.'

Play fighting turning into real fighting

Sometimes practitioners clamp down on play fighting, because they think it often leads to real fighting. This appears to be a misconception, perhaps based on the behaviour of a small number of children. Both interviews with children, and observations in playgrounds, show that most of the

*Photograph 9.3   Play fighting is characterized by facial expression such as a 'play face',
laughter or smile*

time rough-and-tumble play does not lead to real fighting (Schafer and
Smith 1996). During the primary school years only very small proportions
of rough-and-tumble episodes, about one episode in 100 or 1 per cent,
turn into real fighting. Many teachers and lunchtime supervisors think it
is more, about 30 per cent.

Although the great majority of rough-and-tumble is really playful,
occasionally things can go wrong and a fight does develop or someone
gets hurt. According to a study by Pellegrini (1994), this is much more
likely in 'rejected' children – those who are disliked by many peers and
seldom liked much. He found that these children often respond to rough-
and-tumble aggressively (to around 25 per cent of episodes, compared to
1 per cent as the usual norm); indeed, this behaviour could contribute to
their dislike by classmates.

Why should some play fights turn into real fights, especially when
'rejected' children are involved? This could happen for two main reasons.
One has been called 'honest mistakes' and refers to a lack of social skills: a
child lacking appropriate social skills incorrectly responds to a playful initiation, such as a playful punch, as if it were hostile. The other would be
deliberate manipulation or 'cheating' – a child, sophisticated in understanding and manipulating playground conventions, deliberately misuses
the expectations in a play fight situation to hurt someone, or display social
dominance while 'on top' (Fagen 1981; Pellegrini 1988; Smith 1997).

The benefits of play fighting

Is play fighting just a 'useless' activity, or is it really important in children's development? Does this differ for boys and girls? Because play fighting often looks like real fighting, Symons (1978) argued that, for rhesus monkeys at least, play fighting served as relatively safe practice for real fighting skills. It is relatively safe due to features such as self-handicapping, choice of friends as play partners, and choice of safer spaces and surfaces for play fighting. Smith (1982) argued a similar case for play fighting in children. The argument is consistent with age trends (with real fighting becoming more important by adolescence), and sex differences (both play fighting and real fighting more frequent for males). However, there has been an absence of confirmatory evidence from individual differences (are children who play fight less, less good fighters?), or from enrichment or deprivation studies.

Pellegrini (2002) proposes a developmental change in the function of play fighting, especially for boys. During childhood it may function as safe practice in fighting skills and as an enjoyable activity that helps maintain friendships and develop skills of emotional control. In adolescence, however, it is hypothesized to function more to assert, display or maintain social dominance. It may help children realize their own strength and that of others and establish their position in a dominance hierarchy.

Cultural differences in play fighting

Play fighting has been seen in a very wide range of societies, including hunter-gatherer communities such as the Kalahari San, South American Indian communities and a range of modern industrial societies. It thus appears to be a cross-cultural, universal aspect of human behaviour.

However, its expression can vary by culture. Fry described a particularly clear example of this amongst the Zapotec people of Mexico. Fry (1987) made observations of children's play (and adult behaviour) in two villages, which he called San Andrés and La Paz. In San Andrés, children engaged in more play fighting, and there was also more real fighting and aggression in this community; in La Paz, fighting was avoided amongst adults, and in children too there was both less fighting, and less play fighting. It seems that in so far as fighting and aggression are valued or not valued, children's play fighting may also be encouraged or discouraged.

Sex differences in physical play

Boys and girls obviously differ substantially in play and social behaviour, especially in the school years. This starts at preschool if not before, although many activities do not show a sex preference at this age. Even in nursery school, children tend to select same-sex partners for play and by the time children are getting into team games at about 6 or 7, sex segregation in the playground is much greater. Boys tend to prefer outdoor play and, later, team games, often of a vigorous nature; whereas girls prefer indoor, more sedentary activities, and often play in pairs (Lever 1978). Maccoby (1998) has summarized these sex differences into three main phenomena: segregation (a strong tendency for children to play with others of their own sex, from 3 years onwards); differentiation (different styles of interaction in boys' and girls' groups); and asymmetry (boys' groups are both more cohesive and more exclusionary than girls' groups).

Boys more frequently engage in physical activity play, and especially in play fighting (as well as in actual fighting). Boys, more than girls, engage in rough-and-tumble play in virtually all human cultures (DiPietro 1981; Humphreys and Smith 1984). These differences hold for both parent–child play (Roopnarine *et al.* 1993) and peer play, and are more robust for play fighting than for chasing.

Part of these sex differences can be explained by social learning. Fathers engage in rough-and-tumble play more with sons than with daughters, and more than mothers do (Parke and Suomi 1981; Carson *et al.* 1993). In schools, girls' play is supervised more closely than that of boys (Fagot 1974), and this may inhibit physically vigorous play, which practitioners consider inappropriate for girls. In addition, peer group processes are important, as emphasized by Maccoby (1998): boys and girls have clear ideas of what is gender-appropriate behaviour, and peer pressure will increase the tendency to conform to these.

There are also hormonal influences to consider. Hormonal influences on physical activity and play typically centre on the role of androgens on neural organization and behaviour. Normal exposure to androgens during foetal development predisposes males, more than females, towards physical activity generally, and exercise play and rough-and-tumble play more specifically. It has been suggested that excessive amounts of these hormones during foetal development lead to masculinized play behaviour in females (Collaer and Hines 1995). Experiments in which human foetuses are exposed to abnormally high doses of androgens support the androgenization hypothesis, as androgenized girls prefer male activities and more vigorous activities such as play fighting, than matched control girls (Hines and Kaufman 1994; Berenbaum and Snyder 1995).

Conclusion and implications for teachers and other practitioners

The research discussed in this chapter is of relevance to those working with children. A first, clear message is that physical activity play in children should not be ignored or undervalued. There are implications here for a policy regarding school break times. A second message regards attitudes to play fighting, and ways of managing play fighting in children of different ages and backgrounds.

Physical activity play in the form of exercise play is clearly enjoyed by children. Younger children especially appear to have a 'need' for such play, in that when deprived of opportunities for it there is a 'rebound' and they do more of it. It is very likely that this 'need' is because exercise play does indeed have a valuable function for young children, in strengthening muscles, improving endurance, and practising skilled movement. In short, it improves physical fitness. This is a particularly important consideration when there is currently rather widespread concern in the UK, the USA, and some other European countries about declining levels of physical fitness and increasing obesity in young people. Increased television viewing and internet use can produce more sedentary lifestyles. In this context, moves by many schools to reduce play times or sell off school playing areas seem remarkably short-sighted and counterproductive so far as the longer-term benefits for children and society are concerned. Even regarding immediate benefits for concentration in lessons, there is some evidence that suitably spaced break times actually improve attention in lesson times subsequently.

There is also a pressing need for more research in this area. The research base on the effects and benefits of school break times is scandalously thin, and supported by only a few investigators. The 'cognitive immaturity' hypothesis deserves more rigorous testing (Pellegrini and Bjorklund 1997). We also need more research, probably of an experimental or quasi-experimental nature, on the effects of length and timing of play time breaks on children's behaviour, both at play time and subsequently in class times. We can expect such effects to vary by sex and by age. At present, length and timing of break times – an activity affecting virtually all children for some ten years of their lives or more – is based on no research but on tradition, often dating from around the 1920s when widespread schooling was established and, one suspects, on the time that adults feel they need for a coffee break.

Play fighting, or rough-and-tumble play, also deserves more serious consideration by all practitioners. Many children enjoy this, especially boys; and many parents enjoy it with their children. But views of many teachers and playground supervisors, in schools at least, are ambivalent if not hostile. This ambivalence is not entirely without foundation, but it does deserve moderating and more careful thought than it seems to have generally received hitherto.

In younger children – say up to the age of 10 or 11 – play fighting appears to be predominantly a safe and enjoyable activity done with friends. It is a form of physical activity (beneficial in itself) and one way for children to express friendship and affiliation. They show restraint and take turns in being 'on top', so it is likely that useful social and role-taking skills are being practised (just as they can be practised in other kinds of play and social interaction). These findings strongly suggest that play fighting should be tolerated. Of course, play fighting can be noisy and active, but so is much exercise play – it is for the playground or outdoor areas usually, rather than the classroom. Occasionally, a play fight will turn into a real fight, but for most children this should be regarded as a small risk that can be managed without requiring or justifying negative attitudes to play fights generally.

It is clear that there may be a few children who do not handle play fighting well. These children are likely to be sociometrically 'rejected' by classmates. They probably lack some social skills and do not know how to interpret or respond to playful initiations, or possibly ambiguous situations, in an appropriate way. They may hit back hard when it would be appropriate to hit back playfully, and as a result a fight may start.

In my view, the remedy for this is not to ban play fighting, but to watch out for and identify such children and give them help, perhaps through social skills training or some other form of therapy or support. These children are likely to need help in forming friendships and maintaining relationships generally, and the support could focus on this. It may also be the case with younger children that parent–child play fighting should be encouraged (as proposed by MacDonald 1993), provided parents do so appropriately, themselves. In this way children can learn about restraint and reciprocity in play fighting, and perhaps manage this better with peers.

Questions to set you thinking

1 How useful do you feel playground breaks are during school time for children?
2 What are the positive and negative features of play fighting in children?
3 Do the interests of children and teachers coincide so far as this is concerned?

10 Outdoor play and the pedagogic garden

Stephanie Harding

Summary

This chapter explores how a newly developed outdoor learning area has influenced the play of the children and the pedagogical practices of the adults. It looks particularly at how the impact of the variation and diversity within the environment, the increased space, the flexibility and the real tasks have supported the development of children's emotional, social, physical and cognitive skills. It also considers how the adults are responding to the new space and the ways in which they are adapting their practice.

Introduction

> To me the meanest flower that blows can give
> Thoughts that do often lie too deep for tears.
> William Wordsworth, 'Intimations of Immortality'

The reflections in this chapter have grown from observations made of and by adults and children in the recently redeveloped outdoor environment – the pedagogic garden – of an early years centre. The centre has developed from a nursery school built on the Margaret Macmillan model that valued physical and outdoor play as key to healthy child development. It was opened in 1939 and by 2002 it had become an Early Excellence Centre providing sessional daycare and education for 2- to 5-year-olds. As part of the Early Excellence programme it was chosen to be one of 19 centres in England providing models of outdoor provision for the early years. Recent improvements have included an extension to the existing nursery garden and the redesigning of the whole garden space by specialists in outdoor environments for children.

This has given the centre a very large and diverse resource for learning which includes areas for cultivation, storytelling, sand, water, climbing, balancing, pathways, an amphitheatre, and a variety of surfaces, perspectives, landscape and vegetation (see Photographs 10.1 and 10.2).

Photograph 10.1   The pedagogic garden

Play in the context of the pedagogic garden

Our understanding of play is very much informed by the work of Tina Bruce (1991; see also Chapter 18 of this book) and by Froebel, Macmillan and Isaacs. This is partly because of the centre's own history, architecture and core function as a nursery school and also because of the influences on my own learning about young children's development and learning. From reading Froebel (see Hereford 1901) my interest in play and spirituality and the rooting of learning in real, first-hand experience of the natural world has been developed. Macmillan (1919) has also been an influence through her focus on physical play and the benefits of outdoor play for health, as Peter Smith also emphasizes in the previous chapter. Isaacs (1929) highlighted the importance of observing, documenting and analysing children's play, particularly investigations in the outdoors, in

Photograph 10.2   The pedagogic garden

order to understand their thinking. Colleagues and I have used this to inform the development of our practice in the outdoors. More recently the ideas of Pramling-Samuelsson (2004) on playing and learning have been useful in supporting reflection on managing the constant variation and change of the outdoor learning resource and the spontaneous adult responses needed to support the demands of child-initiated and child-directed play, a point taken up further by Siân Adams in Chapter 15 of this book.

The children's responses to the pedagogic garden

At the centre, we work from the stance that there are three interrelated aspects to children's development – cognitive, affective (emotional) and physical (Davies 1995). Play in the outdoors is able to support each of these aspects in a particular way that is different from play in an indoor environment. It also allows the adult as observer to appreciate the ways in which these aspects interact with each other. Martin's story offers a good example:

Case study: Martin

Four-year-old Martin loved physical activities outside and especially enjoyed rolling down the hill we call the Magic Mountain. One day he spent some time with two friends running up the hill and rolling down, running up and rolling down, running and rolling until one time he rolled to the bottom of the hill and ended up on his back. He stopped to look above him at the sky. 'Look, look,' he said, very excitedly. 'Look, it's moving.' He was looking up into a blue sky at the white cumulus clouds making their way across his field of view. He lay for some time watching and calling his friends to come and see.

For Martin an intensely physical activity had led to his important observation and discovery about the world around him, one that he enthusiastically shared with his friends. Later he was able to make the connection between his experience and pictures of clouds projected onto a wall indoors. He was able to identify and question the circular movement of the projection as against the linear movement he had observed outdoors.

The importance of variation and diversity

Play outdoors provides opportunities for learning and other forms of development. It encourages observation skills, as Martin illustrates, because of the inherent difference and variety in terms of what the natural world provides to stimulate the senses, for example the difference in colour, shape, smell, feel and sound made by different vegetation, topography and weather conditions. As Howe and Davies point out in Chapter 11 of this book, we know how important these are for children's development, particularly in science understanding. Pramling-Samuelsson (2004) talks about knowledge as an internal relation between the child and his or her world and how variation is the source of knowledge for the playing, learning child. The outdoors is a rich source of provision for variation within a stable context, as the story of Anita shows.

Case study: Anita

Two-year-old Anita is very observant of the plants in the garden. One day she walks up the lavender path and stops at each container to look, touch and smell the different lavenders. At each container she looks first at the flower and then rubs the leaves, looking to the adult occasionally for affirmation. She is acquiring knowledge about the sameness and the difference in types of plants which she will be able to use and transfer to any further interest in plant life. She also has the opportunity to develop ideas around classification and organizing information about what are common characteristics and what are differences in the things she observes.

The outdoors provides a richer context for the movement of materials and people than indoors. Different surfaces – soft, gravel, sand, bark, water, soil, concrete, grassed, sloping, stepped, flat and uneven – specifically support particular interests and schemas (repeated patterns of behaviour across different contexts; see Athey 1990). Children who enjoy a 'transporting schema' and those who are interested in wheeled vehicles are provided with an array of real problems to experience and solve in moving themselves and their loads across the garden. For example, on the textured path Brandon was observed to pull Tom along in the cart. He pulled his passenger along the flat and around the corner following the path. The path began to slope. Tom jumped out and held the back of the cart to stop it from rolling too fast while Brandon guided it, still pulling it down the slope. At the bottom Tom jumped back in the cart and they continued their journey.

Using the space

A large outdoor area with paths of various kinds and a variety of perspectives from different heights provides opportunities for children to enhance and consolidate their spatial awareness and mental mapping skills through physical play, transporting and role play (Athey 1990; Palmer 1994, and chapters in Part 2 of this book). The role play that takes place in the outdoors is often wide-ranging and can engage large numbers. Consider Carl:

Case study: Carl

Carl is interested in pirates. He takes the role as lead pirate and searches for treasure, ably assisted by two friends. He ranges high and low along paths, through wood, across water and over hills seeking for treasure, escaping crocodiles and looking out for baddies. His journey lasts about thirty minutes. In the course of his travels he uses the whole of the very large space of the garden (0.815 of an acre) and he narrates his travels, calling on help to fight the foes and then engaging passers-by in his search for treasure. The band of pirate children gets larger but they continue to follow Carl and occasionally contribute gifts of detail for him to add to his story. At one point, as they follow the path to the treasure, there are up to ten children engaged in the hunt!

There are few indoor spaces that could accommodate heights, surfaces and variations in cover in the same way. This wide-ranging role play is evident in quieter, more domestic-focused play as well, as when Sue and Tanya are taking their babies for a walk.

Case study: Sue and Tanya

Sue is pushing an empty buggy and Tanya is holding her baby. They walk up the waterfall steps. This is quite hard for Sue as she has to lift, push and pull to get the buggy up and over the steps and puddles. They stop at the top of the waterfall and Tanya makes a call on her toy mobile several times. She turns and calls to a friend at the bottom of the hill. After this they both walk down the waterfall to the base. Tanya is still clutching her baby and they amble over to the bird hide about twenty yards away. In the bird hide Sue finds a baby and puts it in her buggy. Tanya takes off again, walking along a small path to the main green lane. Sue follows. The buggy is difficult to manage so she has to lift it with its baby inside and carry it to the green lane. At the lane they stop to rearrange their babies and then to follow the green lane to 'the house' area. Tanya goes up and over the style and Sue continues along the path.

They reach the bark-covered area where Mandy is sitting on a log seat with her doll. Tanya puts her baby down next to Mary and walks around the bark area. Sue sits down next to Mandy, still holding onto her buggy. Tanya returns to the log, picks up her baby and proceeds through the gate at the other entrance to the area. Sue and Mandy get up and follow her through the gate. They struggle with their buggies and continue to follow Tanya across the long grass to the top of the hill where she is lying. They manage to meet at the top and talk to Tanya before Mandy moves off.

Although there are very different narratives in the two examples, the space and variety of contexts within this area of the garden allows children actively to explore the journeying aspects of their role play. There may be gender issues around the form of the journeying that the role play takes and this would make an interesting subject for further research at the centre.

A flexible and open-ended environment

The garden environment has open-endedness in terms of what it is able to represent for the children. There is evidence above of both domestic and fantasy worlds being represented within the same space. This open-ended potential is also true of the objects in the natural environment and encourages creative thinking. In her case study, Harrold (2004: 4–5) found that Sophie, the 2-year-old child she was observing, used a natural resource – a stick – as a tool in a variety of different ways.

> Firstly she used the stick as a prop in an imaginative play scenario when she was playing at being a dog. Then she used it to help her stand up after sliding down a slide. Then she used it to hit the grass and a dandelion clock. She then used the stick to open and close a gate. Later, she used the stick to hoe wood chips, saying 'I'm raking.' Then she returned to using the stick to make sounds on wood before finally using it to point to an aeroplane in the sky.

The examples of Carl, Sue and Tanya's role play illustrate how children use the different areas of the garden to represent different role play contexts. They also show how the large space enables children to move in and out of each other's narratives and also enables different leader/follower relationships among the children. It is clear that opportunities for such physically wide-ranging role play would be more difficult in an indoor environment.

Children as teachers

An important aspect of making such a large area available to the children is the role of children as teachers to their peers. The space allows the children to be away from the adult gaze if they want to be and offers more space for children to interact with their peers. Harrold's observations of Sophie show the importance of children as teachers and models. She reported that Sophie observed her peers closely and used them as models for her own play – 'I observed her intently watching another child filling a bucket with water, and then she imitated the child's actions exactly.' Sharing discoveries like this is very important in such a large area as adults cannot always be in close enough proximity to give immediate feedback.

Sophie went on to show how sometimes children actually prefer support from their peers rather than from adults. She developed a particular interest in balancing and knew when she needed help and when she could succeed on her own. At one point she forcefully rejected adult support, a rejection accepted by the adult, and later she asked for help from an older child. She sustained the balancing with help from her older friend for quite an extended period.

Developing an understanding of the natural world

An increased understanding of the natural world springs from closer experiences of it and links very much with what has been written previously about observation skills (see also Janet Moyles's Introduction to this book). Outdoor provision that is diverse and varied includes support for this area of knowledge at a sensory level as well as at a knowledge and skills level. Children are able to feel ice melting, to experience the sensation of hailstones falling and the fragility of flowers; they can smell rain, flowers and herbs. Young children can gain an understanding of the food chain by planting seeds, watching their development, harvesting the crop and preparing vegetables and fruit to eat. They can hear the wind in the grass or the trees and can see shadows moving, leaves changing colour and compost decaying (see Howe and Davies's examples from science teaching in Chapter 11 of this book). The world outside is very 'immediate' and children can observe, handle and care for living creatures. Opportunities can occur unexpectedly. An example of this was when two girls were playing on the hurdles and wooden 'stepping stones'.

Case study: Sally and Molly

Sally and Molly were challenging themselves and each other in different ways of balancing on a sloping hurdle. Suddenly Molly saw a red coloured bee. She was very interested and observed it for some time. Sally was at first a bit afraid and daunted and not very interested but Molly was persistent and focused on the bee. This engaged Sally. They both watched the bee. Molly called me over after a while to show me that she had found the bee's home. She had observed it going in and out of a very small raised hole next to one of the wooden 'stepping stones'. She continued to observe the bee, accompanied by Sally, for some time.

This opportunity for observing and learning about insects was unplanned. Molly modelled being a scientist for Sally and was able to sustain her friend's interest through her own enthusiasm. The outdoor environment provides many opportunities for children to make spontaneous observations and discoveries about the natural world for themselves.

Supporting children's emotional and social understanding

Emotional and social understanding in children is supported by outdoor play specifically in terms of confidence, cooperation, spirituality and solitude. Developing confidence is related to the diversity and variation provided by the garden which allows perfectly for children to challenge themselves at their own level and allows them to succeed as they are working within their zone of potential development (Vygotsky 1978), as with Hazel.

Case study: Hazel

Hazel walked around the textured path pushing the blue, small pram, holding it with both hands. She stopped, looked up and around, and then continued to push the pushchair to the bottom of the waterfall steps. She looked up and pushed the pushchair to where it caught on the bottom step. She used her knees and leg to lift the pushchair up two steps, then, still holding on to the pushchair with one hand, she turned her body sideways to face the trees and managed to pull the pushchair up two more steps.

These challenges are meaningful for the child and are complex, requiring problem solving and creative thinking rather than an outcome that can only be judged right or wrong. Angela Anning in Chapter 1 of this book highlights the need for a different perception of the curriculum in this way. In striving to achieve these self-set tasks children come to understand the limits of the resources and gain confidence to manage their own learning in that environment. The outdoors therefore is supporting what Craft (2002: 1) describes as 'little c creativity' and 'lifewide resourcefulness', which underpin more formal approaches to learning and managing one's life.

Increased cooperation has been observed particularly in two areas: the use of wheeled toys and the care of the garden. Previous research at the centre (Harding 1999) identified children's use of wheeled toys as being an area of concern. They often seem to be the refuge of those who have limited oral skills because it is possible to enjoy such toys without having to interact with another person. They also allow children to explore and enjoy self-generated speed. In the pedagogic garden there is a textured path with both slopes and cambers which offers a range of surfaces – including fords over streams and bumps and humps in the path – grass, concrete, gravel and a soft surfaced area. The concrete path has planters arranged in such a way that wheeled vehicles cannot coast down the slope but must be manoeuvred carefully around the obstacles of lavender beds.

Real and meaningful tasks for children

Maintenance of the garden and cultivation of simple crops gives the opportunity for children to take part in real and meaningful tasks (see Tina Bruce's discussion in Chapter 18 of this book). As Carr (2001:

167–72) found in the 'gate project', these real tasks give opportunities for authentic questions, collaboration and the co-construction of ideas between children and adults. For example, a large delivery of bark mulch was made by lorry to the garden and dumped in the middle. For the next week staff and children spent hours digging, transporting and spreading the mulch around trees and shrubs. On another occasion children worked hard and with enthusiasm to help an adult cutting down weeds; he was beset by helpers cutting, hoeing and transporting weeds to the compost heap. There are many opportunities for adults to model activities, for the children to imitate and at the same time to contribute to the development and maintenance of the garden. This model of the adult role is acknowledged in Steiner Waldorf education in that it supports positive social skills and the development of self-identity and self-esteem (Oldfield 2001: 61–9).

The outdoor area, because of its size and the varieties of space it provides, also offers very good opportunities for solitude. For some children the furniture, noise, enclosed space and busyness of the classroom limits their access to quiet space in which they can be actively engaged in imagining, representing and exploring – or just being quietly alone. The importance of a place for solitude in terms of the development of the imagination and in allowing for changes of mental attitude is outlined by Storr (1989). The outdoor area is able to provide solitude and tranquillity because of its space, location (surrounded by gardens and a playing field) and openness to the sky.

Children making connections

A recurring theme in adults' observations of the children is the importance of making connections. This is shown in the child who saw clouds outside and then connected them to those he saw projected on to a wall indoors. In the case of Sophie, an observer wrote that she appeared:

> . . . very involved in making connections between her new experiences in the garden and what she already knew. For example, she accidentally hit a dandelion clock and was very interested in watching the seeds fly away. She attracted the adult's attention and said 'Look, look', and then 'Flower fly.' A few seconds later she said 'Bubbles', demonstrating that she had made the connection between the seeds flying and bubbles flying in her previous experience.

Rather than bringing the inside out or the outside in, practitioners need to highlight the relevant and meaningful connections between them. One way to do this is through using music and story inside and out, by reading the same stories in both contexts and by actually using the physical landscape to follow and imitate the journey in a story like *We're Going on a Bear*

Hunt (Rosen and Oxenbury 1993). It is useful to repeat activities with the children outside and inside to make the connections so they can see and feel the differences. It is certainly more difficult to manage the water xylophone indoors!

Exploring boundaries

The outdoor area allows for a greater degree of self-challenge and self-management in play (see also Bernadette Duffy's account in Chapter 13 of this book). Because of the size and nature of the vegetation and topography of the space, adults are not always able to be in close proximity to the children and this allows them a degree of autonomy not enjoyed indoors. Opportunities to explore the bounds of the resources where adults have to observe rather than physically intervene has created an opportunity for the children to develop strategies to manage themselves and the resources safely, as we saw in the example of Brandon and Tom. This has been assisted by the determination of staff to stand back and observe how the children manage their own experiences rather than to intervene, as in the case of Karen.

Case study: Karen

Karen is outside. She has the hose and is watering the 'baby' garden. She is surrounded by a group of four other children. The wind is blowing strongly and the shower from the spray is blown across the area. The wind catches the spray and blows it over Karen. One of the children, Linda, runs off and returns dressed in a water apron. She stands and waits patiently for a turn. Karen turns around and sees Linda has an apron on and asks for one for herself. Linda rushes off and returns with four more aprons – enough for the whole group of bystanders who are all protected from the wind-blown spray.

Opportunities for release, celebration, using their own voices and exploring the limits of their own bodies are also vital. Being able to run, skip, shout, scream and yell without harming, frightening or upsetting others is a great facility of the outdoors. It provides for emotional release and an understanding of children's own strengths and capabilities as in Mary's case. Mary had been having a difficult time at home and her way of expressing her discomfort was to make very loud sounds. These were not directed communications but intense releases of energy. Indoors this often alarmed other children because of the unexpectedness of the out-bursts but outside Mary could be as energetic and loud as she wished without upsetting her peers. After a few weeks her need for this mode of release lessened and she was able to develop communication that was more direct, using words, with adults and peers.

Supporting children's tactile and physical learning

As we have seen, outdoor provision supports physical learning in a very different way from the classroom, allowing for a greater diversity of tactile and aural experiences. The vegetation provides infinite and changing opportunities to experience and discover anything from prickly thistles to downy grasses and rough bark. The variety of surfaces for play allows for a more immediate understanding of materials and of how children's own bodies respond to them, as in the following example.

Case study: Tony and Kara

Tony and Kara like splashing in the puddles and exploring the water. They decide to wade through the rill (a small man-made stream) to see how deep it is. This is such fun that they try crawling through the rill and at the end of their crawl they sit down, lying across the stream, feeling the water flow around and over their bodies. For the next week they take great delight each day in repeating this sequence.

Outside there are increased opportunities for climbing, rolling, swinging, balancing and running, which provide a broader and more concrete experience of exploring space safely. Through daily opportunities children exercise their whole bodies to build up an increasing physical robustness, strength and control (as Peter Smith emphasizes in Chapter 9 of this book) while at the same time exploring concepts of space, height, width, distance and proximity (Davies 1995). These scientific and mathematical concepts relate well to those written about by Howe and Davies, and Griffiths, in Chapters 11 and 12 of this book respectively.

The adults' developing role in the garden

Among the staff there is often a personal/emotional response to the garden which focuses around words such as 'magical', 'tranquil' and 'relaxed'. Colleagues' comments on the garden give evidence of this:

The garden is extremely tranquil. I feel very relaxed here . . .
I love the peace and quietness of the garden . . .

On the day we had to close because of the snow, I went outside and made new footprints in the snow and climbed to the top of the Magic Mountain. The garden looked magical and the stillness and quiet was very noticeable.

These responses are related to the expanse of space on the ground and above in the sky, the predominance of 'natural' sound over noise and the organic nature of the forms and shapes that combine to create the landscape of the pedagogic garden.

Linked to this experience of peace and tranquillity is the spiritual nature of experiences in the outdoors. For me this is especially true of the experience in the snow or standing on top of the 'magic mountain'. Other staff have also articulated this – 'I find the outdoors very restful. For me it's about enjoying the space and tranquillity. I think I project this in my manner and enjoyment of strolling about and enjoying the environment.' This role of modelling an enjoyment of the space and tranquillity of the environment is an important one and brings to mind Froebel's reflection on spirituality and nature.

Therefore the Human-being, and especially in Boyhood, should be made intimately acquainted with Nature; not in her Particulars, the Forms of her Phenomena only, but in the Spirit of God as it lives and moves in Nature. The boy feels this deeply, and desires it; therefore Nothing so binds together Educator and Pupils, whose feelings are unspoiled, as their being occupied in common with Nature . . .

(Froebel, in Hereford 1901: 75)

The impact of space and structures

The size of the outdoor area changes the nature of communication and is much more dependent on non-verbal forms to convey messages across distances. Gesture and volume are more important in this context than facial expression or a large vocabulary. This benefits our community as it acknowledges a local strength, as research (Harding 2000) has shown that non-verbal strategies are often used in preference to verbal ones. This gives the adults more opportunities to model a wider range of communicative strategies and also allows those who need to express their emotions through loud sounds a space to do this without upsetting other people, as we saw with Mary.

Children really enjoy an area at the back of the garden they have named 'the house'. It is a bark-covered area where there are logs with small areas scooped out to make seats for the children. It often attracts children in pairs or occasionally threesomes as it is out of the way so that they can play away from the adult gaze. The children have especially enjoyed the gate to this area. In a discussion with the contractor who built the structures, he revealed that there are often safety issues for the adults around structures that move and yet these are often the most popular for children. In response to the popularity of our gate we commissioned another sort of gate opposite the first to complement it. This is in the style of a 'kissing gate', a gate set in a U-shaped enclosure that allows only one person to pass through at a time. We hope this will provide and promote opportunities for social discussion, problem solving and increased communication. Adults need to consider ways of incorporating safe moving structures into the garden to allow children to explore how things can be constructed to allow for movement.

Supporting learning

Observations and anecdotal evidence have produced conflicting impressions around the level of adult intervention and adult presence with which children feel comfortable, echoed in Neil Kitson's work in Chapter 8 of this book. While the garden was in the process of enlargement, adults observed that children wanted to be where they could see an adult and that they moved around the garden as the adult moved. In research conducted at the centre (Harding 2004; Thomas 2004) one child, when asked what he would like the adults to do in the garden, said 'Look at me on the slide', corroborating this idea. Other responses to this question indicated that children enjoyed being on their own in a variety of outdoor areas and activities.

There seem to be a complexity of factors influencing when children like to explore on their own and when they want adult support. Home and parental expectations may affect how confident and autonomous a child might be in exploring the outdoors independently (Dowling 2000: 33–40). This underlines the importance of the dialogue between home and school to inform observations made by staff of children. Familiarity with the environment and feeling safe and secure with the adults in the setting so that they feel happy and enabled to challenge themselves are other factors that affect children's confidence in a new environment (Roberts 1995: 80–1). Alternatively, children may see the adult's presence as desirable because the adult, by explaining, commentating, orchestrating (Claxton and Carr 2004: 94) and making connections, is able to enhance, extend and make their play more meaningful.

A safe garden

The historical idea of 'play time' as a special time to let off steam (Spencer 1898), separate from the time of learning, and the present emphasis on risk associated with legal liability has led to a view of the adult as a supervisor, which we have struggled with but which still informs some individuals practice.

As a staff group we have made an effort to observe before creating rules so that any restrictions on use of the garden come from observed risks rather than perceived risk. As a result of this, during the development of the garden there has been a shift away from adults wanting to 'supervise' and concerns around physical safety to a more stand back and wait approach to observe how the children are self-managing and self-regulating. This has been cultivated by using a risk assessment procedure to document and address actual and perceived risks as they occur. By using a Leadership Research Bursary (Harding 2004 and Thomas 2004) we have been able to create opportunities for all staff to voice their observations, feelings and thoughts and to make all feel that they are actively part of the development of the garden.

Management of the new space is daunting but not overwhelming. Staff have developed strategies that combine some of the 'supervisory' role with their role as observers, documenters and facilitators. This has meant nurturing a habit of waiting to see if the child can find his or her own solution to a problem before intervening (see Vea Vecchi in Edwards *et al.* 1998: 188 for a description of a similar dilemma). An illustration of how attitudes have changed is that originally we thought all staff would have to carry walkie-talkies and each individual would carry around a first aid bag when outdoors. As the adults have managed the expanded area they have developed strategies, assisted by its thoughtful design, to support learning in a safe but challenging and stimulating way. For me, with familiarity and growing confidence, the pedagogic garden has diminished in size and does not feel nearly as big or at all daunting.

Support from experts

Because the garden is so rich but also so detailed it is useful to have experts to support in terms of knowledge and skills and to model for the adults and the children. To accommodate this we have engaged environmentalists regularly to support the staff and children in the management of the environment and in exploring the many habitats for wildlife. We also have the support of a musician and music educationalist through the ELM Music Project to model for us how to support children's spontaneous musical play and how to use sound makers and instruments outdoors, and we have also developed planned activities that use the outdoors as a source of inspiration and creativity. (More ideas for music education can be found in Chapter 14 of this book).

In the future, it is hoped that the benefits from observing, exploring and interacting in the garden will impact on how the adults perceive their role indoors especially in terms of observing and facilitating rather than intervening and directing. We want to be sure that we can continue to construct an environment that is informed by the mixture of flexibility and challenge that is found in the pedagogic garden.

Questions to set you thinking

1 How can we share with parents the benefits of the outdoor learning environment?
2 How can we help children make meaningful connections between the outdoor and indoor learning environments?
3 How can we support children to self-manage and assess risks?
4 How can we overcome our inclinations to supervise outdoor learning rather than to document and facilitate it?

11 | Science and play

Alan Howe and Dan Davies

Summary

In this chapter we explore ways in which young children learn scientific concepts, attitudes and skills through play and how science can contribute to a rich early years curriculum. We focus on a number of key ideas including the relevance of recent research into children's cognitive development, the role of the practitioner, science in the Foundation Stage and how assessment can inform planning of an appropriate play-based curriculum. We offer practical advice for the practitioner on how to promote children's scientific learning, based on principles that emerge from theories about how children learn through play. We begin by discussing these theories.

Introduction: children's scientific learning

Bruce (1994) identifies three main views of childhood that have informed educational thought through the last century: empiricism, nativism and interactionism (see also Chapter 18 of this book). The empiricist view is essentially a deficit model of childhood that emphasizes gaps in knowledge and skills, which teachers need to 'fill'. This notion of 'filling gaps' has been prevalent in much science education to date. Nativism suggests that children's development is biologically pre-programmed and there is little that educators can do, so we believe that an interactionist account offers keener insights into children as scientists. This account (Norman 1978) explains children's development in terms of interactions between their own mental structures, the environment and the ideas of other people.

This interactionist account of development is consistent with the prevalent social-constructivist perspective of learning in science. Social-constructivism draws particularly on the work of Bruner and Vygotsky to explain that learning in science depends on what learners already know and how they can build on this through social interaction with others. These existing concepts are likely to be 'alternative' to the 'scientifically correct' view but provide children with sufficient working understanding for their needs. (See also Tina Bruce's examples in Chapter 18 of this book.) For example, a child may think a puddle 'disappears' during a warm day because it soaks into the tarmac, rather than have any concept of evaporation. It is these alternative frameworks (Driver 1983) that provide the foundation for future learning. The role of the adult is crucial in this account of learning; the child will learn in a social context and interactions with 'more knowledgeable' people will be vital encounters along the way to scientific learning.

Play and the scientific brain

Much is made of the supposed gulf between the sciences and the arts (Snow 1959) with its apparent validation in 'left brain–right brain' thinking patterns. As adults, we often define ourselves in these categories, excusing ourselves from grappling with 'hard' scientific concepts because we 'haven't got a scientific brain'. Are these differences biological and immutable (our 'nativist' model above) or is the situation more complex than that? Recent studies of the brain (e.g. Greenfield 2000) and of the ways that computers appear to 'think' and solve problems ('artificial intelligence') have led to sophisticated 'network' models of learning (Gardner 1999b). In such models, the brain behaves like a 'wet' computer, forging links between neurons to increase the number of pathways along which electrical signals can travel – our 'parallel processing' capacity.

When we think, patterns of electrical activity move in complex ways around our cerebral cortex, using the connections we have previously made through learning. This has clear relevance for children as scientists, since it is the ability to make links between apparently unrelated ideas (e.g. the motion of the planets and a falling apple) that lies at the heart of both creativity and understanding (Howe *et al.* 2001; Duffy and Pound, Chapters 13 and 14 of this book respectively). As children explore materials and physical or biological phenomena through play, physical changes are actually occurring in their brains! The more of the right kinds of experience they have, the more complex their neural networks will become, but conversely these connections can decay or atrophy through lack of stimulation – 'use it or lose it'!

Every time children pick up, squash, slide or roll objects, arrange them in lines or build them into towers, they are exercising those parts of their brains concerned with spatial and logical-mathematical thought (Gardner 1983); they are *being* scientists. Some may be better at it than others (aspects of our brains concerned with space and logic may be 'pre-programmed' to an extent) but the incredible plasticity of young children's nervous systems means that all can improve. The role of 'emotional encoding' (Gardner 1999a) here is crucial; children need to feel good about themselves in order to learn and the emotions are just as fundamental to the functioning of the brain as is 'logical' thought. Many scientists – unlike their stereotype – will admit an emotional content to their work; a scientific theory 'feels right', and the emotional energy needed to overcome setbacks is sometimes immense. Since play is a low-risk, inherently enjoyable activity, the associated emotional encoding will tend to be positive. With the requisite play experiences, there is no reason why any child cannot develop a 'scientific brain'.

Photograph 11.1   With the requisite play experiences, there is no reason why any child cannot develop a 'scientific brain'

Exploring the practitioner's roles in enabling 'scientific' play

Perhaps the first stage in enabling the sorts of play likely to lead towards the development of scientific learning is to recognize where in our settings science may be going on. Our definitions of science may be too narrow! If, from our own educational experience, we see science as a factual body of knowledge about the world, concerned with laws and formulae and 'discovered' through complex experiments, we will find it difficult to recognize the scientific significance of 4-year-olds pushing each other around on wheeled toys, as detailed by Harding in Chapter 10 of this book. If, on the other hand, we regard scientific knowledge as shifting and tentative – inherently rooted in the 'here and now' of everyday things and events – early years science will appear as a natural component of young children's play. The images we have of science in the world beyond the classroom will inevitably affect our attitudes towards children's scientific activity, and will in turn be transmitted to the children with whom we work (Harlen 2000).

Many activities in which young children spontaneously engage are intrinsically scientific: blowing bubbles, playing with sand and water, and looking at flowers or spiders' webs. For some children many important early experiences will be gained at home, whilst for others, early years settings must provide them with the first opportunities to explore materials, resources and ideas. This observation suggests a principle for early years science – that it should build on children's existing experiences and understanding and that using 'everyday' resources in new ways will provide a bridge between learning at home and at school.

Photograph 11.2   Using 'everyday' resources in new ways will provide a bridge between learning at home and at school

Scientific processes (exploration, observation, asking questions, trying things out) are very important aspects of early years science. Indeed, we would argue that the younger the child, the greater the emphasis on the *procedural* ('doing') aspect, in comparison with the *conceptual* ('understanding') components of scientific learning. Not that we would wish to separate these elements; for young children doing is intimately bound up with knowing, and both depend fundamentally upon the development of scientific *attitudes*. Children's emotional disposition towards learning and their responses to natural phenomena can serve as the starting points for developing the attitudes of curiosity, open-mindedness and respect for evidence.

Recognizing science in play needs to be a shared understanding across the setting. Teaching staff, nursery nurses and classroom assistants need to meet as a team to identify the areas and activities where science is already happening. A typical list might look something like this:

Activity	Scientific learning
Water play	Forces, gravity, buoyancy, density, flow, capacity, surface tension, light, colour, reflection
Sand play	Forces, properties of materials, flow, mixtures, evaporation
Malleable materials	Forces, properties of materials, drying, plasticity
Dolls	Human body, nutrition (if feeding), evaporation (if washing clothes)
Construction	Colour, forces, movement, friction
Musical play	Sound, vibrations, and properties of materials
Role play	Human body (hospital, dentist), mass, nutrition (shop), mixing materials (kitchen)
Cooking	Materials, nutrition
Outdoor play	Forces (large apparatus, wheeled toys), ecosystems, habitats (playing in natural environment), light, shadows

Potentially one of the most scientific parts of any early years setting is the role-play area. Even if this is set up as a traditional 'home' environment children can explore the properties of liquids and solids in the 'kitchen' – mixing and moulding, washing and drying. However, when we involve children in setting up the role-play area we can provide a genuine context for creative thinking, planning and action as they decide with their teacher what the new space might become and how it might be organized. The notion that, simply by providing a set of resources within a stimulating environment, children will spontaneously 'discover' scientific principles has been discredited (Harlen 2000). Even non-directed, child-initiated activities need to be part of a carefully planned sequence, and the value of any experience we set up should be judged on the basis of its potential future pathways. For example, a water tray activity in which carefully chosen objects float at different levels may be more productive than one in which all have equal buoyancy, depending on the prior experience and observation skills of the children.

Most scientific play in early years settings falls under the general heading of 'exploration' (Foulds *et al.* 1992; Johnston 1996). Exploration can take different forms; all of it is carefully planned and provided for by the practitioner, but the degree of focus and structure can vary as implied by the following terms:

- 'free' exploration (child-initiated, adults may join in to play alongside);
- 'guided' exploration (either child- or adult-initiated, in which the adult intervenes to question and suggest ways forward);
- 'structured' exploration (adult-initiated, with deliberate scaffolding of scientific skills, concepts or attitudes).

Even within apparently 'free' exploration, there is a role for the practitioner to '. . . feed spontaneous structures with content, not necessarily found at home, or in the street or playground' (Athey 1990: 41). David (1999) reminds us that careful questioning, explaining and telling are not inconsistent with play as the main 'vehicle', though Bruce (1994) warns against using all play as an excuse for adult input. Playing with children can have several purposes (Edgington 1998):

- to encourage imitation (e.g. to demonstrate appropriate use of equipment);
- to broaden knowledge (e.g. sitting in the dentist's chair and asking: 'Can you look at my filling?');
- to challenge and extend thinking (e.g. by introducing incongruity as discussed by Neil Kitson in Chapter 8 of this book).

The *types* of talk we use when intervening in play are important (as indicated by both Jane Hislam and Neil Kitson in chapters 7 and 8 of this book respectively). Sigel (1993) suggested that certain types of talk, referred to as 'distancing strategies', are better at producing mental conflict or 'disequilibrium' than are other types. Disequilibrium might seem like a strange objective for adults intervening in play – surely inducing mental conflict is likely to destroy the play by spoiling the child's enjoyment? This is certainly a possibility, but we need to remember that children learn by having their existing concepts challenged, a process Piaget (1929) described as 'accommodation'. For example, a child playing with model farm animals who has grouped them into two fields – 'animals' and 'ducks' – may have to redefine their classification when the participating adult asks 'can my hen join your animals?' Of course, the child may spontaneously have to rethink his or her classification of animals through the play, but the adult as a 'more knowledgeable other' can scaffold this step through a deliberate action within the play scenario, potentially leading to sustained shared thinking about whether a hen is an animal, a duck or some new category of living creature.

Science and the Foundation Stage

In their analysis of the *Curriculum Guidance for the Foundation Stage* (QCA/ DfEE 2000), Siraj-Blatchford and Siraj-Blatchford (2001) find that the document supports the idea that practitioners should make effective use of unexpected and unforeseen opportunities for children's learning and that there is a general acceptance of the appropriateness of 'emergent learning'. This is good news for early years science educators who believe that the best science begins with children's curiosity and that therefore the child's interests should determine the content. This is consistent with the fact that the curriculum guidance does not state *which* specific scientific knowledge is to be gained during the Foundation Stage and this, in our opinion, is to be applauded.

It is also appropriate that science is not a 'subject' in the *Curriculum Guidance for the Foundation Stage*. It is often said as a kind of shorthand that 'science is *in* Knowledge and Understanding of the World'. This is a reference to the sentence in the Guidance that states that 'Knowledge and Understanding of the World forms the foundation for later work in science, design and technology, history, geography, and ICT' (QCA/DfEE 2000: 82). However, in our view there is not a straightforward correlation between 'subjects' and 'areas of learning'. As we shall see below, science-based experiences can provide appropriate contexts for all areas of learning whilst experiences from *all* areas of learning contribute towards later work in science.

There is a close relationship between *communication, language and literacy* and science. Black and Hughes (2003) suggest that the construction and use of narrative is a vital part of coming to understand the world. Scientific understanding has been passed down through cultures by making use of narrative. This approach is ideally suited to Foundation Stage practice, where children encounter stories, songs, rhymes, fantasy and scientific phenomena daily. Children can be encouraged to tell the story of what they have done, what they have found out or what they plan to do. They can play with new language that they learn (the names of dinosaurs or trees) or invent vocabulary to describe the properties of materials. In turn they can be told stories about how things came to be as they are. Practitioners need not worry if the stories are 'correct' or fantasy. There is still plenty of debate about 'how the zebra got its stripes' amongst biologists. More importantly, children will wish to follow up stories with their own questions or play around with their own ideas; this is the beginning of the scientific skill of hypothesizing, as well as developing their language abilities, as outlined in Chapters 4 and 5 of this book by Whitebread and Jameson, and Broadhead and English, respectively.

Science and *mathematical development* can be combined by using the learning potential from collections of objects that lend themselves to description and classification; central to science at all levels. Such collections should include natural materials for children to explore. In Reggio

Emilia settings, one principle is that children have access to real materials at all times. Children are not given miniature, sanitized versions of the real world, but are immersed in the real world just as it is. Brightly coloured 'play dough' bears little resemblance to clay; plastic food is nothing like the real thing. 'Through natural playthings children come to learn about the world of which they are part, rather than forever be at a rehearsal of it' (Howe 2004: 2). A collection of pebbles or shells or sticks carefully selected to include a range of shapes, sizes, textures or colours will lend themselves to individual and small-group play. This way of guiding play could be seen as an extension of the 'heuristic play' approach of providing 'treasure baskets' of natural objects – stones, bones, fruits, feathers and so on. Children may want to order the objects in patterns, line them up, roll or rotate them or make them into pictures dependent on their schematic interests (Nutbrown 1999). These actions will lead to the development of ideas about shape, space, colour, cause and effect. Different collections will appeal to different interests – papers and flexible materials for wrapping, mechanical toys for cause and effect schemas – so variety of provision is essential. Productive adult questions can also emerge from the children's actions: 'I wonder what would happen if . . .'; 'I wonder if all these will behave in the same way. . .'; 'I wonder if this object could be bent, folded, stretched . . .'. Observant practitioners can then extend these questions through intervention – by showing what else an object or material can do, or tests that could be performed to find the hardest, softest, stretchiest or fastest. Cause and effect can be articulated: 'So when you do that . . . look what happens to this!' Communication skills and specialist vocabulary will emerge from such activities.

Sorting games may be an appropriate next step to developing children's mathematical reasoning through the use of scientific collections (see also Rose Griffiths's suggestions in Chapter 12 of this book). Sorting can also be used to develop questioning skills and as a way of introducing children to concept areas of science such as the properties of materials where children are encouraged to test for the criterion they suggest. For example, does it float or sink; is it hard or soft; is it magnetic? Of course, children may not articulate their ideas in quite this way. Less curious children may be encouraged to sort objects by a practitioner modelling this behaviour. Figure 11.1 shows some suggestions for sorting games that may provide meaningful contexts for work with materials.

Children's *physical development* can be considered at fine-motor and gross-motor levels, as outlined by Peter Smith in Chapter 9 of this book. Science contexts offer considerable scope for the development of both. When children are 'playing the scientist game' (see below) they will be taught to use special equipment such as magnifying glasses, 'bug boxes', 'pooters' (a tool for collecting insects and the like), liquid droppers and cameras. When exploring objects children will improve their dexterity and learn new skills, such as sieving, pouring, mixing, cooking and constructing.

These games can be played with a collection of packaging: the collection can be added to by the class but should include items that are made from card, paper, metal, wood, plastic.

Games should begin after all the children have had a chance to handle each object.

1. **Where Shall I Put It?** The practitioner begins by handling and sorting the collection, perhaps to 'tidy-up'. S/he may need help to decide whether an object should go in this group or that. S/he may make mistakes that the children could help correct.

2. **It's a Mystery:** Put one object from the collection into a 'feely bag' or closed box without giving the children a chance to see which it is. Pass the box round the children and give them the opportunity to feel, shake and listen before asking one question about its hidden contents. A small group each with a box ensures the children's interest is maintained. Even if the object is identified, carry on allowing everyone to make up his or her mind.

3. **Give Us a Clue:** An adult selects an object in their mind from a collection but does not reveal the choice. S/he provides clues one at a time until children identify the object.

4. **Domino Game:** This can be used to identify similarities or differences (differences are easier to begin with). Each child holds an object from a collection. One child is asked to place his or her object on the floor; the others are then asked if their object is different in any way from the object on the floor. One child is asked to place their object alongside the first and say why his/her object is different. (This is hard and that is soft, etc.). The process continues until all objects are on the floor. The game can also be played like traditional dominoes, where two items are placed end to end because they are similar (e.g. both are red, both are hard, both are made from plastic). This continues until a linked chain of objects have been placed on the floor.

Figure 11.1   Science games with collections of materials

Stevens (2002) outlines a number of activities for children to do on a windy day that will encourage gross motor skills and full-body activity. She suggests that a 'windy day box' might include assorted streamers, windmills, balloons and pumps. This idea can be extended by the provision of 'weather boxes' that contain resources to encourage outdoor play whatever the weather (see Figure 11.2).

The *Curriculum Guidance for the Foundation Stage* has a number of references to children working outdoors. It is suggested that practitioners 'make good use of outdoor space so that children are enabled to learn by working on a larger, more active scale than is possible indoors' (QCA/ DfEE 2000: 15). Both Peter Smith and Stephanie Harding show in Chapters 9 and 10 of this book the value of outdoor, physical play.

Sunny day box

Chalk for drawing around shadows

Silhouettes or shadow puppets

Brushes and water for painting

Washing lines, pegs and washing

Sunglasses and hats (N.B. never allow children to look at the sun)

Transparent and opaque materials

Windy day box

Washing lines, pegs and washing

Streamers of cellophane, string/wool

Windsocks

Windmills

Balloons

Parachuted toys

Kites

Rainy day box

Washing lines, pegs and washing

Rain catchers/ rain gauges

Umbrellas

Solids to sprinkle (talc, flour, paint, salt)

Absorbent and waterproof papers and objects

Figure 11.2   Weather boxes

Planning in a regular time when children are taken outside to explore an aspect of the environment can ensure this. One important reason for making time for outdoor play is the contribution it will make to children's developing sense of place. This in turn will lay foundations for children to develop an appreciation and understanding of the natural world.

Play is widely associated with children's *creative development* (Claxton 1999; Howe *et al.* 2001; Robinson 2001). Scientific knowledge can also be developed in the mix between creativity and play. Much of children's creativity will begin with an interaction with resources and spaces (see Bernadette Duffy's observations in Chapter 13 of this book). Sand, water, construction kits, recycled materials, bits and pieces of all shapes and sizes will elicit creative activity and scientific learning. By providing new

Photograph 11.3   Science contexts offer considerable scope for the development of both fine and gross motor skills

resources children can be encouraged to play in a new way and find out new things about the world. For example, water provided for play can be warm, cold, icy, frozen, bubbly, coloured or perfumed, whilst sand can be supplemented with a wide range of tools and toys or replaced by other materials such as leaves or compost. Art materials lend themselves to a number of scientific explorations. For example, working with clay can lead children to discoveries about reversible and irreversible change; wax resist techniques (e.g. painting with cooking oil and powder colour wash) can reveal that oil and water will not mix; drawing and painting on different surfaces and papers can demonstrate absorbency properties.

Transition to Key Stage 1

It is of course a mistake to regard children's early experiences as merely a preparation for later learning (see discussion by Fabian and Dunlop in Chapter 16 of this book). However, we should acknowledge that a smooth transition from scientific exploration to enquiry is desirable, provided children do not lose their playfulness in the process (Johnston 1996). As children move into Key Stage 1, their motor skills will become finer so they can begin to be introduced to appropriate equipment for observation and measurement (hand lenses, balances, timers). Their thinking skills will also become more sharply defined and sequenced: the beginnings of what the National Curriculum describes as scientific enquiry. Particularly for young children, activities focused upon one or two skills, such as observing a spider carefully, are likely to be more developmentally appropriate than 'fair-test' type investigations that may be very time-consuming and teacher-intensive.

In developing young children's scientific observation skills we need to remember that observing has a strong cognitive element (Nicholls 1999) – what we see is determined by what we know. Children may differ from adults in which aspects of an observed object they consider to be important (e.g. focus on a part of a flower that 'looks like a face' rather than the anther and stigma) or bring in other information (e.g. pictures from storybooks). Whilst we may wish to draw children's attention to particular features that we consider of interest it is important not to override their more imaginative approaches to observation. Scientific observation can be about the whole shape, form or outline of an object, not just specific details. It is also not just about looking; there should be opportunities for children to explore tactile properties and use their other senses (with regard to health and safety considerations!).

Once children have had plenty of experience of guided and structured exploration, we can begin to 'scaffold' their planning of a scientific enquiry by 'playing the scientist game' (Siraj-Blatchford and MacLeod-Brudenell 1999). If children can take on the roles of scientists – whilst avoiding stereotyped accessories such as white coats – they are more likely to become engaged with the enquiry and see it as relevant to their lives. The scientist game then involves a set of 'rules' or steps to be followed. Goldsworthy and Feasey (1997) introduced a technique for teachers to model planning an enquiry, involving a brainstorm of factors that could be changed (variables) jotted onto 'Post-it' notes, which children then select from and transfer to sheets which help them to structure a question, prediction, recording table and chart. Versions of this technique aimed at young children have been developed by Devon Curriculum Services (1998), using shapes or symbols to denote particular thinking skills or phases of the planning process. Our ideas for shapes that symbolize the different stages of an enquiry are shown in Figure 11.3.

The shapes we have used for each stage are intended to convey something of what that particular thinking skill involves, which should appeal to visual learners. Other shapes can be used, but it is important to maintain consistency throughout the setting so children become familiar with the activity denoted by each symbol. Some teachers make a display or mobile of the shapes for the classroom, or even use giant versions on the floor for children to move between when playing the scientist game. 'I've moved to the think cloud so now I'm predicting what will happen' is a kinaesthetic way of remembering the process.

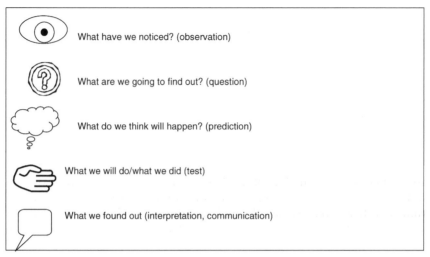

Figure 11.3   Shapes that symbolize the different stages of a science enquiry

Gender differences in scientific play

Girls and boys may be acquiring different scientific ideas through gendered play. Through their recreation of domestic and medical scenarios in
the role-play area, girls may be learning more about biological and – to an
extent – chemical concepts (e.g. mixing, drying and changing through
heat). In this respect boys may be disadvantaged: Walkerdine (1997) has
observed that boys clearly do not feel at home in domestic imaginative
situations, as girls have the controlling hand, and that girls are more likely
to treat 'work' activities as play, so classrooms tend to be more geared
towards their interests. However, since early years practitioners may not
recognize the role-play activities as 'science' there is, conversely, the risk
that girls feel disengaged from scientific learning.

Boys, on the other hand, may be developing more understanding of
forces and movement through their domination of construction activities
and wheeled toys in the outdoor area. Girls, when playing outdoors, tend
not to modify the toys or equipment as boys do, and prefer to use fixed
rather than moveable features (Walkerdine 1997). Because this physical
and constructional play is perhaps more obviously 'scientific', practitioners may inadvertently convey the message that science is a 'boys'' area
of the curriculum. So, girls are disenfranchised from physical sciences – an
inequality which shows up significantly in secondary education – whereas
boys may be more generally disadvantaged in the educational setting,
since the (predominantly female) staff appear to show little interest in the
areas boys enjoy (Davies 1991).

In order to introduce greater gender equality into children's scientific play, we need a two-pronged approach. For girls, we need both to validate the science content of their existing play, and enable them to access those areas of play which may tend to have been dominated by boys:

Helping girls recognise their scientific understanding within applications where they have confidence, gives these activities status and also provides a basis for enabling them to transfer their knowledge to other contexts which may lie within 'male' domains.

(Browne and Ross 1991)

So, once girls have learned to recognize themselves as scientists when playing 'doctors and nurses' they can be encouraged to 'be scientific' in areas such as construction play. This is where the second part of our strategy needs to come into play, because unless practitioners appear to value construction activities, through making with children and celebrating the outcomes, girls will not see the activity as worthwhile and boys will feel that their interests are being marginalized. So paying attention to construction actually benefits both sexes. Remember the power of role models; female practitioners who demonstrate an active interest in scientific phenomena and join in with children's scientific play will both encourage the girls and validate boys' interests.

Science, play, observation and assessment

To gain a holistic overview of a child's scientific concepts, skills and attitudes, observation should be carried out over a range of science-related activities in a variety of social contexts, e.g. when the child is with an adult, a group of peers, or working independently. Sometimes the activities should be teacher-initiated as this can provide a broader range of experiences than children may encounter on their own. At other times the observed activity should be something the child has initiated herself because it is when she is fully engaged and interested that she is likely to demonstrate her most creative behaviour and deep understanding.

Angela, teaching a Reception class, had set up a display of magnets for the Reception class to explore in their first term at school. On one occasion she worked with groups of children to focus their attention on the display and assess their understanding. Angela played alongside the children whilst another adult made notes about the interactions in a 'floorbook' using a different coloured pen to record each child's ideas. Essentially, a floorbook is a large format 'home-made' book of plain pages, made of sugar paper or flip-chart paper in which an adult or the children write and draw ideas, observations, predictions, questions and explanations. With young children the book is compiled on the floor so the group can all have a good view and opportunity to contribute. It can be completed during one session or revisited during a number of sessions. In analysing the information gathered from the play with magnets afterwards it became apparent to Angela that children in the group had responded quite differently. For example, Louise made a number of comments indicating the kinds of observations she was making during her exploration:

The big magnets stick to each other.

They are wobbly (two 'polo-mint' magnets on a dowel); they won't stick.

From these and other comments it was clear that Louise was on her way to reaching the Early Learning Goals for exploration and investigation and would benefit from encouragement to find out about a wide range of things that interested her. Damien made the following observations:

When I stuck a magnet to another magnet they stuck really hard.

The can has metal on the back.

Yet most of his utterances were questions:

What happens when you spin (the magnet)?

What's under (the display) sticking to the magnet?

What happens when you slide them on each other?

These indicated to Angela that Damien was achieving the following Early Learning Goal: 'Ask questions about why things happen and how things work' (QCA/DfEE 2000: 88). She anticipated that he would benefit from support to be more systematic in his explorations in order to satisfy his curiosity.

Ellie made little comment during the session, although she was engrossed with the resources. Rather than make notes of what she said, the observer had sketched some examples of the ways in which Ellie had arranged the magnets – in 'trains' and 'ropes'. It was clear to Angela that she would need a lot of encouragement during the year to put her ideas into words and express them confidently in a group.

Another powerful tool for recording science play is the digital camera. Pictures can be taken by adults and children and used in a range of ways. Pictures can record the activities or the events that seem of interest: the tower or shadows we made, the pet that visited or the way we played. Children can review what they have made, seen or done during the day. These pictures can be shared with parents to promote a discussion about children's attitudes to science, including curiosity, perseverance and enjoyment in their scientific play.

Questions to set you thinking

1 Would a practitioner with little knowledge of science be in a position to plan appropriate provision to promote children's scientific learning?
2 Do the disadvantages of using natural materials with young children outweigh the advantages?
3 What new opportunities for scientific learning can you identify in your current planned provision?

12 Mathematics and play

Rose Griffiths

Summary

Teaching maths through play has many advantages. Play can increase the child's motivation to learn by providing sensible and enjoyable contexts, and by allowing children to direct their own learning. An emphasis on using and applying maths with young children can build the confidence of children and the adults who work with them. This chapter includes many practical examples which illustrate how this can be done and demonstrates links between children's learning at school or nursery, at home and in the world around them. Some examples were teacher-initiated, and some child-initiated. I emphasize that children need time to experiment, and to see that maths can be enjoyable and useful. Making and doing, talking and listening, with writing or drawing used in a purposeful way, provide a better route to understanding in maths than premature formal methods of working.

Introduction

To many people, mathematics and play seem to be mutually exclusive activities. As one teacher said to me, 'If I enjoy doing something, then I know it can't be maths. I was never any good at maths when I was at school. I hated it.' Like many others, she assumed that it was her own lack of ability that caused her difficulties with the subject. She had never considered the possibility that her feelings of inadequacy may have stemmed from the methods that were used to teach her.

Many people use the way they were taught as the basis of the way in which they then teach, whether in an educational setting or as part of family life. For example, my mother taught me how to tell the time as a child in an effective way, and I did the same with my children. But what about other people who have been taught in ways that have left them confused, miserable or lacking in enthusiasm? Should they use the methods by which they were taught, if they are working with children? It obviously makes little sense to do so, yet it is difficult for adults in that position to generate other useful strategies simply because they will almost certainly lack confidence in their own abilities. So a vicious cycle is perpetuated.

There are, unfortunately, many ways of teaching mathematics badly. The Cockcroft Committee (DES 1982), set up in response to concern about the standards of mathematics teaching in England and Wales, considered that many teachers used too narrow a range of both mathematical content and teaching styles. The Committee also echoed the concern of many employers and teachers that children (and adults), when faced with real-life, practical problems, often had difficulty in making effective use of the mathematical skills they actually possessed.

This emphasis on the importance of children being able to use and apply mathematics was evident in successive versions of the National Curriculum (see DfEE/QCA 1999). Subsequently, the *Curriculum Guidance for the Foundation Stage* (QCA/DfEE 2000: 69) states firmly, 'Mathematical development depends on becoming confident and competent in learning and using key skills' and expresses the view that effective teaching requires '. . . practitioners who develop children's thinking by showing an interest in methods, not just solutions' (p. 72).

Providing children with opportunities to use and apply mathematics is not always easy: it is difficult to provide 'real-life' experience within the classroom, and teachers need to be wary of presenting contexts that oversimplify the real world, without acknowledging the pretence to children. For example, I know of no shop where you can buy a teddy for a penny, but I have seen a classroom shop where this was possible. The teacher's desire to make the arithmetic manageable had undermined the link to the real world. At the same time, a child from that class was beginning to hold coins on a visit to a shop with her parent, and was struggling to understand how much money was enough to buy a teddy. This real-life problem was ignored in school (although coin recognition *was* tackled, but not with any discussion about what you could buy with each coin).

As Hughes, Desforges and Mitchell (2000: 115) state:

. . . it may be helpful for teachers to think in terms of a continuum. At one extreme, there are activities that are basically classroom exercises, and where the 'real-life' content is minimal . . . At the other extreme are activities that are firmly rooted in real life, and where the constraints of the classroom have been reduced as far as possible. In practice, activities at this end of the continuum are likely to be much messier and harder for the teacher to control: however, they may have greater value in promoting application.

How can children learn mathematics successfully through play? First, I shall explore some of the advantages of learning maths through play, and second, offer a range of examples of successful play activities that promote the development of mathematical skills and understanding.

The advantages of learning mathematics through play

There are five key factors that I believe are worth exploring: purpose and motivation; context; control and responsibility; time; and practical activity.

Purpose and motivation
All of us learn better when there is a clear purpose to what we are doing. When children (or adults) play, a clear and significant purpose is enjoyment, and fun is often sufficient to encourage us to concentrate on a task for long enough for learning to occur.

Sometimes we teach children skills and then look for ways of practising them, but sometimes it is much more effective to use problems which children are interested in, to motivate them to learn new skills in order to use them immediately (as Nigel Hall demonstrated in Chapter 6 of this book). For example, we can ask children to practise drawing straight lines with a ruler – or we can begin work on making stripey patterns, and then talk to children about improving their skills at using a ruler, to help make their patterns.

Context
One of the things which make maths a difficult subject to learn is the fact that some elements of mathematics are very abstract. Paradoxically, this abstraction is also what makes maths such a powerful tool – the same abstract piece of mathematics can be used to solve problems in many different contexts. Ways need to be found of helping children to see the links between concrete and abstract ideas (Hughes 1986). This can often be done using a starting point that makes human and practical sense to children in a context provided by play (see comments by Fabian and Dunlop in Chapter 16 of this book). A context that makes sense to children will also be one which makes sense to the staff working with them (no matter how little confidence those adults have in their own mathematical ability), and to the children's parents or carers at home.

Control and responsibility

Many adults find it much easier to encourage children to make their own decisions when they are playing than when they are in a more formal learning situation. Allowing and positively prompting children to take control of their own activity is a very important aspect of teaching mathematics. It is difficult to become more skilled at problem solving, investigating or discussion if the teacher is always telling children what to do and how to do it. Adults need to strike a balance between providing structure or direction and expecting children to take responsibility for themselves. Children who are used to organizing themselves in play and learning activities are more likely to become confident and creative mathematicians than those who are continually 'spoon-fed'.

Time

Time for mathematical play provides children with a welcome and valuable opportunity to repeat things and gain mastery over actions and ideas, to raise questions, to discuss things with their peers and to clarify ideas, free from pressure to progress too quickly to the next mathematical concept. (Time for playful and creative approaches is also a theme in Chapter 13 of this book by Bernadette Duffy.) Everyone needs time for new ideas to be assimilated. This is especially important with those aspects of maths that are hierarchical, where understanding each new idea depends on having understood its precedents.

Practical activity

Play ensures that the emphasis rests on practical activity, not written outcomes. For children to increase their mathematical understanding, it is important that their written recording should serve a purpose which is useful to each child and is linked to activity and discussion. Written recording for its own sake will not help children with understanding. As Hughes (1986: 170) asserts:

> If they cannot tell how many bricks result from adding five bricks to nine, then there is no advantage to be gained by writing down the problem as '9 + 5 =': this gets them no nearer the answer.

Thinking about these five key factors may be especially helpful for adults who do not feel very confident with maths themselves. Liz, a teacher of Year 1 children, expressed her own anxieties: 'I want to let the children learn through play, but I worry that there's not enough maths in what they are doing, so I ought to be doing something more formal.'
This raises two possibilities:

1 Adults may not always recognize the mathematics in a play-based activity, and may need time to analyse it carefully, preferably with a supportive colleague. For example, a teacher who was concerned about the mathematical value of playing with a railway layout was reassured

when she realized the children were, among other things, gaining experience of comparing distances, using straight, curved and parallel lines, discussing position and movement, using diagrams and building in three dimensions.

2 The activity may *not* provide much opportunity for mathematical learning and it may need planning again to make mathematical activity more central and more explicit. For example, a teacher who had hoped that playing in a pretend shop would lead to sorting, categorizing and counting soon realized that this was not actually happening. Although the shop was full of things to sell, there was generally only one or two of each item – unlike a real shop where, for example, there would be 10 or 20 tubs of margarine, not just one or two. The teacher increased the amount of sorting and counting the children could do by providing a larger number of a smaller range of items.

Playing *with* children obviously provides educators with time to discuss children's own ideas and, in addition, gives opportunities to share information and to teach them in a more direct way. For example, some mathematical facts are rules or agreements that people have established in the past, such as:

• We call a shape with exactly three straight sides a triangle.
• This is how we write the number five: 5.
• When we count things, we count each thing once; we don't miss any out or count any twice.

Children might eventually realize that these things are true by observing other people, but it can be more straightforward for learners to be given this kind of information as and when they need it or want it.

Some mathematical facts, however, are ones which children need to be able to work out for themselves, if they are to gain understanding and are to be convinced by them. For example:

• When we count a group of things and we do not add any or take any away, then there will still be the same number when we count them again.
• 3 add 5 makes 8.

Frequent use may lead to children knowing facts like '3 + 5 = 8' off by heart, but if they forget, they should be able to work each fact out again from scratch, because they understand the process. Play can provide the variety, repetition, motivation and interaction with peers and adults that is needed to establish both understanding and fluency in an enjoyable way.

Helping children learn mathematics through play

Play can give children the confidence to tackle quite complex ideas. The role of the teacher is to suggest new possibilities, to give information, to support children's ideas and to encourage discussion. The rest of this chapter will focus upon examples of play-based activities that were both enjoyable and mathematically useful. They include both teacher- and child-initiated activities, something emphasized throughout this book. As Siraj-Blatchford and Sylva (2004: 720) state in a report on the Researching Effective Pedagogy in the Early Years (REPEY) project:

> Our findings suggest that the most effective settings (for enhancing child development) . . . achieve a balance between the opportunities for children to benefit from teacher-initiated group work and in the provision of freely chosen, yet potentially instructive, play activities.

The examples are grouped under two main headings: *play and counting* and *play and shape and space*.

Play and counting

Learning to count groups of objects accurately takes a surprisingly long time for young children, and counting underpins children's understanding of arithmetic. For example, if a child cannot count ten objects consistently, then it makes little sense to ask her what 4 add 6 makes, since she is likely to get a different answer each time she tries this question. But as soon as a child is confident about counting a group of, say, six objects, and knows that the number will still be the same if he counts them again, then he is ready to think about any problems involving addition or subtraction within that range.

Children who are learning to count need frequent practice in a variety of contexts in which they are genuinely interested in finding out how many objects there are. There is no incentive to count accurately if you really do not care whether there are 8 or 9 counters! Children also need someone else to check their counting sometimes while they are learning, but that does not always need to be an adult.

Helicopters
Children like making things to play with. Using a piece of paper folded in half lengthways, and cut across from one long side to the middle fold to make flaps (see Figure 12.1), Shaun decided to draw helicopters. Other children drew teddies, dogs, fish, cars and babies, among other things. Shaun played with his strip by himself, with friends of the same age and with younger children in the class, and then took it home to play with his younger sister. They enjoyed taking it in turns to turn down some of the flaps and ask each other, 'How many helicopters can you see?' Sometimes

Figure 12.1   The helicopter game

they counted to get the answer; sometimes they did sums: 'Two there, and one there, that's three.' Children who made a longer strip could work with larger numbers. Whichever number they had chosen, they very quickly became familiar with the combinations of numbers which made that total.

Teddies' teatime

Children helped to set up the home corner as the bears' house, and made a variety of food for the teddies to eat. It was important to make a good quantity, so that there was enough to count when a group of children played together. The children cut cookie shapes from salt dough for their teacher to bake at a low temperature until they were hard enough to play with. Jam tarts were made in the same way, with a small-sized cutter and 'jam' painted on after they had been baked, using red or orange acrylic paint. Corrugated card became sandwiches and crackers, and a variety of beads and bricks were used to represent nuts and fruit.

Some children needed no prompting at all to count as part of their play; others only started to do so after watching and listening to the adult or other children. For example, Kerry mostly used none, one or two. 'What do you want, Blue Bear? Two cakes?' Anna set herself much more complicated tasks: 'I don't know about these jam tarts, if I can give them all five each or if there's not enough.'

Sitting with children who are playing and talking often gives us the chance to review their achievements and think about what they might benefit from doing next, in a way that is more accurate than more formal methods of assessment.

Monsters in the bath

The adult made four cards showing Monsters having a bath (see Figure 12.2). Monsters love playing with sponges, and these were made by cutting two sponge kitchen cloths (one blue, one orange) into small pieces. Children played with the cards and sponges in a variety of ways. Some children wanted time to play on their own to start with, without any suggestions from an adult or their peers. Others wanted an idea to get them started.

For counting practice, the first step was to choose a number that the child needed to practise counting. Suppose it was six. Just for the first go, the adult would count six sponges on to one card to show what was wanted. Then the child would give the other Monsters six sponges each, too. The most popular way of playing was in a pair, when each child had four Monster in the Bath cards and they rolled a dice or picked a card from a pile of number cards to choose which number to count. When they had given their own Monsters their sponges, they would count each other's to check. In the course of one turn of the game, each child had counted the practice number eight times.

Children could also make up sums for each other. 'Monster had four blue sponges and five orange ones. How many did she have altogether?' or 'Monster used to have ten sponges but she's lost two. How many has she got now?'

Figure 12.2 Monster in the bath game

Some children liked using the little sponges to wash Monster's face or to polish the bath taps, and some little sponges turned up in the bath in the dolls' house! Children liked drawing or painting pictures of Monster, and some wrote captions for their pictures or wrote on a number to say how many sponges there were. They wanted to represent the maths they had done on paper, and they did so in ways that made sense to them, which only gradually moved closer to using numerals and other symbols.

As they gained in experience, when children made up problems for each other about Monster and her sponges, they found they could solve them without needing to re-enact the whole problem. Using play-based materials had helped them imagine the scene 'in their head' – the beginnings of mental arithmetic. Using a calculator alongside their game, to check or reassure them, was also useful. It provided them with a real reason to learn to recognize each written number and the symbols +, – and =, so that they could press the right keys on the calculator, and that gave them a model to write down: for example, $2 + 3 = 5$.

Monsters in the Bath was one of a group of similar counting games, including Ladybirds in Gardens and Elephants in Blankets (Griffiths 1988, 2004).

Mobile phones and remote controls

Young children who are used to organizing themselves, taking the initiative and improvising or making props for their own play will often surprise the adults around them with their ambition, ingenuity and skill.

Gemma and Kyle (aged 4 and 5) decided to use small boxes to make 'mobile phones' and asked their teacher to show them how to write a 2, 6, 7, and 9. (Between them, they already knew how to do 0, 1, 3, 4, 5 and 8). Interestingly, Kyle positioned his numbers in the order of his mum's phone number, but Gemma realized that the numbers should go in order, 1, 2, 3 and so on. They also used calculators as pretend mobile phones, and tried hard to learn which number was which, to phone each other up. When their teacher found an old mobile case (with numbers intact), they noticed that the calculator and the mobile had their numbers in a different arrangement, and spent some time discussing whether one of them was 'wrong' or whether it did not matter what order the numbers were in. Their motivation to learn how to read and write numbers was high because they wanted to *use* them.

Dylan (aged 4) was good at number recognition. His motivation was cable television – he wanted to use the remote control to choose Channel 608, or 144, or 102. I suspect he would soon be telling the time very competently, too, as he told me, 'This programme is on again at five thirty, so I'm going out to play in the garden now, and I'll watch it later.' When he started school, would his teacher recognize the skills he already had, or would it be assumed these were things he still had to learn?

Dogs and bones

Children who have used counting games like Monsters sometimes come up with ideas of games they can make themselves (see Figure 12.3). 'Dogs and Bones' was Kelly's idea. She drew and cut out one dog, and fixed it to another piece of card so that it would stand up. Her friend Jo (aged 5 – a year younger than Kelly) made the other dog, and both children cut 'bones' from little pieces of card.

At first the children used the bones in the same ways as Monsters. Then they invented a simple new game: they took it in turns to throw a dice on behalf of each dog, and gave the dog that number of bones, so that each dog gradually accumulated more and more. Every now and then they counted to see how many bones each dog had altogether. When they ran out of bones they made some more, and only stopped playing when each dog had such a large pile that they were finding it difficult to count them.

I was keen to use Kelly and Jo's own context to explore division, using problems where they had to share different numbers of bones between the two dogs. This was prompted by watching a children's television programme where two puppets were sharing five apples between them. 'One for you and one for me. One for you and one for me. Oh, there's one left over!' said the puppet, 'What shall we do?' The 3-year-old who was watching television with me shouted excitedly 'Cut it up! Cut it up!' The puppet, sadly, ignored this possibility, and said, 'We'll have to put it back in the bowl.'

Why was the writer of this programme apparently so frightened to

Figure 12.3 Dogs and bones game

introduce halves as an obvious solution to a real problem? We should not have such low expectations of children when presenting ideas in a context that makes sense to them. Fractions may be difficult to deal with when the expectation is one of calculating with them using pencil and paper, but this does not mean we should ignore them at earlier stages.

So I talked with Kelly and Jo about sharing bones fairly between their two dogs. It was agreed that, if we had four altogether, each dog should have two bones. But what if we had five bones: how could the dogs share the extra bone? Kelly thought the dogs should just take it in turns, and have a lick each, but Jo said they wouldn't like that because they might want to crunch it up. He thought we could try hitting it on a rock, or sawing it up with an electric saw, or possibly running it over with a steam roller. Then Kelly produced scissors and snipped it in half!

The children were told that a half is written like this – ½ – and were given a blank dice with the numbers ½, 1, 1½, 2, 2½, 3 written on the faces. At first, the children counted up parts of bones separately: 'This dog's got 4 and a half and a half', so I showed them that it is possible to fit two halves together and count it as one bone. They played their Dogs and Bones game again, with adult help at first on how to say the numbers. They had no difficulty in counting out the right quantity, with the aid of scissors if appropriate. After a few sessions of playing on their own, they were happy to work out in their heads the answers to questions such as: 'If your dog had three and a half bones, and you gave him two more bones, how many bones would he have altogether?'

Board games

In theory, many board games should encourage children to count, match and follow rules. In reality, children often play these games without gaining much in terms of mathematical experience. For example, when children play in a group, those who most need counting practice frequently have their pieces moved for them by more experienced players, or they are told where to move to. If the main purpose of the game is to become the 'winner', there can even be good logical reasons for counting badly! Games where children compete against each other are often less likely to encourage them to explain things to each other, and to discuss what they are doing, than cooperative games with a common purpose.

Making up a board game for oneself can involve a considerable amount of maths but the whole process can be too daunting for children whose skills at drawing and measuring are still at an early stage. A preliminary stage of providing the children with a teacher-made blank playing board and some component play pieces can, however, produce some very interesting ideas.

Playing boards made by drawing grids with a permanent pen on pieces of plastic table covering or large pieces of card are a good start. The most popular board I have made was a rectangle of four squares by eight, where each square measured 10 cm. (One of the advantages of making your own game is that it can be made to a large scale.) The simplest way of using this board was for 'race games'. For example, four plastic people, animals or toy cars were lined up, and one or two children took turns to throw a dice and move the pieces to see which one would get to the end first.

Variations are plentiful. Using the same board, one group of children made 'ghosts' from cotton wool and had ghost races. Taking up the idea, a second group invented a new version where toy people raced, each with a ghost just behind them. For each turn, a dice was thrown twice – once for the person, once for the ghost – and the person had to try to get to the end before the ghost caught them. The children experimented with different rules to give the toy people a reasonable chance of escaping. After a great deal of discussion, they decided that giving them one extra throw of the dice to start was best.

Numbers were made for the board by writing them on separate 3 cm squares of card which children could fasten on to the main board for themselves, using Blu-tak. Sorting the numbers into order and deciding where to put them is quite challenging for many children, but it helped them understand the layout of numbers on other board games.

We used these numbers, along with cardboard cut-out snakes, and ladders made by glueing lollipop sticks together, to make our own snakes and ladders games. Before playing, agreement had to be reached as to where to fasten the snakes and ladders: it was possible to have only ladders, but the children usually decided it was more fun to have at least one snake.

Designing a board game uses many aspects of mathematics, not just number. Measurement, shape and ideas about probability are also important.

Play and shape and space

Many activities which children enjoy use shape, pattern, movement and position. Building, threading, sewing, printing, dancing and climbing are just a few examples. Children learn more when they have problems to solve than when they are just asked to name shapes or describe what someone else has done: they need to use and apply their growing mathematical knowledge.

Towers for tortoises

Katie sometimes made small piles or lines of wooden bricks, but she never seemed to be very confident or enthusiastic about building. The turning point came after she had spent some time talking about how (especially at age only 4) it is possible to see much more when you stand on a chair. At that time, Katie often played with two wooden pull-along tortoises, which we decided must sometimes get fed up, because they could only see people's ankles. Katie decided to build them a tower, to give them a different view. Katie's building now had a definite purpose, and she returned to the problem several times over the next few days. At first she did not want anyone else to copy her or help her, but then she relented and enjoyed working with other children, getting ideas from them in return. For example, she started to think about ways of making bridges so that the tortoises could get from one tower to another. She learned by trial and improvement, becoming quicker, more skilful and more imaginative with her constructions. In quite a short space of time, Katie's new confidence with wooden bricks encouraged her to be more adventurous and thoughtful with other construction toys.

Sleeping bags

Talking with a group of 5- and 6-year-olds, I discovered that they had all, at some time, slept in sleeping bags. They were very keen to take up the suggestion that they could make little pipe-cleaner people and sleeping bags for them (see Figure 12.4). When they had each made a person, we discussed sleeping bags before they started to make them. How big should they be, and what shape? They decided that a sleeping bag is cosiest if a person can stretch out and still have her shoulders covered, but it should not be so big that the person disappears completely inside it. Most sleeping

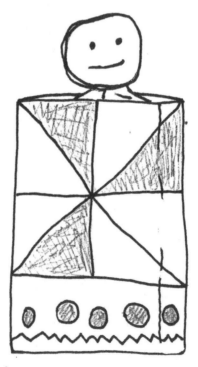

Figure 12.4   Sleeping bags game

bags that the children had seen were rectangular, and most had patterns on them.

Cutting out a rectangle proved to be more difficult than most of the children had thought it would be. Trying to judge how big to make the rectangle so that it would be the right size for their person once it was folded over was challenging, too, and called for a great deal of trial and improvement. (One child decided that changing the sleeping bag to fit the person was much too hard, so she cut her person's legs shorter instead.) The children were reminded not to fix their sleeping bags together with sticky tape until after they had decorated them. They used a variety of designs, sometimes like ones they had seen themselves. Some drew on pictures (dogs, fairies or racing cars); others did spots, stripes or geometric patterns. Some of the children made tents from folded card, or chalets from small boxes, but many preferred to make another little person and another sleeping bag, the second time much more expertly than the first. They enjoyed playing with the things they had made, and they had developed their knowledge of shape, size and pattern.

Fish and chips

It is important to remember how much children learn outside school or nursery, and how they can link their play in an educational setting with the real world.

Michelle (age 3) was playing in the 'fish and chip shop' at her nursery. When her first customer came she shovelled a portion of plastic chips onto a sheet of white paper and pulled the paper around them. As she handed them over, all the chips shot out of the front and fell to the floor. Michelle kicked them to the side with her foot, said, 'You can't eat them, they're dirty' and served another portion. This time, she wrapped the paper the other way round, and this time the chips fell out of the side. Michelle gave up at that point, and skipped off to play in the sand.

Two weeks later, I visited again and saw Michelle in the 'chip shop' again. She served a portion of chips, wrapping them diagonally side to side then rolled front to back, as though she had worked in a chip shop all her life. I talked to her mum when she came to collect Michelle. 'She's been driving me mad – we walk home past the chip shop, and I have to take her in and hold her up so she can see what the lady does, how she wraps up the chips. And she's been wrapping up her toys at home, too. I've said to her, we'll have to have pass the parcel for your birthday, won't we!' It seemed evident that Michelle had not seen her initial problem with wrapping as a 'failure', but as a prompt to find out more from an expert, and to experiment for herself.

Wrapping involves many complicated mathematical ideas which children can work on intuitively, including size, shape, surface area, position and sequencing. Michelle's teacher made sure that Michelle had a chance to talk about her new skill, and to think about *why* this way of wrapping works. As Michelle said, 'I did it before, and chips fell out because there was holes. Now I do it and they can't get out.'

Gymnastics

Sometimes children's spontaneous play from lunch or play times gives them ideas they want to pursue when they come back into the classroom. So it was with Emma and her friend who had been playing 'gymnastics' during the lunch break. Emma wanted to count up how many different gymnastics positions she had tried. She tried describing them and counting at the same time, but lost track after just two or three, and said impatiently, 'Oh, give me some paper, I'll write them down and count them.'

Representing something from real life (i.e. in three dimensions) on to paper (in two dimensions) can be quite difficult to do, but Emma managed very well. Before she did each new drawing, she checked to make sure she had not already drawn herself like that before. She numbered her drawings as she went along, and was very pleased to find 15 positions altogether (although I have my doubts about number 12 – see Figure 12.5). Emma's concentration was remarkable – except if you realized how much she wanted to know the answer to her own question.

Physical activity is an important part of learning, as Peter Smith emphasizes in Chapter 9 of this book, and, in particular, learning about shape and space – there is usually no reason to record what you do with pencil and paper. Just as with number work, children's written work in shape and space is most likely to be successful if the children can see a purpose in it for themselves. It should build on practical activity and play, and never become an end in itself.

Conclusion

Maths and play are very useful partners. If we want children to become successful mathematicians, we need to demonstrate to them that maths is enjoyable and useful, and that it can be a sociable and cooperative activity, as well as a quiet and individual one. We must be careful, too, to remember that play is not just a way of introducing simple ideas. Children will often set themselves much more difficult challenges when we give them control of their learning than if it is left to adults.

Questions to set you thinking

1 How can you support colleagues who lack confidence in teaching maths (or improve your own confidence, if needed)?
2 Could you introduce some new and more varied ways for children to practise counting in your setting, where children will be keen to be

Figure 12.5   Emma drew her different gymnastic positions!

accurate because they are interested in the materials or contexts provided?

3 How could you use role play more effectively to provide opportunities for mathematical thinking?

4 How often can children in your setting follow their own line of mathematical enquiry? How can you make sure this is valued and encouraged?

5 What links do you make at the moment between learning at home and in your setting? How could you strengthen these links?

13 Art in the early years

Bernadette Duffy

Summary

In this chapter I will explore what is creativity and why it is important to the child and the wider society. I will examine the links
between creativity and the arts and ways in which adults can foster
creativity through their interactions with children and the environment they create. Planning, recording and documenting art experiences will be discussed, alongside working with parents and carers
to gain the richest experiences for all children. The chapter will
emphasize that we, the practitioners, are the most important
resource children have: in our hands lies the power to hinder and
curtail children's creativity or to nourish it and watch it grow.

Introduction

This chapter will emphasize the importance of creativity and the role of
the arts in promoting this, drawing on our experience at the Thomas
Coram Centre in Camden. The Centre is a partnership between Camden
local authority and the charity Coram Family and is situated in south
Camden on the Coram Community Campus. The Centre serves a culturally, religiously, linguistically and economically diverse community.
Twenty per cent of the children are referred to the Centre as children in
need. This site has been a special place for young children for over 300

years and a place where the arts have always been seen as important in the life of young children. The practitioners currently working on the campus are continuing this tradition. We are committed to creativity and are trying to develop an approach which ensures that children are encouraged to develop their own personal creative responses, using a wide range of media and resources.

What is creativity and why is it important?

In recent years the importance of creativity has frequently been stressed. 'Creativity is good for the economy, good for the individual, good for the society and good for education' (NACCCE 2000). 'The government knows that culture and creativity matters' (Tony Blair in DCMS 2001). Creativity is seen as important because it enables us to respond to a rapidly changing world and to deal with the unexpected by extending our current knowledge to new situations and using information in new ways. It encourages us to take risks, think flexibly, be innovative, play with ideas and respond imaginatively.

The 2000 review of the National Curriculum recognized creativity as an important aim for education and stated that the curriculum should enable pupils to think creatively and critically, to solve problems and to make a difference for the better. In response the Secretary of State for Education and Skills asked the Qualifications and Curriculum Authority (QCA) to conduct a review on how schools could promote pupils' creativity through the National Curriculum: the results have been published in *Creativity: Find It, Promote It* (QCA 2003a).

The importance of creativity in the early years has also been recognized. *'Birth to Three Matters'*, the DfES guidance for supporting children in the first three years of life, stresses the importance of promoting children's creativity from their earliest years (DfES 2002; see also Chapter 2 of this book). Creativity is emphasized in *Curriculum Guidance for the Foundation Stage*: 'Creativity is fundamental to successful learning. Being creative enables children to make connections between one area of learning and another and to extend their understanding' (QCA/DfEE 2000). *Excellence and Enjoyment: The Primary Strategy* suggests that 'promoting creativity is a powerful way of engaging pupils with their learning' (DfES 2003). Clearly creativity is seen as a 'good thing' and an area that should be developed in early childhood settings.

However, defining creativity is not easy and there is much debate about how it is characterized and identified (Bruner 1962; Gardner 1993a; Fisher 2003). Part of the difficulty is that the term is applied to individuals, to a process and to products. For some, creativity is reserved for a few very gifted individuals; for others it is a human characteristic that we all possess.

Recent thinking distinguishes between 'big c' and 'little c' creativity

Photograph 13.1   Is creativity a human characteristic that we all possess?

(Craft 2001). 'Big c creativity' involves invention and a break with past understanding, for example the creative process engaged in by Einstein. 'Little c creativity' enables individuals to find routes and paths to travel. It is a process of conscious invention and describes the resourcefulness of ordinary people rather than extraordinary contributors. Such creativity involves originality, seeing things in fresh ways and learning from past experiences. It involves thinking along unorthodox lines, breaking barriers, using non-traditional approaches to problems and creating something, whether an idea or object. Creativity means connecting the previously unconnected in ways that are new and meaningful to the individual concerned, to make real something that you have imagined (Duffy 1998).

Creativity across all aspects and areas of learning

There has been a lot of discussion about the nature of creativity in young children. Children's creativity is best defined as creativity with a little 'c'. Children are being creative when they use materials in new ways or combine new materials; they are creative when they make discoveries that are new to them. When children are being creative they go further than the information given to create something new and original for them. For young children, the process of creativity – which includes curiosity, exploration, play and creativity – is as important as any product they may create.

Children are born with a strong desire to explore the world around them and from this innate curiosity creativity develops. Creativity is part of every area of the curriculum and all areas of learning have the potential to be creative experiences. The creative process is as applicable to Personal, Social and Emotional Development; Communication, Language and Literacy; Mathematical Development; Knowledge and Understanding of the World; and Physical Development as it is to art, music, dance and imaginative play. *Birth to Three Matters* and the *Curriculum Guidance for the Foundation Stage* stress creative development. Access to the arts supports development in all areas and aspects of learning. For example, in *Birth to Three Matters*:

- 'A Strong Child' includes the component 'Me, Myself and I', which is about children's realization of their own individuality, recognizing personal characteristics and preferences and finding out what they can do. The creative process emphasizes open-ended experience and offers children the chance to make their own choices and reach their own conclusions. It enables them to discover their own individual preferences and find out what they can do.
- 'A Skilful Communicator' includes the component 'Making Meaning', which involves understanding and being understood, influencing others, negotiating and making choices. Creative experiences bring children together and offers meaningful opportunities to listen and respond to others. Children are able to understand the importance of negotiating and understanding each other and realize that relating in this way is beneficial to all.
- 'A Competent Learner' has many links with the arts and creativity: indeed, one component is 'Being Creative'. This includes responding to the world creatively and is about exploring, discovering, experimenting with media and movement, developing competence and being resourceful. Through the arts children are able to respond creatively. There is no right or wrong way to use the materials or resources and the emphasis is on exploration and discovery.
- 'A Healthy Child' includes 'Emotional Well-being', which involves emotional stability and resilience, and being able to express feelings. Children are able to use the arts in their own way to express their feelings. For example, pounding a lump of clay when frustrated or the soothing sound of music when upset helps children to regain their emotional balance. Creative experiences encourage the ability to solve problems and to persist with challenges. It helps to develop a sense of mastery or resilience in the child which is closely linked to well-being. (For a fuller explanation, see Langston and Abbott in Chapter 2 of this book.)

The *Curriculum Guidance for the Foundation Stage* continues this process. For example:

- 'Personal, Social and Emotional Development' includes dispositions and attitudes, relationships that build self-confidence and emotional development. Creativity builds on children's curiosity and encourages a positive approach to new experiences. Children display high levels of involvement and are able to select and use resources independently. Through the creative process children can develop concentration, problem solving, planning and seeing things through to completion. Working together encourages a sense of self-respect and valuing of others.

- 'Communication, Language and Literacy' includes language for communicating and listening, and the arts offer plenty of opportunities to speak and listen, for example when sharing resources or creating a shared dance. Reading development builds on representation through making marks. Ascribing meanings to these marks helps children to understand the symbolic nature of written language. The fine motor skills needed for writing are best developed through meaningful, enjoyable experiences which the arts provide, for example through manipulating materials and equipment. The narratives children develop through their imaginative play provide the basis for writing stories (see the chapters in Part 2 of this book).
- Mathematical development is supported as concepts of shape, size, line, and area are used to classify and sort objects in the visual arts. Dance provides many opportunities to explore spatial concepts, and sequencing events and objects, for example creating a pattern on a piece of clay, helps children to understand patterns.
- Knowledge and understanding of the world is developed through the investigations that occur when children are presented with unfamiliar materials and resources and exposed to a variety of materials and their properties.
- Physical development is encouraged by the many opportunities to develop and practise fine motor skill, for example through sculpting, play equipment and materials. Gross motor skills are also encouraged (see Peter Smith's comments in Chapter 9 of this book) as children involve themselves in movement and dance and develop body control, balance, coordination and poise.
- Creative development is an area of learning in its own right and the guidance emphasizes the link between creativity and the arts. Children are encouraged to use all their senses to explore and take part in a wide range of visual and performing arts.

The role of the arts in promoting creativity

Frequently creativity and the arts are seen as the same thing. However, involvement in the visual and performing arts does not necessarily mean involvement in creativity. Many art experiences offered to young children are dull, repetitive and far from creative, rather a way of occupying children and covering the walls; creating something does not necessarily indicate creativity. The arts do have a particular contribution to make and when they are introduced to children in appropriate ways can enrich and stimulate. *ARTS alive!*, the QCA curriculum development project, has identified ways in which the contribution of the arts to pupils' education can be maximized. The key message to emerge from this research is that investing in the arts can transform schools, raise standards, change attitudes, improve behaviour and increase the quality of teaching and learning. The 2002 Arts Council of England national study of the arts in the early years also found a strong belief in the value of the arts in early years settings. By using the arts we are supporting the development of positive dispositions and providing meaningful links across the curriculum.

Creativity through the arts enables children to communicate their feelings in non-verbal and pre-verbal ways and to express their thoughts. Through the arts children can comprehend, respond to, and represent their perceptions. They can develop their understanding of the world, experience beauty and express their cultural heritage. Such experiences help children to gain self-esteem and create a view of the world that is uniquely their own.

Music gives practitioners a vehicle for getting to know the children and for bringing children together as a group, which reinforces a sense of community (Young and Glover 1998). At Thomas Coram we have been fortunate in receiving support from the National Foundation for Youth Music to develop a music programme aimed at encouraging the innate musicality of adults and children (Linda Pound expands on the concept of musicality in Chapter 14 of this book). As an example, 'Finding our Voices' is one such project:

Photograph 13.2   Through the arts children can comprehend, respond and represent their perceptions

Case study: Finding our Voices

The starting point for this programme is the belief that musicality is an innate human characteristic and that involvement in music making not only gives children a chance to develop musical concepts and skills but also encourages self-esteem and well-being. As a staff team we were aware that music making was an area in which many of us lacked confidence and we needed a confident music maker to support our own musical development alongside that of the children. We wanted music to be embedded into the life of the Centre, not to be something a music teacher does once a week with the children. Children and staff attend regular music sessions with an experienced music maker and as staff confidence develops they take over the sessions with the support of the music maker. The sessions are linked to the ongoing work of the Centre and the songs and music from the sessions become part of the day-to-day life of the Centre. The children also have the opportunity to listen to and work with visiting musicians from a range of musical traditions and to share their music making with their parents and the wider community.

The voice of the child

The arts have an important role in ensuring that the child's voice is heard (Lancaster 2003). For example, drawing is about looking – the particular things children choose to look at and to draw will be those that have special relevance. Drawing offers us an insight into children's thinking. The content of children's imaginative play also gives us an insight into their preoccupations (see Chapter 5 of this book), for example the superhero play in which many young boys often engage (Holland 2003). But we need to be aware that our attitudes may stop us listening to the voice of the child (a point taken up by Jane Hislam in Chapter 7 of this book). Anning and Ring (2004) found that boys' use of drawing for meaning-making was unacknowledged by practitioners until they were at the stage of visual realism. Holland (2003) also found practitioners reluctant or unable to accept the child's voice in superhero play. Children with disabilities and special needs can also remain unheard. In some cases, access to the arts is limited because programmes for the children focus on what they cannot do and practitioners concentrate on plugging the gaps. In other cases, lack of imagination on the part of the adults leads to children not having access because the additional support they may need is not forthcoming. Hearing children's voices can occur in many different contexts, such as the following example:

Case study: Camden Dance Festival

During the regular music and movement session we had found that for many children the medium of dance enabled them to express themselves in a way that words alone cannot do. Children from Thomas Coram were invited to take part in Camden's Dance Festival. This involved working with dancers to create a dance and then performing this at a local theatre alongside children and young people from Camden's primary and secondary schools. Initially we had concerns about such young children taking part in a public performance, as we did not want the children to feel pressurized to live up to adult expectations. However, since taking part in the Festival we have revised our ideas. For the children the experience of being performers in a proper theatre with a real audience has been a magical one. There has been the excitement of going backstage and finding out what happens behind the curtain. Then there has been the pleasure of appearing before an appreciative audience, sharing their work with the wider community and knowing that their voices have been heard. The increase in confidence and self-esteem has been marked.

The role of the adult

While there are common aspects in children's development (Duffy 1998), the sociocultural context they experience has a strong influence on their development (see Chapters 17 and 18 of this book). The way in which the adults frame an activity is crucial to how the children perceive it and how it motivates them to join in or to avoid the activity. Learning is a communal activity and children's dispositions are very influenced by the adults around them (Anning and Ring 2004). In order for creativity to flourish it is necessary for the child to be actively involved in the process of learning (Prentice 2000). Creative teaching is an art; it involves practitioners in using their imagination to make learning more interesting, exciting and effective. Creative teaching involves taking risks, leaving the security of structured lessons behind and learning from the children (NACCCE 2000), such as in the Dolls' House Project example.

Case study: Dolls' house project

Tom, a teacher at the Coram Centre, was discussing presents with his key group of 3- and 4-year-olds. The children decided that they would like to make a dolls' house as a present to themselves and the other children at the Centre. While this was not what Tom had planned to do with the children, he felt that he should capitalize on the children's enthusiasm for the project. With Tom's help the children spent time researching how to make a house – what did they need to include in their design? How did the different pieces fit together? What were the best materials to use? They used the woodwork skills they had previously acquired to construct the frame and during the process had plenty of opportunity to understand why accurate measuring is important. Once the structure was complete they used their knowledge of paint to create wallpaper for each room and designed and made furniture. Tom documented the process as they worked, especially the children's comments. He used this to plan retrospectively, to look at what the children had learned and relate this to the different areas of learning demonstrating the cross-curricular nature of creativity. The children had meaningful opportunities to develop mathematical concepts and real reasons to communicate clearly. Working together was essential and the particular skills of different children were used. Boys and girls worked collaboratively on the project and once the house was complete it was interesting to see how much the boys in particular enjoyed playing with it, developing and acting out their own stories.

The Effective Provision of Preschool Education Project (Sylva *et al.* 2003) stresses the importance of adult–child interactions. A child's freely chosen play offers many opportunities to promote learning when practitioners recognize its importance and interact with children while they play. We can support learning through modelling possible ways to explore the materials and demonstrating to the children how they might use the new materials and equipment. Open-ended questioning is also very important as are pondering comments or thinking out loud – for example, the adult pondering 'I wonder why that happened?' or 'I wonder what would happen if I add more water?' These comments draw the children's attention to possibilities but do not put them under pressure to find a right answer.

However, when it comes to interacting with children about their art representations many practitioners are not confident (Ofsted 2004). There seems to be a reluctance to intervene based on a fear that this may adversely affect or curtail natural creativity (Burton 1980). When adults intervene with sensitivity and understanding (as Neil Kitson emphasizes in Chapter 8 of this book) this can deepen children's understanding. To intervene effectively we need to have an understanding of creative and artistic concepts, developments and processes and the vocabulary to discuss them with children. It is also crucial that we tune into children's preoccupation and understand what they are tying to do. Are they interested in the properties of the materials or resources and their possibilities? Are they exploring concepts such as shape, colour or pattern, pitch, or texture? Is their interest in the capturing of a feeling, movement or image from the world around them? It is also important to know when to be silent, pause before speaking and give children the opportunity to speak first (as Nigel Hall also emphasizes in Chapter 6). We may help by focusing their attention on a particular part of their representation, recalling experiences to encourage them to make association and introducing them to the work of others. Hypothesizing or making suggestions can also be helpful, especially when the child seems to be experiencing frustration and needs support towards the next step. It is important to give children time to reflect on their work by not taking away work too soon and remembering that it is never too early to discuss with children how their images work (Matthews 2003).

The creative environment

Both *Birth to Three Matters* and the *Curriculum Guidance for the Foundation Stage* point out that practitioners should pay particular attention to creating an environment that stimulates children's creativity, originality and expressiveness inside and outside. Each setting will offer its own possibilities. As practitioners we need to look at our setting and maximize its potential for creativity. Creativity is about making meaningful connections, using ideas and materials in new ways (as practitioners did outdoors in the account provided by Stephanie Harding in Chapter 10 of this book). Practitioners' organization of space and resources will largely determine whether children can do this.

Children need a space in which to be creative. It is important that there is sufficient space to work and easily accessible material and tools. Without access to resources it is hard for children to demonstrate their creativity, especially when trying to create two- and three-dimensional representations. The range of resources and organization we provide will determine what and how the children can create and how creative they can be. Access to a range of resources enables children to choose the best medium for a particular representation.

The creative process also takes time. Children need sufficient time to explore, to develop ideas and to finish working at these ideas. This means that we need to think about the organization of the available time to ensure that the children have as much of it as possible to engage in

Photograph 13.3   Practitioners need to think about time to ensure that children have as much of it as possible to engage in creative experiences

creative experiences. Lack of time is often cited as a reason for curtailing children's creativity, especially in the Reception year when the perceived demands of the numeracy and literacy strategies seem to eat into the time available (see Adams *et al.* 2004). This is an opportunity for practitioners to engage their own creativity! A cross-curricular approach allows us to draw on the appeal and potential of the arts to encourage learning and development in all areas of the curriculum. Such an approach enables children to deepen understanding and make creative connections, and helps practitioners to 'join up' the curriculum. Through the arts children acquire a range of skills and understandings that are transferable to areas such as literacy or numeracy (see particularly Rose Griffiths' playful and creative approach to maths in Chapter 12 of this book). Whatever the circumstances or restraints under which we work, practitioners need to look at the time available and make sure that it is put to the best use.

The setting alone cannot provide all that children need and it is important to recognize the role of the wider community in developing children's creativity. Children are very much part of the wider creative community and the *Curriculum Guidance for the Foundation Stage* highlights the value in children having the opportunity to work alongside artists, musicians and crafts people, as in the following example.

Case study: The sculpture project

The children at Thomas Coram have had the opportunity to work with artists from our local gallery, the October Gallery. The starting point for this particular project was a practical one – creating seats for the courtyard entrance to the nursery. Artists from the October Gallery worked with the children to create designs for the seats based on animal forms. The practical aspects (how to make the seats stand up) and the aesthetic aspects (how the create pleasing shapes) were both explored. Drawing up prototypes to try out ideas was a new experience for the children, as was the process of selecting the best designs from a range of designs. Working with the artists gave the children a chance to develop new skills, such as drawing up designs, and to work with new materials, such as concrete and tiles. The opportunity to work with a group of artists for over a year meant that children, staff and artists developed an understanding of each other and real relationships were formed. While the process was important the end results are also very important to the children. The animals they have created to sit on are very precious to them and have become part of the nursery – a number of children greet each animal in the morning and say farewell at the end of the day.

Planning for creativity

There is no single system of planning that suits all settings and all children all the time – it is not a case of 'one size fits all'. But there are principles that should underpin the systems we choose to use. Too often young children are given access to a narrow, limited and superficial range of creative experiences. For example, opportunities to paint can be restricted to using a small number of ready-mixed paints, with no choice of brush or paper texture, size or shape. Freely chosen play activities often provided the best opportunities for adults to extend children's thinking (Sylva *et al.* 2003). Planning for creativity should include time for extending child-initiated play as well as time for adult-initiated group work.

Practitioners need to differentiate the experiences they present and to match the learning experiences to the needs of the individual children. The arts offer children the freedom to use the materials in an open-ended way. As there is no prescribed end product, individual children are able to use the materials and ideas in a way that matches their own learning needs. The adult's expertise is in enabling children to develop mastery and the freedom to explore at their own level by finding ways to develop the skills and concepts children need at the time they need them.

Planning should be based on observations of individual children's needs and interests, relate to their previous experiences and actively involve the children. The experiences need to be introduced to the children in ways that excite their curiosity and allow plenty of time for exploration and play. When reviewing the experiences offered, practitioners should reflect on how the children have responded to them, why they have used materials or ideas in a particular way and how to extend the experiences offered.

Recording and documenting

It is as important to record and document children's artistic development as with any other area of the curriculum. It is especially important to record the processes as well as any end products. Portfolios for individual children enable progress to be tracked over time and offer the children an insight into their own learning. Documenting the ways in which groups of children work together on common projects is also important. Digital photography can be used to record individual children's progress with accompanying notes and to create displays complete with children's comments on their learning. If practitioners have access to a video camera, it is also useful to record episodes of play to reflect on with others – the children, in team meetings and with parents. Video offers the opportunity to stand back and view the bigger picture: watching a video makes it possible to see things you missed at the time. Recording and documenting children's work in this way enables us to use evidence to complete the *Foundation Stage Profile* (QCA 2003b).

Working with parents and carers

The importance of working in partnership with parents is a key theme in *Birth to Three Matters* and *Curriculum Guidance for the Foundation Stage*, and this is especially true when it comes to the arts. Some practitioners express concern and, on occasion, annoyance at certain parents' unwillingness to allow their children freely to explore materials such as paint or clay. In turn some parents are confused by the practitioner's view that making a mess is important, especially when it involves doing things that are often actively discouraged at home! It is important that practitioners develop a dialogue with parents which enables them to discuss children's creative development and work together to support and encourage it. Hands-on joint workshops for parents and children are a good way of introducing parents to painting and drawing and enabling them to experience at first hand the pleasure and learning children acquire from these materials.

Inviting parents to come and make music with their children not only gives parents an insight into the benefits for their child but also strengthens the adult–child bond.

Questions to set you thinking

1 Think over the last week – how have you supported and developed your own and the children's creativity?
2 Think of three things you can do during the next week to develop:

  • your creativity as a teacher;
  • the children's creativity.

3 What kind of creative arts projects within the community might children in your setting engage in over the next year?

14 | Playing music

Linda Pound

Summary

In this chapter the term 'playing music' is considered and compared with the language used to describe other playful and creative experiences. The biological functions of play and music are discussed and their role in learning and development explored. These include a sense of group cohesiveness, supporting memory and the reflection or representation of mood. The importance of including playful music in the curriculum is emphasized, including physicality which is an integral part of music-making in young children. I discuss the ways in which music can be made more playful by giving more opportunities for improvisation, rather than simply playing the music dictated by others; song-writing, an activity which most young children engage in spontaneously but which disappears since practitioners largely ignore it; and physical action, now recognized as essential to all learning.

Introduction

In an effort to convince parents and policy makers that play is of value in school, there was a period during the later part of the twentieth century in early childhood education where everything that happened in the nursery or other early years setting was described as work. Children were asked whether they wished to work in the sand, work in the home corner or work with the blocks. It was hoped that this strategy would give essentially playful activities status and enable them to be seen as serious and productive. It did nothing, however, actually to present play itself as either serious or productive. The lessons of neuroscience and developmental psychology are supporting educators in seeing not only that 'play is fun with serious consequences' (Greenfield 1996: 75) but that play, along with music and interaction, appears to be part of every child's learning repertoire from their earliest days (Trevarthen 1998). In essence, play (and, as this chapter will demonstrate, music) is not just fun, but it is also of fundamental importance.

The way in which we describe musical activity in everyday life gives some interesting clues to its relationship with play. Our choice of the term 'playing music' contrasts with the language we use in relation to other subject areas or areas of the curriculum. We would not talk of working with musical instruments nor would we suggest playing painting. Although we use the expression 'playing music' in everyday life for a vast range of activities ranging from concert pianists to a rap CD, we do not generally describe many of the music-making activities that go on in the classroom as playing music. While we talk of children playing instruments, we generally describe other activities simply as singing, dancing or listening to music. We do not generally ask if they would like to play with songs or play dancing. In other areas of the arts, while we may talk to children about playing or (working) with clay, we are more likely to describe their artistic endeavours as painting, drawing or dancing. Artists do not generally talk about playing painting, playing sculpture or playing dance, although we know that engagement in these creative acts involves a great deal of playful activity. Picasso and Mozart, for example, are frequently characterized as essentially childlike in their passionate and playful behaviour.

Perhaps less surprisingly, people rarely talk about playing mathematics or playing physics. Yet it is said that Richard Feynman's Nobel prize-winning work in physics sprang from playing in the canteen with paper plates. Shakuntala Devi, acclaimed by the *Guinness Book of Records* as the world's fastest human computer, states that at the age of 3 she 'fell in love with numbers'. She continues: 'Numbers were toys with which I could play' (Devi 1990: 9). Seymour Papert, inventor of Logo – software which in his words enables 'the child (to) program (*sic*) the computer' (1980: 5) – describes his childhood passion for gears. He writes that 'playing with gears became a favourite pastime. I loved rotating circular objects against one another in gearlike motions' (1980: vii). He goes on to describe his excitement and to generalize this to all learning – the exploration and passion being seen as vital components.

Small (1998) suggests that the word music should be used as a verb – musicking – to remind us that being engaged in music (either playing it or listening to it) is an active process which involves others. The term 'playing music' does of course denote action but is not in everyday language applied to all areas of musical activity in the comprehensive way that Small envisages. Although as indicated above we *play* recorded music, we do not play live music – we merely listen to it! Small would describe all such activities as musicking. Since music appears to have a particular place in our vocabulary we can speculate that music may also have a particular place in our living and playing.

What is music for?

Since musicking is a universal feature of human endeavour we can speculate that it has a biological purpose. In all societies, music plays a number of important functions or roles in human living and learning (Pound and Harrison 2003).

- Music supports group identity. This can be seen in places of worship and at football matches, in armies and in the performance of school songs. It is evident in the way in which educators use song in particular to hold the interest of a group of children coming, for example, to sit on the carpet for story time. Bowman (2004: 44) describes music as essentially a matter of identity 'as much a matter of who (children) become as what they do'. This is also evident throughout life – both in the fiercely defined types of pop music and in the clientele attending the opera house. Music is culturally specific and even very young children recognize and enjoy music that has cultural significance. Siegel (1999) suggests that cultural awareness is amongst our earliest memories.
- Music helps to create and express or reflect particular atmospheres or moods. Again this is evident in everyday life – at funerals, parties, hotel lobbies, or supermarkets, the choice of music helps to put even the apparently passive listener into a particular frame of mind. As adults we are often highly discerning about whether a particular piece of music will suit our mood – either in reflecting it or in helping us to overcome it. We may choose music to relax, revive or rally us. This function is also evident in the universal use of lullabies and soothing songs with young children. Not even babies and toddlers are exempt from the energizing influence of music – even before they can move independently, a piece of lively music will have them bouncing and waving excitedly.

  Hargreaves (2004) has described music as 'a sound track to life', suggesting that around forty per cent of our time is accompanied by music – listening, singing, whistling and so on. (The use of iPods and Walkman means that for some people virtually one hundred per cent of their time must be lived to the sound of music!) That suggests that for a significant part of our lives, our responses are being shaped by the choice of music – some of which will be made by us but much of which will be selected by others.

- Music supports memory. Certain pieces of music can conjure up memorable situations – just hear the opening notes of a particular song or piece of music and you are transported to a particular time or place. Advertisers exploit this. The rhythm and cadences of their jingles (whether or not they are set to music) remain lodged in the brain, often to our annoyance when we no longer wish to think about toothpaste or chocolate. But educators are also aware of music's potential – rhymes work because learning a string of apparently unrelated words (one, two, three or Monday, Tuesday, Wednesday) or letters (A, B, C) and being able to recite them in a helpful order is made easier if they are set to music. Helen MacGregor's (1998) songs set to familiar tunes exploit this link, in describing circles, triangles and squares in memorable ways. Mention triangles and a group of children familiar with the song will be away – singing the song to the tune of *Three Blind Mice*.

These important functions of music as being about mood or atmosphere, social cohesion and cooperation, memory and thought are reflected in schools and early years settings. These functions are reflected in the way in which early childhood practitioners commonly use music to:

- draw together a group of children at specific times of the day, attracting their attention and maintaining a group focus;
- create a warm positive atmosphere at the beginning or end of the day;
- celebrate events such as religious festivals and birthdays which may draw attention to diversity as well as social solidarity;
- move children from one space or one activity to another in an orderly fashion, perhaps using a tune or song to signal clearing-up time;
- help children to learn letters and numbers or other similar information by heart;
- help children to learn social values and behaviours which might include taking turns or saying 'good morning' to the group (based on Hildebrandt 1998).

This emphasis on group management and conformity was openly acknowledged by Robert Owen who, when setting up his innovative and philanthropic venture at New Lanark in the early part of the nineteenth century, gave music a focal place in the curriculum, for children from 2 years of age. He viewed music and dance as a means of 'reforming vicious habits . . . by promoting cheerfulness and contentment . . . thus diverting attention from things that are vile and degrading' (Donnachie 2000: 170). More recently Hildebrandt (1998) reminds us that, all too often, despite the rich potential offered by music the main use made of it is in getting children to conform – all doing the same thing at the same time. That same thing might be focused on the music – all singing the same words or doing the same actions – but it might equally be to do with discipline; all lining up nicely to go out to play or march into assembly. Hildebrandt suggests that this contrasts with other areas of the curriculum, where exploration and experimentation are more effectively encouraged. With painting and drawing we welcome idiosyncratic responses, valuing the importance of the imagination, which underpins children's work. With music, however, we are anxious about keeping in time, about getting the tune, words and actions 'right'.

There are other functions of music that are much less well developed in the curriculum. These are related to its role in communication and to its place as a component in the development of creativity. First, music eases communication in situations where it would otherwise be difficult (Papousek 1994). The difficulties may be of three particular kinds:

1 Where the difficulty is because of the distance between those trying to communicate, musical elements are used to make words or sounds more easily heard and understood. Yodelling, whistling and drumming are familiar examples of this. However, the technique is put into practice in day-to-day situations where the distances are less great but still a barrier to communication. When wanting, for example, to call children from the far side of the playground, adults commonly adopt a rhythmic chant or exaggerate the intonation so that it has a music-like quality.
2 Music has a perhaps unique role in aiding communication where the feelings expressed would be difficult to put into words in everyday contexts or using everyday language. Music can enable us to vent anger, and to describe love, joy or sorrow, can in short enable us to express 'that which cannot be said and on which it is impossible to be silent' (Hugo, cited by Exley 1991). As Bowman (2004: 32) aptly writes, 'Music sounds like feelings feel.'
3 Music plays a part in supporting the vital but potentially difficult job of drawing babies, who have not yet learned language, into the culture by 'reducing the distance and highlighting the emotions'; capturing the baby's attention; developing shared meaning; and communicating feelings (Pound and Harrison 2003: 13). Hearing, the first of the senses to develop (Bowman 2004) and the last to leave us (Pound 2002, citing Storr), is first stimulated by the 'intrauterine symphony' (Bowman 2004: 37) which surrounds the unborn child.

The role of musicality in supporting development and learning continues throughout infancy. Adults and even very young children raise the pitch of their voices and use a sing-song melody in their talk with babies. Babies' hearing allows them to differentiate languages and voices – their preferences being their mother's voice and her first language. They also prefer complex sounds, including music and 'highly intonated speech' (Eliot 1999: 228). The intonations chosen by adults are now known to convey a range of emotions which show an apparently universal pattern. Thus the tunes used to communicate approval, disapproval or comfort show significant similarities whether the language used is English, French or even a tonal language such as Mandarin (Fernald 1992).

From three or four months of age, babies and adults engage in playful musical interactions which involve songs, rhymes and chants that may be traditional but increasingly may also be versions of popular music adapted to display the features common to these games (Trevarthen 1998). The common features (Pound and Harrison 2003) include the fact that the musical form of what Trevarthen (1987: 189) has called 'baby songs' and 'baby dances' appears to be essentially the same despite different languages and different cultures. They provoke interest through repetition with variations in tempo and pitch. They have a story-like structure and invite an emotional response, often associated with a delayed climax.

To these three aspects of communicating with the help of music we should add a fourth, which is widely acknowledged in early childhood education. Music is often well used to support communication with those for whom it would otherwise be difficult, namely children with special educational needs. Even children with severe expressive speech difficulties can sometimes join in songs on cue, carried as they are by the rhythm of the music. This has been described by Bowman (2004: 38) in the following words: 'Sound seldom reflects the periphery of the body . . . It circulates in, around and even through us, both individually and collectively.'

Music is also of great value in supporting communication with young children in the early stages of learning English as an additional language. Vocabulary is rendered memorable in song; sounds are often exaggerated and can therefore be more readily identified and actions support the meaning. In common with storytelling, the high level of repetition (which would be unacceptable in everyday conversation) supports the development of understanding.

Finally, but by no means of least importance, music has a role or function in supporting the development of creativity (see also Bernadette Duffy, Chapter 13 of this book). The early development of individual babies (Trevarthen 1998) and that of the species as a whole (Devereux 2001; Lewis-Williams 2002) owes much to music and the physical action that accompanies it. The playfulness of music and dance appears to have a vital function. Since play and music are embedded in human development at both an individual and at a universal level then, suggest Papousek and Papousek (1994), it must be the case that both have a biological role to play in the development of the species as well as the development of the individual. The evidence from recent work on creativity seems to indicate that the biological function of play, music and dance is to support the development of creativity that enables our remarkable brains to develop flexibly (Pound 2003 citing Papousek).

Music and play

Having considered the functions of music it is now important to link music and play. Music is not just important in its own right: it can make a unique contribution to playful learning. Papousek (1994) suggests that the voice is the baby's first plaything and, in the development of humans, dance was probably the precursor or herald of our humanity. It is likely that we were unable to use our voices to sing or our hands to play instruments before we had risen up on to two legs. Since Storr (1989: 12) suggests that 'human beings danced before they walked', is it possible that the playful, emotional excitement and physical exuberance which we now associate with dance caused us to rise up on our hind legs?

In Figure 14.1, links are made between music and the learning that is associated with play.

How can we make music education in the early years more playful?

Of the many possible or desirable changes, I have selected three as of particular importance. These are musical improvisation, song-writing and physical engagement. Renewed emphasis on these three things could transform music education in the early years.

1 Improvisation is frequently associated with jazz musicians but in fact it has a firm place in most musical traditions, including western classical music. It fulfils the role of play – in promoting the rehearsal of ideas, exploring boundaries, drawing on and transforming familiar themes. It can be the doodling which leads to the masterpiece or the transitory chatter. Just as learning to talk involves play, alone and with others, so learning to musick needs to involve playful improvisations – alone and with others. We do not think of spoken conversation as of less value than printed words – different but with different functions. We do, however, refer to improvised music – the 'talk' of music (Harrison and Pound 1996) – often in a disparaging tone as being just 'made up'. In fact we should be encouraging children to engage in musical chatter, to take risks and to make up songs and music.

2 Song-writing is a form of improvised music which most children engage in for a time. Although children as young as 2 years of age can be heard improvising songs as they engage in other forms of play, often by statutory school age this creative music-making has disappeared. Coral Davies (cited by Pound and Harrison 2003) has identified three types of song produced by children and believes that with more active encouragement children would continue to make up songs. She identifies (Pound and Harrison 2003: 32–3):

   • 'story songs, where the emphasis is on the narrative and the melodies follow the pattern of the words';
   • 'frame songs in which there is a recognizable musical structure often derived from familiar songs'; and
   • secret songs – or 'free vocal play in which children explore a wide

Curriculum Guidance for the Foundation Stage (QCA, 2000: 25)	Playful music – with an emphasis on expression, creativity and physicality
Explore, develop and represent learning in order to make sense of the world	Learning and experience may be represented by songs related to current interests. Where there is an emphasis on creative or expressive music-making children are encouraged to make up songs and music about current enthusiasms, exploring the different sound-making potential of a range of instruments and everyday objects.
Practise and build up ideas, concepts and skills	Practice does occur in the repetition of songs, but generally the amount of time that children are given to explore sound freely is insufficient to enable them to develop ideas or skills. In addition to whole or small-group periods of music-making, children need time and space to 'play about' with sounds. In theory, music areas should provide this, but all too often the music area gathers dust as adults are uncertain about how to interact with children using the resources. In order to ensure sufficient time for children to really practise and build up ideas, concepts and skills, children need similar levels of time and space as they would for other aspects of provision such as role play or block play. A large area for music-making, space to dance and a mirror to see yourself dancing, together with adults who are confident to support children's explorations, are essential.
Learn how to control impulses and understand the need for rules	Many adults worry about managing group music sessions. Even the music area can be seen as likely to erupt into uncontrollable noise. Adults are often too quick to step in and put the instruments away instead of discussing with children how noise levels can be managed – or better still engaging with children dancing, singing and playing. Children will learn better how to control noise levels and interactions and to understand the need for rules if adults are not constantly imposing the limits but working with children to ensure that their play is purposeful and satisfying.
Be alone, be alongside others or cooperate	Music-making offers unique opportunities to engage with others. Musical conversations and improvised group performances (in addition to the regular singing times) enable children to develop a sense of group cohesion. Opportunities to seek out a quiet space, where a child can really explore what a particular instrument can do, or to listen alone to a favourite piece of music, are also of value.
Take risks and make mistakes	The traditional emphasis in education on getting music right has led generations of adults to claim that they can't sing or can't play an instrument because they can't read music. It's time to restore the play to musicking and encourage children to take musical risks – have a go at picking out a well-loved tune, try and see if you can drum like the drummer who came to school or play the recorder like your big brother.
Think creatively and imaginatively	Music is creative and imaginative. Playing with sounds, listening to a range of music, responding through dance, painting or other creative media all promote creativity and imagination. Reggio Emilia's hundred languages of children must include opportunities to translate ideas into and from music.
Communicate with others as they investigate or solve problems	Music is communicative – as long as adults encourage children to use it in this way. Since music and movement offer what Odam (1995: 19) describes as ' a unique schooling for the brain' in using both hemispheres and in encompassing both space and time, they support the kinds of thinking and dispositions which promote problem-solving (Pound and Harrison 2003)

Figure 14.1   (continued overleaf)

| Express fears or relive anxious experiences in controlled and safe situations | John Sloboda (1994, cited in Pound and Harrison 2003) has identified common characteristics of the childhood experiences of those who go on to become high musical achievers. These include important lessons for early childhood educators. They include early musical stimulation; opportunities for long periods of engagement in musical activity; family support; and an early emphasis on having fun with music. His list also includes something which is less well tackled in early years settings or indeed in education as a whole. Those who went on to succeed in music had had opportunities as young children to express emotions. In a study by Sosniak (cited by Pound and Harrison 2003) one concert pianist describes coping with his fear of thunderstorms by creating loud, fierce noises on the piano to emulate the sounds around him. Much of the music we use with young children is quite bland and if emotions are mentioned at all they tend to be of the happy-clappy variety. |

Figure 14.1   Making links between music, learning and play

range of sounds and effects without concern for conventions of story', or often, indeed, of music.

If early childhood educators were to give more active support to children's creative songwriting, their development would be enhanced. As Hildebrandt (1998: 68) reminds us, '. . . we don't always appreciate children's invented songs as music. Although we strive to honour children's creativity in all areas of development, sometimes music gets lost in the process.'

3 Physical engagement is an essential part of all learning. As the neuroscientist Susan Greenfield (1997) tells us, if we did not move we would not need a brain. Sadly, the importance of the body is not always acknowledged. Ross (2004: 173) asserts that 'progress through the educational system brings with it increasingly less time and permission for the physical participation of the body. The student body's presence in the classroom from kindergarten to twelfth grade gets quieter and quieter until it is effectively mute.' This might be read as suggesting that all is well in the early years. In fact as Tobin (2004: 111) points out, 'the body is disappearing in early childhood education'. Not only, he claims, has there been a kind of moral but misguided panic about physical contact with children but the emphasis 'on academic over social development' has had the effect of drastically reducing the amount of time that children spend in physical activity, creating 'an imbalance which favors (*sic*) the brain over the body and skill acquisition over feelings and more complex thinking' (Tobin 2004: 123).

While acknowledging that some similar pressures are beginning to create some similar responses in Japan, Walsh (2004: 97) highlights the importance given to physicality in Japanese early childhood education. In Japanese culture young children are viewed as essentially and importantly physical. Their physical development is central to early schooling. Many Japanese early childhood educators believe that intellectual development requires a balanced body and that physical play aligns the body (see also Peter Smith's reflections in Chapter 9 of this book).

Walsh suggests that physical competence gives children a sense of agency – of being able to take risks; to explore and to control their bodies and environment. He reiterates Tobin's view that this has been lost from much early childhood education, citing Japan as 'a last best place in early schooling across the world' (Walsh 2004: 107).

Music, with its inherent physicality, offers an important mechanism for reclaiming the body in early childhood education. Bowman (2004) describes the way in which arts educators have embraced Howard Gardner's Multiple Intelligence Theory (see for example Gardner 1999b) because it offers some kind of vindication of the importance of the arts. He points out that although this has given some academic respectability to the arts in general and music in particular, it has been counter-productive. In deciding that there is 'more strategic clout to be found on the rational side of the cognitive/emotional divide' (Tobin 2004: 29) music educators have missed opportunities to reconstruct the meaning of ideas such as mind, intelligence and cognition. We have in short neglected what Bowman regards as the most important aspects of music-making: 'experience and agency, the bodily and the social' (Bowman 2004: 33). This, he contends, means that we have failed to 'highlight the co-origination of body, mind and culture' (Bowman 2004: 46) and to 'create a model of education in which music's role might be seen as a continuation and enhancement of precisely what makes all our intellectual achievements possible' (Bowman 2004: 34) – namely the body.

While it is true that music for young children necessarily involves movement, it is a physical impossibility for them to listen without moving. Early childhood educators can take two simple steps to re-embody music education, making it more playful. First, we can ensure that music areas have enough space for children to move freely, with or without instruments and that mirrors are available so that children can see what their bodies look like when they are moving. This is difficult in many classrooms where there is a shortage of space – but we can at least try to make it possible sometimes. Secondly, we can offer more musical opportunities outside. While physical development does not have to happen outdoors, the space and freedom it can offer make it more likely that gross motor activity will occur. There are in addition opportunities to explore loud sounds and natural sounds.

Conclusion

Foremost amongst the reasons music truly matters educationally is its participatory, enactive, embodied character and its consequent capacity to highlight the coordination of body, mind and culture.

(Bowman 2004: 46)

Like play, music is of fundamental importance in human development and learning. Early childhood educators have a grave responsibility to ensure that its social, creative, physical and, therefore, cognitive benefits are made available to young children by letting them play music.

Questions to set you thinking

1 What steps do you need to take to make music in your setting more playful?
2 What do you need to do to help parents appreciate both the long-term and the short-term benefits of musical activity?
3 What support do you need to feel sufficiently confident in your own musical ability to intervene successfully in children's musical play?
4 What spontaneous opportunities do you provide for child-initiated 'musicking'?

Part 4
Play, culture and playful practitioners

15 Practitioners and play: reflecting in a different way

Siân Adams

Summary

Much has been written about the dislocation and tensions between practitioners' principles and practice. Research suggests that bringing to the surface the values and beliefs of even experienced practitioners proves to be challenging; even with informed support, articulating the principles of practice which are grounded in activities and narratives is difficult. The process of adopting a reflective approach to practice – benefiting from informed support within a culture that values and celebrates pedagogical thinking – appears to prompt the intellectual stimulation required to analyse practice critically. This chapter questions whether reflective practitioners think more deeply about playful practice – at philosophical, ethical or political levels – or whether the values of early years practitioners continue to be embedded in the practical care of the young.

Introduction

Until you're with other people and talk about it in any depth, you just carry on doing your day-to-day business of doing your own thing: filling in your tick-lists and all the rest of it. I don't think we've reached an understanding [of play] yet, but that's part of the excitement. I'm not suggesting that I reflect on my practice more than I did, but I reflect in a different way.

This chapter recounts the story of Too Busy to Play (TBtP) – a research project in which nine practitioners (teachers and nursery nurses) and two researchers worked together for over three years (Moyles and Adams 2001). Throughout this period, the group of 11 met regularly and frequently for opportunities to discuss the ways in which they supported children's learning through play within the early years and Key Stage 1 of the National Curriculum. During these meetings, they challenged each other about how they valued play and explored ways in which playful experiences might be used to further children's development and learning. The outcome of the project was a comprehensive set of Statements of Entitlement to Play (StEPs: Moyles and Adams 2001) with clear frameworks identifying ways in which practitioners might ensure children's developmental needs are in harmony with teaching and learning experiences.

Most of the meetings were university-based, whilst some occurred in each other's schools, providing opportunities to appreciate the range of settings represented by the TBtP group. Videos were taken of practitioners teaching and children playing, interviews between researchers and practitioners were recorded and documentation provided by each member of the group was collated, including:

- photographs of children engaged in a variety of activities within each setting;
- journals maintained by the group during their involvement with the project;
- each setting's mission statements and policy documents;
- curriculum planning and evidence of evaluation of children's learning;
- children's profiles.

All these resources were later examined and analysed in order to understand the different ways in which everyone worked and determine how each interpreted 'learning through play'.

The process involved the development of a deeper, effective, reflective approach to teaching and learning – *reflecting in a different way*. Through telling the story of the Too Busy to Play Project, this chapter will also illustrate the ways in which reflective practice can be developed, thus enhancing practitioners' work and play with children.

The images that are used to illustrate this account are taken from the video of one of the practitioners whose children are preparing for an Eid party (Moyles and Adams 2001). Quotations are taken from the transcripts of the research.

Setting the scene: background and the early stages of the project

It has been long accepted that even the concept of play remains elusive (McLane and Spielberger 1996). Establishing conceptual understanding of play is highly complex: determining its definition and principles defies both practitioners and academics – and proved to be particularly challenging for the practitioners and researchers in the Too Busy to Play Project.

Compounded with the intrinsic complexities of play are contradictory beliefs and the personal, implicit values often held by practitioners (Berlak *et al.* 1975). Even the small group of nine practitioners who considered they shared similar philosophies about play found that they did not all hold similar values and beliefs about the way in which their shared principles might inform practice. Each practitioner brought different experiences, understandings, perceptions, and priorities for the diverse needs of the children and the wider communities within their responsibilities. Many meetings were required to reduce the initial set of over one hundred dearly held principles listed by the group to a more manageable set of six statements. It follows that if the principles of play are elusive then ensuring that practice is informed by such principles will be similarly complex and problematic.

During the early days of the project, the TBtP practitioners recorded a sense of uncertainty in defining their practice for, although play continued to be proclaimed as the way through which children's learning and development may be promoted, practitioners were conscious of the difficulties in ensuring that children do actually learn through play. One practitioner expressed the uncertainty she experienced in ensuring that children's learning – and the evaluation of that learning – was underpinned by a playful philosophy: 'I want my [learning] objective in the back of my head, and I want to be able to find out if they've got there or not – which is the hardest part.' It is easy for children to remain occupied, 'to have fun and to have a good time', but not so easy to ensure they are also learning. Hence, the feeling of tension – and uncertainty: how can we know if quality learning takes place when teachers support playful practice in the Foundation Stage? Exploring beliefs and understandings about play was a very challenging and rewarding process that resulted in practitioners becoming more articulate, better informed – and more reflective.

So, *how* did these practitioners become more reflective about play? Deepening thinking and becoming more critical in the approach to practice involved several developmental stages (see Figure 15.1).

These five stages will be explored in the following account of the Too Busy to Play project.

Stages	Processes	Examples
1 Review of past practice	Initially including anecdotal recall of significant events	Talk about situation in which children are drawing with a range of writing materials in the home corner.
2 Confrontation of issues	Acknowledge area to be explored – at pragmatic level	Examine quality and relevance of resources in home corner. How can play be developed in order to support and challenge learning? Discuss opportunities and interests with children.
3 Conceptualization	Acknowledge area to be explored – at developmental level	Consider ways of promoting social and emotional development in children's play. Build on ethos of trust and respect.
4 Deconstruction	Critical analysis of learning	Question what children are learning when they are playing in home corner. Ensure resources are linked to children's learning and developmental needs.
5 Reconstruction	Plan for change in behaviour and areas for professional development within setting and at senior management levels. Examine wider ethical and political implications.	Provide adult support for children's play. Explore ways in which children's culture is valued. Discuss ways in which school policy supports practice.

Figure 15.1   The stages and process of the TBtP project

Review of past practices

The early discussions with the group were characterized by practitioners talking about recent significant pedagogical events – examples of teaching or learning which they wished to share with other like-minded early years practitioners. Most of the early discussions related to the dilemmas and uncertainties experienced in planning for effective, playful learning experiences. Practitioners may find themselves on the one hand planning for experiences that are fun and enjoyable – for doesn't 'interest promote learning'? – while on the other hand struggling to ensure that planned, predicted learning also occurs in a playful context. Practitioners have the responsibility of reconciling their understanding of children's responses in play, based on early models of play, with the direct instructional method-ologies supported in the current climate. Hurst (1994a) suggests that the adult role in supporting autonomous behaviour in play is a subtle and increasingly challenging one partly because of the polarization of playful principles with today's more structured curriculum. The practitioners considered that valuing the processes of spontaneous learning could be overshadowed by the emphasis on the products of learning – that it was difficult to encourage children to be spontaneous and creative when they were expected to 'produce displays' or '30 Easter cards', conduct 'assessment schedules' or 'fill in your tick lists'.

Fein and Wiltz (1998) questioned whether spontaneous, flowing play does occur in schools, for when children do play in school it is structured by times, curriculum areas, routines and practitioners' provision of materials. The type of play that might promote children's development might not necessarily be the type of play required by teachers who are expected to plan, record and predict learning outcomes within often inflexible timetables. During discussions with the nine practitioners, many repeated concerns were raised that the demands of the curriculum are incompatible with teaching and learning through play (Blenkin and Kelly 1994; Hurst 1994a; Wood 1999). More specifically, despite evidence of the value of playful learning, concern was expressed that not all children have the opportunity to learn through play, and not all practitioners really know how to teach through play (Wood and Attfield 1996). Consequently, identifying learning through play was problematic.

Within this context of uncertainty about play the group began to talk about their experiences, although initially this was at a very practical level with an emphasis on talking about resources and the different ways in which materials were used by the children. During these early stages, the elusive qualities of play, being so hard to define, resulted in practitioners speaking with more confidence about what children were *doing* rather than ways in which children *learn* through play.

Using Photograph 15.1 as an example, these early stages of discussion,

Photograph 15.1   Practitioners were more concerned with situations in which children are holding a pencil and making marks on paper

focusing as they were on the pragmatic – were concerned with situations in which children are holding a pencil, making marks on paper, writing, drawing: a positive step in identifying areas for further discussion and development.

It was expected that as the project progressed the group would begin to explore the following questions:

- What do practitioners need to know in order to interpret what children are doing when presented with playful choices?
- What might children be learning when engaged in playful activities?

For instance, in addition to what children might be doing – making marks on paper – they might also be learning how to concentrate, to persevere, to imagine, to work alone, to relate to others, to make decisions, to develop autonomy, to be confident and to develop an increasing awareness of self as writer, communicator and initiator.

Confrontation of issues

Lack of pedagogical knowledge

Increasingly, the group was provided with open-ended opportunities to talk about practice, which included comparing routines, discussing recently acquired resources and sharing successes and concerns about individual children in their settings. These anecdotal discussions, discussing the details of activities whilst reviewing practice, also provided identification of contemporary issues that became the basis for further reflection. This involved, for example, considering at a more critical level the quality and relevance of resources in the home corner. Increasingly, discussions focused on *how*, as well as *what*, children learn.

Bruner (1986) considered the need for philosophical discussion are really important; for instance, he commented that it is difficult for children to engage in metacognition if practitioners do not know about or understand how to promote its development. One practitioner confessed: 'I think it's very easy to provide play activities, but whether the children are learning anything from what they're doing is a completely different matter!'

One response to these play-related concerns suggested by Gipps and MacGilchrist (1999) is that in order to develop an articulate primary pedagogy which encourages children's effective learning, we need primary teachers who have good subject and curriculum knowledge with classroom management skills. Also, primary teachers must have a good understanding of how children learn and be able to use this understanding to inform the teaching strategies they employ. Consequently, talking about practice – teaching and learning, beyond the practical level – is an important phase in developing an articulate, critical, reflective pedagogy able to determine, for example, the most appropriate, effective teaching strategy in a given situation or explore *how* play can be developed in order to support and challenge children's learning.

There was an initial reluctance to engage with deeper issues, practitioners adopting a preference to focus on the practical (Hord *et al.* 1998). However, this interest in what children were doing in the home area provided the group with an area to be explored: they were surprised at their reluctance and inability to articulate at a deeper level what children were learning. As one practitioner acknowledged:

> I ought to think about this [how to support play in the home corner] . . . because it's something I take for granted and I'm a bit horrified and, I don't mind you quoting me on this, I can't answer it.

Confronting the black hole

In order to encapsulate the concerns about the emerging evidence of limited pedagogical knowledge, an image of a 'black hole' was developed which represented the ways in which practitioners were hindered by their insecure knowledge:

> . . . basically we had no knowledge [before the TBtP project], just intuition at the beginning. Because we did it then [teaching and learning through play] because that's what we did, whereas now it's the case of there's a sound reason behind it. So we've all grown in confidence because we are professionals.

Confronting their 'not knowing' motivated the group to construct a positive route out of their 'black hole': through talking about practice, questioning each other, reading, learning, researching, being critical, probing, challenging within the context of focused, informed support the group developed a more constructive, informed and critical approach to their practice. The scaffold of confident articulate understanding of practice helped to lift them out of confusion and feelings of inadequacy to a state of confidence, efficacy and empowerment: 'You've got more insight into the reason why you put that equipment out and what you're getting out of it . . . because you can see the value and purpose of it.'

Conceptualization

Simmons *et al.* (1989) suggest that the process of articulation and problematization – confronting a focus for reflection – involves making explicit the taken-for-granted aspects of pedagogy. As already suggested, there were occasions when practitioners were almost flummoxed by relatively simple questions such as 'Why do you have a home corner in your setting?', especially when asked such questions in the context of philosophical discussion. 'Well, we have it because it's there . . . we've always had a home corner' were typical responses.

Discussing classroom experiences with each other promoted a fluency of discourse as they presented, listened and related to each other's accounts. These opportunities for pedagogical discourse occurred within planned, structured discussion but opportunities were also grasped for informal, spontaneous dialogues during breaks, over lunch, or at the ubiquitous photocopier – and so the process of articulation of values and beliefs was developed. The content of their discussion progressed from practical concerns about the provision of resources to deeper conceptualized deliberations: moving from: 'What are the children doing?' to 'What are they learning?'

Once the group had established an ethos in which discourse was valued they began to share immediate concerns, and articulate the successes, celebrations, delights, frustrations, concerns and dilemmas encountered each day during their interactions with children. The practitioners' anecdotes later became the source material for analysis.

> What attracted me to it was the thought of people involved in Early Years, talking about what we do in our practice and what we believe in. I enjoy doing that; I thought it was a really nice experience – you don't get the chance to talk about what you do with children.

It has been established that practitioners do not readily identify and articulate pedagogical values and beliefs (Turner-Bissett 1999). In order to help them locate their own voices, to articulate pedagogical values and beliefs, they need opportunities and time to recount the anecdotes and stories of the daily activities in which they are engaged (Jensen *et al.* 1997). Within the TBtP project it was found that using practitioners' own experiences was the most effective way of exploring theoretical understanding, values and beliefs. Their own experiences were meaningful and relevant and, more importantly, helped the group to focus on and conceptualize deeper issues. For example, at a pragmatic level, a discussion might focus on the appeal of new resources – maybe introducing a new set of pens in the writing area (see Photograph 15.2). But at a deeper level, considerations may also include:

- introducing choice of materials so that children can decide which type of crayon/pen/pencil to use;
- developing creativity – through exploring different textures of different resources;
- developing self-awareness and confidence though being presented with choices;
- ownership of learning while exploring the process of playing with colours;
- making decisions while selecting one item and discarding another.

This deeper level of thinking leads to thoughtful, considered practice. For example, in Photograph 15.2, having recognized children's interests in Literacy and Celebrations, the practitioner consults with the children.

Photograph 15.2 Practitioners show respect for children's play, through determining various ways in which they might write invitations for their Eid party

She shows respect for their play, through determining various ways in which they might prepare for their Eid party using their interests in writing invitations as a starting point for further learning.

The children suggest that they will need food, clothes and party invitations. This party preparation then developed to a deeper discussion with the children. The practitioner explores the reason for the party – celebrating Eid – whilst also acknowledging and respecting the other different faiths in the community. The activity of the Eid party provides opportunities for children to demonstrate and build on what they already know about their own and others' cultures and religions (Moyles and Adams 2001: 26).

The video of this play episode and its underpinning philosophy was used as the basis for further questioning – a process which involved deconstructing many of the understandings practitioners held about their role in children's playful learning. The group began to ask the following questions:

- How can imaginative play be supported and developed in order to support children's learning and development?
- In what way might our principles – the values and beliefs in play – inform the ways in which we playfully support children's learning?
- What does 'respecting other children' actually look like?
- How can we build on our existing ethos of trust and respect?

And so began the process of deconstruction.

Deconstruction

There is much evidence suggesting that engaging in reflective practice requires support, challenge and confrontation (Goodfellow 2000). However, no one within the group was prepared for the anguish which resulted from questioning firmly held values, beliefs and understandings. Confronting their insecure pedagogical knowledge was uncomfortable and resulted in the following responses:

> I felt the last session was quite hard; I thought that was quite challenging – to make you really think.

> I still think I don't know enough about children's development.

> You don't necessarily like to identify it, but you're not really happy with what you're doing.

> I think I thought I knew a lot about practice, but I didn't really have the underlying knowledge – or I had forgotten a lot of it. As the process of deconstruction happens, I feel insecure and isolated . . . I can't see a way through.

> I felt destroyed . . . torn apart . . .

The group began to 'take apart' – to deconstruct – their understandings of how to playfully teach young children. With informed support from each other – both researchers and the other practitioners in the group – they began to identify the areas of pedagogical knowledge which they considered were insecure. These areas became the focus for further focused reflection and questioning, partly because the inquiries took place in a context of trust and non-judgemental, informed, sensitive support (Hord *et al.* 1998). This appropriate context promoted the disposition, enthusiasm and willingness to question and to deconstruct practice (Dahlberg *et al.* 1999).

At a practical level, the group considered ways in which classroom organization might further support learning, or additional resources might facilitate the deepening of culturally respectful play. For example, it was considered that additional resources, supported by informed adults within the community, might enrich children's understanding of each other's cultural backgrounds. In Photograph 15.3 two children take time to help each other change into their party clothes. At a deeper level, the values and ideologies relating to the diverse cultures within the group were considered: some practitioners felt they did not understand enough about the religions and cultures represented in their school's communities, so training to address these needs was established.

They began to talk about the different ways in which they could build on children's interests, strengths, experiences and sociocultural contexts, determining ways in which their pedagogy was informed by respectful considerations of children (Arthur 2001). The practitioners questioned

Photograph 15.3   Two children take time to help each other change into their party clothes

whether existing resources supported their philosophy of respecting and valuing their cultural backgrounds, as in Photograph 15.3, and continued to examine whether the resources really did promote children's learning and developmental needs.

In Photograph 15.4, one child prayerfully prepares for the Eid party; the image represents a celebration of pedagogy in which children and their cultures and religions are better understood, valued and respected.

The questioning became more vigorous through interrogating pedagogical documentation listed earlier, always aiming to make explicit the taken-for-granted aspects of pedagogy – asking such questions as:

- Why? . . . why?
- To what purpose . . .?
- What is the benefit of your interactions in children's learning?
- On what basis do you work in that way?
- What informs your responses to children?
- In what ways does your philosophy make a difference to the way in which you teach?
- How do you further promote play in these areas?
- On what basis do you make this decision?
- What evidence do you have that children are learning when engaged in play?
- In what ways do you show respect for children?

Extensive use was made of cameos – stories told by the group to each

Photograph 15.4   Prayerful preparation for Eid

other during the early stages of the project – and videos, taken in each other's schools of children in playful situations. The cameos and videos were scrutinized openly and constructively by the group in their quest to become better informed practitioners.

Having recognized the pedagogical weaknesses, it was essential that a training programme be developed which would address their identified needs. Strategies were developed to define ways in which future practice would be informed by theory and research as well as being enriched by experiences and established understandings of working with children. One practitioner revealed: 'I felt destroyed – undone all I've ever believed in, . . . I can't believe I didn't know why I had a home corner in my classroom.'

The researchers had a responsibility to rebuild these pedagogical spirits; this led to the fifth stage, a positive conclusion, in which values, beliefs and understandings were reconstructed.

Reconstruction

One of the key conditions required in order to promote reflective practice is that practitioners receive informed, focused support (Hord *et al.* 1998). In the context of the TBtP project, support was made available from the two researchers. Within the context of working in schools, Inch and MacVarish (2003) have explored the benefit of providing collegiate support – with either:

- a colleague in a similar aspect of education, e.g. both early years – with the added benefit of both parties enjoying a repertoire of shared experiences; or with
- a colleague in a different phase, e.g. one early years, the other Year 2, so that both can support and challenge each other without intruding on each other's domain.

Inch and MacVarish document their study in which two practitioners spend time, out of school, talking with each other about their work, sharing the passion and content of their teaching without invasively or intrusively interfering in each other's work. The result was a combination of powerful and subtle changes in the way they work. In talking about how they teach, they were encouraged to question each other and then to question themselves (Inch and MacVarish 2003: 3):

> Working with Judy has made me reconsider, re-evaluate and re-write my teaching techniques. I take nothing for granted now. I used to think that every student should be able to understand my explanations. Now I realize that some students just don't learn that way. I also know that some students won't learn unless I tie these new ideas to practical problems.

A second condition of support is provision of time required to reflect and develop aspects of practice. For instance, the two practitioners above took time to talk about their practice with each other, in this case out of the classroom. Dawson (2003) comments that whilst practitioners are encouraged to develop a reflective approach to practice, in reality little opportunity is provided for opportunities to reflect quietly and critically in a way that is likely to nourish the pedagogical soul.

There is considerable evidence that senior management can be responsible for developing an ethos in which reflective dialogue is encouraged and valued. This can be developed effectively through adopting policies that provide time for discussion, sharing ideas, concerns and examination of all aspects of early years pedagogy (Moyles *et al.* 2002). Contemporary issues, or the deliberation of sensitive dilemmas which face early years practitioners, can also be brought to the surface during these discussions. This might include racist or cultural attitudes which might emerge in children's play, or the consideration of practitioners' values and understanding of broader political issues which might impact children's responses in play. The familiar debate might be revisited on whether to ignore, forbid or encourage gun play or there might be discussion of children's responses to acts of aggression which they observe in the world around them (Adams and Moyles 2005).

Being reflective: does it matter?

Within the TBtP project one of the benefits of reflective thinking resulted in an enhanced sense of self-efficacy in which practitioners began to think differently about themselves.
The following comments were typical:

> The enabling power of knowledge has allowed many in the group to gain promotion in their professional lives (including me) and led to others pursuing higher qualifications (also including me!). The irony is that in aiming to foster a love of learning in the children in my setting, I had forgotten to tend to my needs as a learner. I am responsible for my own lifelong learning. Taking part in this research was a timely intervention, through which I feel, and know, I have become a more effective practitioner. Not only have I survived, I feel as if I have achieved more and am reaching for things I did not know were within my grasp.
>
> (Adams *et al.* 2000: 163)

During this process the practitioners said they began to '. . . discover knowledge I'd forgotten from long ago'; '. . . do things I never thought possible'.

Engaging in reflective practice, questioning, confronting weaknesses, building on strengths, learning and reconstructing pedagogy resulted in thoughtful practice informed by research, theory and reflected-upon experiences. Consequently, the practitioners within the group were better prepared to:

* resource their settings in ways that support children's playful learning and development;
* be articulate, knowledgeable professionals (Moyles *et al.* 2002);
* be informed and more familiar with current initiatives and concerns for young children (Adams *et al.* 2004);
* respond with confident fluency in children's play;
* learn about appropriate playful practice;
* remain true to their own professional values, in spite of different priorities from parents, LEA staff, their own insecurities and personal values;
* be playful practitioners – teachers and nursery nurses.

Conclusion

Earlier in this chapter, I expressed concern regarding the dislocation between practitioners' philosophy and practice that continues to abound (DfE 1990; Education and Employment Committee 2000). Yet recent initiatives increasingly support children's playful learning (QCA/DFEE 2000).

Through reflecting in a different way, informed practitioners may better realize the opportunities to interpret the *Curriculum Guidance for the Foundation Stage* in playful and developmentally appropriate ways.

Questions to set you thinking

1 What is the benefit of your interactions in children's learning?
2 On what basis do you work in that way?
3 What informs your responses to children?
4 In what way does your philosophy make a difference to the way in which you teach?
5 How do you further promote play in these areas?
6 What evidence do you have that children are learning when engaged in play?

16 The importance of play in the transition to school

Hilary Fabian and Aline-Wendy Dunlop

Summary

This chapter considers the importance of play in the transition to school. Whilst there are significant differences in the curriculum for school entrants in England, Wales and Scotland, there are common features of transition and of play that are equally important in each context. Children may enter early years provision and school at a similar age, but the curriculum models vary. In England, the Foundation Stage supports children from 3 to 6 years of age, then a transition occurs on passing to Key Stage 1. In Wales the new Foundation Phase covers the ages 3 to 7 years and a transition occurs at age 7. In Scotland, presently undergoing a curriculum review encompassing discussion of a 3 to 18 curriculum, children from 3 to 5 years in preschool settings experience the Curriculum Framework for Children 3 to 5. However, on entry to primary school the curriculum 5 to 14 takes over. In each country, children are subject to a significant curriculum transition not only in content but also in the style of teaching and learning. This chapter will present evidence to show that, amongst other helpful mechanisms to bridge curriculum transitions between phases, play provides important opportunities for children to make sense of the new and to achieve personal competence and progress in their learning.

Introduction: defining transition

The nature of transition encompasses several theoretical spheres that affect children. The current interpretation defines educational transition as the change children make from one place, stage, state, style or subject to another over time. For children, educational transitions are characterized by the intense and accelerated developmental demands that they encounter as they move from one learning and teaching setting to another. A range of writings (Fabian and Dunlop 2002a; Dunlop and Fabian 2003) propose that the way in which transitions are experienced not only makes a difference to children in the early months of a new situation, but may also have a much longer term impact, because the extent to which they feel successful in the first transition is likely to influence subsequent experiences. Changes of relationships, teaching style, environments, space, time, contexts for learning and demands of learning itself combine at moments of transition.

Ways of thinking about the transition to school

There are two main strands to the transition to school: 'settling in' to the school in terms of getting to know people and the environment, and learning about learning at school. Continuity is the key to both these elements. In the past, there has been an emphasis on the importance of preparing children for school by introducing them to the new situation before they have left the old. Induction approaches ranged from an initial visit to a series or programme of visits and participation in a number of school activities, often in the school term preceding entry. In some situations, children were expected to develop certain necessary skills before school entry, and such development was planned for in the prior-to-school setting attended. Whilst most schools now provide pre-entry visits or programmes, the focus of these is to introduce the child and family to the ways of the school and to ensure that families feel respected. Such approaches aim for adjustment and change and for the child to have an expectation of 'school-readiness' (Broström 2002).

It is informative to consider other ways of conceiving school entry. Corsaro and Molinari (2000) write of the whole of the prior-to-school experience being like a priming event for school. They emphasize the embedded nature of children's growing experience as distinct from specific school preparation. On this model, the expectation would be that the experience of learning, cooperating and working alongside others through play situations, investigation, pretend play, talk and hands-on activity would combine to develop the kinds of skills that children need as their education becomes more formalized. The idea of Rogoff *et al.* (2003) of 'intent participation' highlights the nature of learning in early childhood as being part of the sociocultural activity around them, in which children learn through social participation, the dynamic of being part of social relationships, opportunities to observe others, and chances to participate alongside more experienced members of a social setting. Learning within this model is interactive. Lave and Wenger (1991) write of 'situated learning' in communities of practice. In this model, the extent to which children are able to participate is extremely important. In reflecting on the idea of communities of practice, there is scope to consider how one set of practices may borrow from another. Here, the idea of boundaries and boundary relations (Wenger 1999) between different stages of educational practice can be seen to be important. This raises the spectre of two very different traditions in education – before school and from school entry – and the relative value placed on particular pedagogies and philosophies in each.

Today's children face a future that will require adaptability, flexibility and creativity (Claxton 2000), both for their social well-being and their cognitive development. How then do children themselves negotiate the changes from one type of school setting to another? Here it may be helpful to consider the relevance of the work of van Gennep (1960) on rites of passage, Campbell-Clark's (2000) work on border crossings, Bourdieu's (2001) concept of rites of institution and Bruner's (1996) thoughts on the culture of education, and various authors on agency (e.g. Dunlop 2003). If we conceptualize transition as the passage from one phase of life to another, then it will be important to mark that time of change and to allow children to feel the differences between being a preschool child and a school child. Their identity will change in educational transition, just as it will change if they become a 'big sister', a child of separated parents or a homeless child. Such child and family transitions need to be recognized for their complexity and impact on development. Children, therefore, need support to help them mark, as well as to negotiate, change. The need for negotiation becomes apparent when transition is conceptualized as a 'border crossing'. Day-to-day separations, new experiences, moves from school to out-of-school provision, all involve the crossing of boundaries. It can be argued too that each crossing is likely to involve a new set of rules or rites that belong to the particular institution, and that to become settled and competent in each setting the child will need to absorb and respond to the mores of that setting. The question of children being able to use what they know from one setting to another is intricately woven into this tapestry of different ways of envisaging transition and change. Their power to act, to feel and to be competent will be influenced by how familiar or different the new situation is, what signposts exist to help the child make connections, how well they are able to take account of difference, their resilience and the balance between the recognizable and the new.

Photograph 16.1   How familiar or different are the new situations in transitions?

The place of play in transitions

Play is a common childhood experience. Most children have opportunities to play in ways which have been shown to influence learning, from social competence to cognitive benefits, including the development of language, imagination and pretence (see Part 2 of this book), supporting children's emotional well-being, and gaining physical benefits (as is emphasized in many chapters in this book). Some children miss out on this common childhood experience, either through dint of circumstance or because of their special educational needs (see Chapter 3 of this book).

Many writings on play cite the work of Piaget, Vygotsky and Bruner, as we have seen in the Introduction to this book. Piaget's stage theory of intellectual development focused more on the child's construction of reality than on the social context of learning. Donaldson (1978) emphasized the importance of the human context in children's play and learning and, whilst questioning Piaget's work, added to it by focusing on the need for learning to make 'human sense' to children. Smilansky (1990) extended Piaget's categories by adding a category of constructive play as this was so dominant in early childhood. Children were found to build and rebuild and in the process invent, test and represent their ideas about the world (Hewitt 2001).

Vygotsky (1978) anticipated the importance of using activity as a basic psychological construct: the zone of proximal development is an idea that has been much exploited in terms of the role of the more able 'other' in play and learning. Bruner's (1966) spiral curriculum supported the notion of children returning to their zone of proximal development and progressively focusing, widening and deepening their learning. Drawing further, and more recently, from Bruner, the interrelationships of agency, collaboration, reflection and culture that he proposes (1996) can as usefully be applied to play and playful learning as to teaching and learning, so a picture begins to emerge of the importance of personal agency, collaboration and reflection in play. Play is about doing. Reflecting on learning comes through talking about it, by making what is learned 'make sense': collaboration allows for the meeting of minds, for sharing child-to-child, child-to-adult, adult-to-child in learning and teaching. Culture is the context in which agency, reflection and collaboration can take place. The way of being, of organizing classrooms, of providing for children, will determine whether the particular classroom culture supports the other ideas.

Key changes at transition to school

School brings certain key changes that we have typified by contrasting a social and emotional agenda with a cognitive agenda, as shown in Figure 16.1 (from Fabian and Dunlop 2002b).

We propose that for progress from preschool to early primary to be purposeful from the earliest days, whether at age 4, 5 or 6, account needs to be taken of both social–emotional and cognitive dimensions of learning. The interconnections between home and preschool and school, and between the various phases of school, and the interaction between the

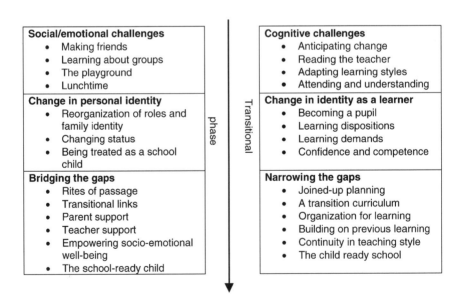

Figure 16.1   Key changes at transition to school

person and the environment, will affect the developmental outcomes of children in transition. Curriculum, relationships and settings are different, but have the possibility of being closely tuned in ways that are favourable for children. The interrelationships developed can be decisive for children in terms of their start in school and their continuing learning, so affecting future outcomes (Fabian and Dunlop 2002b). Such an ecological model of learning stems from the work of Bronfenbrenner (1979) and provides a theory of transition that has the interconnectedness of children's experience at its core.

Social challenges

The 'seriosity' of life (Griebel and Niesel 1999) starts with school when children undergo a change in identity and become a 'school child'. A study by Brooker (2002) outlines how children move from 'child in the family' to 'pupil in the school' and how the values of home and school often differ. These include differences in the way play at home and play at school is perceived according to family and cultural values. These differences may cause emotional difficulties for children. However, starting school means not only having to learn the social rules and values of the organization, but getting acquainted with different adults and children (Thyssen 1997). On entering the wider social world of school there is the possibility of making new friends, but also, entering the world of social comparison, the need to 'read' social situations and have a social understanding, in order to become a member of the school society. Barrett's (1986) study of children starting school highlights some of the lack of control that children feel when they start school, which also impacts on their emotional well-being. Leaving the preschool setting can cause stress due to the loss of friends, adults and familiar routines. Starting school can create times of uncertainty about what to do, where to go and whom to approach.

   A child is less likely to learn well and profit from school without the support of friends but there are complex social skills involved in making and maintaining friends. These include 'the ability to gain entry to group activities, to be approving and supportive of one's peers, to manage conflicts appropriately, and to exercise sensitivity and tact' (Dowling 2000: 23). For example, children might be unaware that they are joining an established class where friendships are already formed (Hughes *et al.* 1979) but are expected to have the social skills to learn in groups within this class. Considerable social understanding is involved in knowing the group culture to gain acceptance, adapting to large group situations where children are expected to learn alongside others, and gaining membership of smaller groups where they are expected to cooperate and work collaboratively (Fabian 2002). Children must learn to work and play in different size groups and also learn to be a member of both informal and formal groups, for example in assembly, during classroom activities and at play time. The playground, with its noise and volume of 'traffic', sometimes moving at high speed, can be a frightening and stressful place (Ghaye and Pascal 1988: 16).

Cognitive challenges

School demands that children often learn to think and reason in 'disembedded contexts' (Donaldson 1978). Instead of dealing directly with situations that make 'human sense', often children have to use symbol systems and deal with representations of the world (in words and numbers, pictures and diagrams). The key to being able to do so is to have an awareness of the mind's activity. Deliberately using talk about thought, or taking another's perspective, or imagining how someone will think or what they should do in a given situation helps people to develop this reflective awareness. The consequence of this discovery of the mind has cognitive, social and emotional importance.

There are substantial changes in the development of representational skills between the ages of 3 and 5, but not all children entering school will have an emerging capacity to understand the teacher's intentions and requests or to pay attention and respond appropriately. The growing understanding of mind that children acquire in the preschool years underlies their social interactions with family and friends and provides the foundation for their cognitive activities in school.

Children who are emotionally and socially ready for school may be better placed to meet the cognitive challenges of a new stage of education and accommodate changes in their status as learners so that they move readily into the changed demands on their capacities to learn. We cannot ignore the mutual influences of social and cognitive change. Nor can we ignore evidence that children 'dip' after transition (Dunlop 2004). However ready for school the preschool child may seem, it is helpful if changes are continuous rather than abrupt, if connections are emphasized and environments and modes of learning are similar. Discontinuity occurs for children when experience is intermittent and separated by time and by space. Progression implies an onward motion, an advance, an integration of the previous into the present. It is proposed that continuity and progression are key elements in school success and that play can help to build a transition bridge.

Supporting children's social understanding through play

Many children find it easier to learn and discover their abilities outside; they feel more comfortable in an outdoor environment and the activities they experience are often more physical and play-based (see Peter Smith's and Stephanie Harding's comments in Chapter 9 and 10 of this book respectively). However, while playing and learning outside is a central part of an early years curriculum, the emphasis on outdoor learning reduces as children move into more formal education at the start of school. While many schools have developed their playgrounds into interesting areas and gardens (see Chapter 10 of this book), learning takes place mainly indoors and is generally a much more sedentary occupation than that found in preschool settings. The outdoors has been shown to benefit boys particularly and can offer experiences, challenges and risks essential to learning. What can schools do to use the playground as a way to ease the transition at the start of school?

Using the playground to promote friendship

One school has developed social, personal and creative education, known as 'SPACE time'. This is a set time every afternoon when each class in the school uses the outdoor areas for an informal learning activity. Pupils in the first year at school said they enjoyed 'SPACE time' where they could flow between inside and out, much as they had done in nursery and Reception, playing with musical instruments, taking part in dance and using a designated area to practise ball skills as part of their outside lessons. While some of the activities were teacher-directed, many gave the children an opportunity to develop their own play situations and ideas.

This use of the outdoors has several benefits. It promotes the use of a large space and reduces the fear that children might have of the playground at transition. The way in which children learn in less formal surroundings helps them to develop friendships, and the outside contributes to their health and well-being. Perhaps the most important benefit is that the children are in control of the way in which they want their play to develop and give themselves tasks in their play, not really for an outcome, but to shape the play-process itself. This helps the children to build a strong identity and gives them a sense of achievement.

Children in the above example learned the social mores of the school through participation in play. The following example illustrates how, through collaborative role play, children can be active agents in bridging the gap between settings.

Using role play to transmit the culture

Children in the nursery painted pictures of their favourite stories and then acted them for the children in the first class in school. These included traditional stories such as The Three Little Pigs and modern classics such as The Hungry Caterpillar. When the nursery children started school, the teacher displayed their paintings in the classroom at the beginning of term. This gave them great self-esteem and a sense of belonging. They then built on their role play by extending the stories that they had demonstrated to the previous year group.

In order to signal to their teachers what is of interest to them, and to learn with their friends, it is essential that the social processes of play take place. By choosing their own stories to paint and act, the children begin to bring their own (nursery) culture to the school setting rather than assuming that the school culture is the norm. They also had a starting point to continue their role play in the new setting, responding to changing storylines and inventing new endings as they acted out their ideas.

Playing with materials not only helps children's understanding of the curriculum but also, if children have a shared interest, this can help them to break into other friendship groups.

Using materials to learn about learning in groups

One nursery put together some Discovery Bags containing materials related to various scientific themes such as magnetism, sound, materials and suchlike that the children played with in small friendship groups. When they moved to school, these same Discovery Bags formed the beginning of a science lesson. The children had joined an established class of pupils and during the lesson they worked in their friendship groups demonstrating to groups in the established class how they played with the materials in the Discovery Bags and what they had observed.

This activity demonstrates the way in which children were able to develop their confidence through playing with materials. This then gave them the confidence to demonstrate their understanding to groups of children with whom they were unfamiliar. It gave them a starting point for conversation and developing further friendships.

Supporting children's learning and transition through play

Adult ideas about children's learning strongly influence the experiences we offer them. If play is considered the preserve of early years preschool settings, children risk being deprived of the very mode of learning which has been dominant for them (see Tina Bruce, Chapter 18 of this book). The nature of the setting is also powerful. The classroom environment reflects the model of learning held by the teacher or the school. If the classroom environment and the modes and style of teaching are recognizable to children then they are likely to 'dip' less on school entry, to be able to demonstrate what they know and can do, and to manage their own social behaviour. If, on the other hand, the environment is more limited than in their previous experience, if play is kept to manageable table-top activities, if talk is discouraged and choice is all in the hands of the teacher, then children will be less able to draw on their previous experience and will lack confidence that things they already know and can do are acceptable in the new setting. Agency, collaboration and reflection as part of play and a playful learning culture would be at risk. Even if play is on offer in these circumstances, changes in forms of play may make it unrecogniz-

Photograph 16.2   Changes in forms of play may make it unrecognizable to children

able to children, and teachers can feel that these children do not know how to play: the distinction between 'play as such' and 'play in schools' (Guha 1988) can be very real.

A picture begins to develop of agency often being more visible in preschool contexts than in early school contexts with greater personal agency in preschool play than in primary. Group activity, choice in play and a lot of first-hand activity characterizes most preschool settings for the main part of each session. Children and adults work or play alongside each other. Sometimes the adults set up activities children could choose to join, sometimes children start out on their chosen activity and are joined by an adult.

Case study: Briarbank Nursery Class[1]

Colin was joined for a lengthy period at the Lego table by his teacher, who built alongside him and interacted conversationally with Colin and other children who came to the table. She noticed how he was using the materials, and discussed with him the bridge building that he was trying to achieve. She followed his agenda asking real, not quizzing, questions and trying to find solutions through his lead. She recognized and respected his competence, but at the same time scaffolded his problem solving. By the time he was ready to move on he had successfully built a bridge that spanned his 'river' rather than running along it.

An increased emphasis on collaboration in primary classes, sometimes with the teacher and sometimes with peers, could lend itself to increased agency. This can be seen in the following example from Colin's primary class. The morning workshops in a number of the classes often closed with a 'show and tell' time in which children talked about what they had done. Where children are encouraged to reflect on their play or playful active learning, it is likely that children's competence as thinkers is enhanced. By encouraging reflection and articulation of learning, reporting back sessions can become much more than 'show and tell'.

Case study: Briarbank Primary School

Colin's primary teacher offered play every day until the morning interval. Children rotated round the available activities during the course of the week. She circulated, supporting and redirecting children in their play, taking time to listen to them and talk with them. Colin found himself at the Lego play one day charged to make a three-storey house and to find a way of getting from floor to floor. Once construction was under way, Colin supported his peers and adopted some of the approaches used by his nursery teacher with him. At one point the building was at risk of collapsing – the children were encouraged to share ideas to make it stable, and to collaborate in finding a solution. At the end of the morning session Colin was asked to report to the rest of the class. His teacher's approach encouraged him to reflect on what had worked and what had not. It was clear that Colin felt good in school.

Group gatherings in preschool rarely made this expectation of children, and whilst play episodes may reflect more potential for complex play than is sometimes apparent in primary classrooms, this can be less articulated than in primary education.

Case study: Grantown Nursery Class

Norrie was invited to help prepare the snack: his spoken English was at this stage very limited, but his comprehension was more developed. He chose jam as a suitable filling, and undertook all sandwich-making tasks alongside his teacher, who talked him through the process. He sometimes paused to watch, sometimes took the lead, until they had filled a plate with sandwiches together. Such support was much more overt when Norrie chose to join Naheem at the computer. Naheem instructed him in the use of the computer: here the two boys shared the game, with Naheem giving directions, placing his hand over Norrie's on the mouse, and telling him when he had been successful.

Both class teacher and another child worked alongside Norrie in his nursery class. The roles of more or less experienced people were shared between adults and children and not necessarily the preserve of one or other. Such collaboration did not extend into school in Norrie's case.

Case study: Grantown Primary School

Norrie often learned by watching: it was the vehicle available to him, but the teacher in his new class did not modify her instruction, nor did she offer the kind of commentary given by his nursery teacher. His friend was placed in the neighbouring class, so he lost the support and intent participation the two of them had shared. He was observed watching two other boys in road traffic play on several occasions in his primary class, but he was not supported actively to enter the play. Whilst most of the time he appeared no less comfortable in his primary class than in preschool, he simply stayed, and was allowed to stay, on the edge.

Once in school, the same children often wait to be told what to do next, have set subjects to paint and draw and play with construction materials according to the teacher's agenda so transforming play into something that has to have an outcome. In some classes, some of the time, play is more similar to preschool, but without the flexibility of resources, time or space. These examples support the idea that there may be change in the forms of play experienced in different situations, and that these can build on children's existing experience to provide progression in play and learning, or can miss opportunities to enhance the competence of the child in the new situation. An increased emphasis on collaboration and reflection, with opportunities to talk about their play, would enhance children's reflection on their own learning and experience.

Opportunities to play with friends, to sit beside known children, and to engage in already known and understood learning styles could have supported Norrie's transition to school more effectively. In Colin's case, the benefits of teacher collaboration between settings and a classroom organized effectively for integrated play and learning opportunities were visible.

Since play often takes place in social contexts an argument may be made that the development of relationships is not only crucial to the development of the sort of reciprocity needed in joint play, but fundamental to being able to reflect on one's own thinking as well as to be able to 'mentalize about others' (Trevarthen and Aitken 2001). Language, too, is variously used in play, for self- and other regulation, for characterization, in switching role, for introspection, to describe and to problem solve, to formulate plans, to reason, to reflect and to collaborate. These varied uses afford children some autonomy and agency in their play and provide an arena for learning. By sharing what we know about effective practice across settings we can also reconsider the role of adults in relation to children's play. Readings in early education variously typify the adult's role as 'stage manager', 'planner', 'scribe', 'mediator', 'role model', 'player', 'scaffolder' and 'companion'. Each of these descriptions can lend itself to playful learning and teaching, most especially within what Trevarthen calls 'companionship relations'.

Play not only has a major role in early childhood development but also in supporting the progression across transitions. We have seen that learning does not happen in a social vacuum but is an interactive event in which children construct their own meanings through being active, through playing with ideas and by being supported by adults. Where learning is collaborative, with children following their own interests and making their own decisions, it has generally started with play. Where learning is meaningful rather than following a set, incremental curriculum, it is an emotional experience, not tied to a goal. It helps with making friends, thus reducing the uncertainty at the start of school, and helps to create resilient and emotionally literate children who have some sense of mastery over their lives. A virtuous cycle develops for those children who are socially skilled, as they are more likely to have a succession of positive experiences with others and consequently develop cognitively.

It is time for the potential of play as part of learning to be revisited. The value of play and its nature must be made explicit, and teachers need to be supported in developing their role in relation to play and playful learning. If a continuum of playful learning is sustained within an ecological model of transitions, taking account of the situated nature of learning, intent participation, and the need for scaffolding and bridging learning, then play can be an important mechanism for supporting the move to school, and an opportunity for continuity and progression in learning.

Conclusion

This chapter has explored the ways in which play can be woven into children's lives and used as a support for curriculum transitions that children make in the UK from early childhood services to school. Continuity and progression are key elements in school success but any abrupt change of curriculum may cause discontinuity. Definitions of transition from a theoretical perspective and key changes that occur from moving from early childhood services to school, both socially and cognitively, have been explored.

Examples have been given of ways that discontinuities might be overcome through the use of play and ways in which play might help to support both learning and social understanding by children gaining control over their lives. We see that learning does not happen in a social vacuum but is an interactive event that helps children construct their own meanings through being active, through playing with ideas and being supported by adults.

Questions to set you thinking

1 How do we assess and record progress made during play?
2 How might this be used to identify children's needs on transfer to school?
3 Should play across the transition be guided by adults or be child-led?
4 What are the resource implications for using play as a transition medium?

Note

[1] All case studies in this chapter are taken from Dunlop (2004).

17 | Play in the early years: the influence of cultural difference

Tricia David and Sacha Powell

Summary

In this chapter we discuss the ways in which culture shapes people's constructions of childhood and how, in turn, ideas about and policies and practices for provision for young children are influenced by these constructions. We present evidence from China and discuss the findings of the OECD's survey, in order to consider if, how or why different cultures adopt particular views about play and learning, and what our answers tell us about that culture.

Introduction

In this chapter we explore the ways in which culture influences the assumptions and expectations held by members of particular cultural groups about the role of play in early childhood settings. We highlight the influences of continuity and change in one particular culture, China, in relation to early childhood education. We present findings from international comparisons of provision and question the motives for, and interpretations of, teaching through play.

What do we mean by culture?

Sanders (2004) considers what we mean by culture particularly in relation to children and their childhoods. He points out that culture is *learned*
and *shared* and relies on symbols to convey meaning. He adds that it is also
patterned – different aspects are linked and each culture is *unique*, while at
the same time being part of the *universal* in the sense that all human
beings live within a culture, or cultures. Some cultures may also include
aspects that link them with other cultures – so there will be a *generality*
about those cultures. Children are *encultured* – they acquire and join in
cultural events and practices, learning how to live within their community's culture by participating. However, some members of a cultural
group sometimes decide they do not wish to follow the 'rules' of their
community's culture. They may defect to live elsewhere, or stay and be
labelled renegades or outcasts. MacNaughton (2003: 14), discussing issues
related to conforming to culture, such as *gender norms*, defines culture as
'what we create beyond our biology. Not given to us, but made by us . . .
what we create of the child beyond their biology.'

Today, with the effects of globalization, different cultures impinge on
one another and there is increasing cultural overlap and complexity.
Further, some cultural practices may be challenged because they do not
promote children's well-being. The Articles of the United Nations Convention on the Rights of the Child (UN 1989 – now ratified by all countries
of the world except the United States and Somalia) are international
standards with which countries have agreed to comply, but they will be
interpreted by each cultural group in ways that make sense according to
their own cultural meanings.

In an analysis of globalization and its impact, Lubeck and Jessup (2001)
warn of the dangers of universal educational goals and argue that early
childhood professionals will need to be more responsive to their local
context. Further, educators will need to understand how people in their
community 'make meaning', as well as being more critical of knowledge
and power relations, more willing to consider questions of value, rather
than simply what works and utilitarian issues. Play approaches and the
curricula that depend on them cannot simply be grafted on to one cultural
'body' from another.

Ideas about play and learning are being constructed, interpreted, or
made sense of within each cultural context and it must be remembered
that cultural contexts are not museums: they are dynamic and changing.
Thus the ways in which a cultural group understands the place of young
children and decides how to provide for them will change over time and
place, and will influence the role and status of their play. However, the
cultural history of a community or nation will also exert a powerful influence, especially if the values espoused by dominant groups or individuals
are embedded in those histories. In some cases a decision may have been
made to try to alter earlier assumptions, as in the case of the community of

Reggio Emilia in Northern Italy. The celebrated and world-famous nurseries of Reggio have provided a model of early childhood education that is characterized by certain fundamental principles. Most central to these is the notion that young children are strong and capable co-constructors of knowledge. The nurseries were founded with the intention of challenging the legacy of the previous Fascist phase in history, when people in the area were subjugated through fear and obedience was demanded. They made a conscious decision to educate their youngest children in such a way that they would think for themselves, express themselves and feel able to disagree with others where necessary – to use the 'hundred languages of children' (Edwards *et al.* 1998).

One of the great benefits of improved opportunities for travel and electronic communication has been the possibility of sharing ideas about policies and practices relating to young children with colleagues from other countries (see for example David 1993, 1998; Anning *et al.* 2004). Exploring provision in other countries is like holding up a curved mirror to ourselves; what we see is similar to but also different from what we take for granted. What this means is that we can reflect on our own assumptions, ideas and practices about play and learning (see Siân Adams's discussion in Chapter 15 of this book). However, in order to make more sense of what we observe, it helps to consider ideas about the cultural constructions of early childhood – what different cultural groups assume about children and their place in society, and how they try to shape them as citizens. Consequently this will have had an impact on whether and how provision is made for play.

How different cultures adopt different models of childhood to serve different aims

Babies seem to be born 'programmed' to participate in the events they find going on around them. They are brilliant observers and have an amazing drive to socialize. They appear to have a strong need to become a member of their own family and community (see for example Karmiloff and Karmiloff-Smith 2001). The ways in which language is used, the rituals, patterns of behaviour, customs, symbols and their meanings, are all eagerly appreciated by these new members of a cultural group. This does not mean to say that young children are passive absorbers of life around them; they are participants who may sometimes actively collaborate in transforming or adapting aspects of their culture, including language. Recognition of this powerful drive to learn about what is going on around them, most recently supported by evidence from brain research, has led many governments to seek to capitalize on this early phase. And neuroscientific research suggests that babies and young children learn best through play and interaction with familiar, loved others – both adults and children (see review by David *et al.* 2003).

Sutton-Smith (1997: 225) studied neuro-physiological evidence and concluded that:

> Play's function in the early stages of development, therefore, may be to assist the actualization of brain potential . . . its function would be to save, in both brain and behaviour, more of the variability that is potentially there than would otherwise be saved if there were no play.

Conclusions like this have led nations with very different cultures to explore whether learning through play might be of more benefit to their young children, and ultimately to their society, than the regimes currently operating.

Rosenthal's (1999) framework for examining the role of early childhood in different cultural groups suggests that highly individualistic cultures adopt free play approaches in their early childhood education and care (ECEC) settings whereas adult teaching and the passing on of knowledge is more likely to characterize a community-oriented culture.

In some cross-cultural research in which a team of us collaborated with a team from Melbourne University, the analysis of the data according to Rosenthal's framework led us to conclude that educators in France and Singapore were operating in largely community-oriented cultures. Australian provision meanwhile seemed to promote individualism. In England we found confusion, a mix of indulgent, child-led free play and highly didactic teacher-led inputs, often with no connection between the two (David *et al.* 2000, 2001).

Learning from China

Earlier in this chapter, the notion of 'culture(s)' was discussed and the importance of recognizing the dynamic nature of cultures was highlighted. This is particularly true in relation to China. The People's Republic of China (founded in 1949 by communist revolutionaries) has a relatively short history in relation to 'Chinese civilization', which is known to have been documented for more than 3000 years. Chinese communist ideologies are built upon long-standing traditions including the teachings of Confucius (551–479 BC) that have dominated the country's philosophies and values for over 2000 years. Therefore, the present political climate that drives for economic reform, modernization and significant social change in China (especially in urban areas) is underpinned by ancient cultural traditions, layered with more recent socialist principles. Studies within and across China and of Chinese nationals living outside the mainland (including people in Hong Kong and Taiwan) suggest, however, that despite the vast geographical size of the country, the extreme differences in living conditions in some urban and rural areas and the exposure to change, or to different social systems and philosophies, many Chinese people retain core cultural values (see for example, Wong 1992; Wu 1996; Li 2002). Pan (1994) identified six key areas:

- Chinese culture emphasizes 'passive acceptance' of fate by seeking harmony with nature;
- Chinese culture emphasizes inner experiences of meaning and feeling;
- traditional Chinese culture is typified by a closed worldview, prizing stability and harmony;
- traditional Chinese culture rests on kinship ties and tradition with a historical orientation;
- traditional Chinese culture places more weight on vertical interpersonal relationships; and
- traditional Chinese culture weights heavily a person's duties to family, clan and state.

These traditional values, meshed together with more recent ideologies, assumptions and expectations, provide a framework within which to explore what constitutes play in Chinese contexts, and whether/how it is harnessed as a means of 'enculturing' children in a society that is experiencing extensive social and economic change.

Referring to the impact of play, Wood and Attfield (1996: 5) state that play may be 'banned, tolerated, encouraged or indulged'. Translated into a continuum (see Figure 17.1), their words provide a useful tool for thinking about the nature or characteristics of play within particular contexts, about changes over time, and about a culture's motivation for locating play, or specific types of play, at different places along the continuum.

During the last five to ten years, early childhood educators and policymakers in China's most politically and economically influential cities, Beijing and Shanghai, have begun to reform the structure of early childhood education (including provision for babies and children under 3 and their

Figure 17.1 Is play . . .

| Banned? | Tolerated? | Encouraged? | Indulged? |

◀───▶

This model raises numerous questions:

- What (if any) types of play are banned, tolerated, encouraged, or indulged, and why?
- What can we learn about the enculturation of children, and about a culture's values and social systems by asking these questions about the (kinds of) play we see and don't see?
- What can we learn about how (or whether) play is harnessed to serve the purposes of an unwritten socio-political or cultural agenda or, indeed, a 'hidden' curriculum?
- What can we learn about the extent to which children are effecting change through their play, and contributing to the development of cultures?

families). There have also been moves to improve early years teacher training and to reformulate early childhood curricula and kindergarten guidelines. In 2001, the state-run news agency, Xinhua, reported that the Chinese government in Beijing was to issue preschool education regulations which, for the first time, had widened the age bracket (currently 3 to 6 years) to birth to 6 years, so that even the youngest children might 'receive systematic education' (*Xinhua News Website*, 31 July 2001). This focus on children from birth to 3 has been instigated partly by recent findings from neuroscience. Another key influence is parental demand for high-quality early years education in settings that provide a 'sound pedagogical foundation' for children whose later education and employment will be in highly competitive contexts (Wei and Ebbeck 1996; Powell 2001).

In early years settings where there is an expectation that children's activities will lead to specific learning outcomes, it is important to consider how play is conceptualized and understood. Fundamentally, there is an underlying question about whether a group of people with shared cultural values believe, for example, in play as an '*ars artis*' activity, in which learning is accepted as inherent (but not predictable), or whether they believe that specific playful activities must be afforded for particular learning outcomes to emerge. In the first instance, children may be afforded greater opportunities to determine when, where and how they play. In the second, adults are more likely to influence the nature of playful activities. Sha (1998) explains that play in China has traditionally been linked to physical development but separated from intellectual development, and that this view stems from Confucian thought (see also Pan 1994). In a study of young children's attitudes to play and those of their families and teachers in China, Sha (1998) discovered that participants saw play as a recreational (rather than learning) experience. However, teachers used children's natural tendency to play as a motivator to engage them in playful but teacher-directed class activities.

Stepping back from providing mostly teacher-directed activities is further complicated in China by teaching style. Several observers (Gardner 1989; Jin and Cortazzi 1998) have described Chinese teachers' practices as similar to a polished theatrical performance, which Potts (2003) argues limits the extent to which practice can be modified to encompass new ideas that demand repeated deviation from the performance.

Nevertheless, as neuroscientific evidence about synaptic development during play (for example, Sutton-Smith 1997) is influencing the emphasis on play in Chinese early years practice, there are attempts to include free play and greater choice for children. Early childhood practitioners are now expected to modify their practice, supported by training and ongoing professional development. But traditional attitudes towards play (as non-intellectual), coupled with parents' beliefs that teacher-directed activities are better for their children's learning, and performance-like teaching styles, do not ease the transition or help to raise the status of free play.

Photograph 17.1   In China teachers used children's natural tendency to play as a motivator to engage them in playful but teacher-directed class activities

References to the importance of play in Chinese early years literature can be found as far back as 1923 when educationalist Chen Heqin developed a 15-point model for the work of kindergartens (Shi 1989). References to play also appeared repeatedly in the first national *Guidelines for Kindergarten Education* (Ministry of Education of the PRC 1981). The most recent *Guidelines for Kindergarten Education* (Ministry of Education PRC 2001), the Beijing Municipal *Guidelines for Kindergarten Education* (BMEC 2003), and accompanying curriculum notes for teachers[1] (BMEC/ British Council 2004: 24) explain that kindergartens should pay attention to 'what society wants and expects children to grow up to be, and to children's physical and psychological development and needs'. Within the parameters of society's hopes and expectations of what young Chinese children will become, play is also expected to 'permeate all activities, in each and every aspect of the lives of three and four year olds'. Teachers are advised that play must underpin activities in the work of kindergartens (see for example BMEC 2003: 24).

BMEC, which has responsibility for overseeing early childhood education in the capital, recently advised that:

> One common problem with preschool education in China is that kindergartens do not have activities designed for young children. The educational approach is mostly copied from that used in primary schools. Children are often asked to sit and listen to lessons and do not learn through play.
>
> (BMEC/British Council 2004: 1)

Furthermore, many kindergarten buildings resemble primary schools, catering for hundreds of young children grouped in classrooms housing 30 or more, and with few possibilities for flexibility and choice in children's movements and use of spaces. Policy-makers, researchers and practitioners are, therefore, enthusiastically working together to develop new ways of providing opportunities for play (including designing new buildings) that reflect the ethos of 'playful everyday life'. Part of their efforts to reform practice involve activities designed to encourage reflection and learning from others' models by, for example, visiting other countries to observe and discuss practice, translating professional books, or inviting foreign colleagues to provide training in China. Returning to Figure 17.1, and following our Chinese colleagues' example, we might usefully consider with them why there seems to be a discrepancy between a curriculum that encourages play and provision that we are told excludes it. Further, what is it about play, or particular types of play, that are either unacceptable or problematic in Chinese cultural contexts – and in our own?

Cannella (1997: 135) warned that 'child-centred pedagogy and play, as central tenets within educational practice, have been created in a particular culture with particular values and biases. Applying the notion of play to all peoples in all situations denies the multiple value structures, knowledges, and views of the world which are created by people in diverse contexts.' Recent calls to early childhood colleagues in the UK and other countries to provide training for early years professionals in China with particular emphasis on 'learning through play' and 'restructuring the physical environment to support young children's physical and psychological development' (BMEC/British Council 2004) have shown the extent to which imported pedagogies, ideas and curriculum models including High/Scope, Reggio Emilia, Montessori and developmentally appropriate practice are being explored and developed within Chinese settings. But the pedagogical models are adapted or metamorphosed to 'fit' Chinese values and expectations. In looking to other cultural contexts for ideas and guidance (perhaps in the form of training or observation) about play or 'learning through play' we can learn much from the critical reflection of our Chinese colleagues about the extent to which non-indigenous, play-based pedagogies and principles are transferable in whole or part.

Reading Chinese early childhood education curriculum documents and literature, carrying out observations in kindergartens and undertaking discussions with early years professionals offers insights into the purposes of EC provision in China. These also help to illustrate why particular types of play or playful activities 'fit' Chinese cultural contexts and others are more problematic. One such example involves 'messy play' activities (see Photograph 17.2).

In October 2004, in discussions between 280 Beijing kindergarten heads and teachers with four English ECEC professionals, the phrase 'messy play area' arose. The Chinese interpreter had great difficulty in directly translating this phrase (and its underlying sense that mess is expected and acceptable). How could provision for play be intentionally

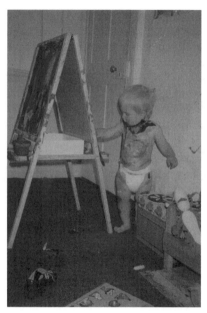

Photograph 17.2   In Chinese cultural contexts some play activities 'fit' whilst others, like 'messy play', are problematic

messy? Why would a kindergarten have an area in which children might be encouraged to get dirty, and equipment become disorganized? What of the health and safety dangers of allowing young children to play virtually (or totally) naked? Some participants explained that parents would be horrified if their child had been allowed or encouraged to play without clothes (for fear of catching cold), or to get so dirty. Beijing kindergartens are expected, they explained, to instil a sense of orderliness and to maintain high levels of cleanliness and sterility. While this may be an extreme example, it serves to illustrate the problems of attempting to 'transplant' provision for play from one context to another without due concern for cultural values and their influence on practice (Goouch 2004).

Play, curricula and different cultural groups

Bennett (2004) reports that the countries whose provision of early childhood education has been reviewed by the Organization for Economic Cooperation and Development (OECD) during the last six years, encourage play-based programmes in their official documents concerned with curricular principles and aspirations. However, he contends that there are two strands in Europe: one is a *social-pedagogic* approach, the other a *pre-*

primary approach. In the former, the development of the curriculum is based on a broad national framework and local democratic consultation, with emphases on the quality of life in the setting, children's well-being and social development and a play-based, flexible pedagogy involving much choice and autonomy for the children.

The OECD teams found social pedagogic approaches in the Nordic and central European countries, where:

> the pedagogical project is firmly play-based, with much movement, choice and child autonomy in evidence . . . The guiding national curriculum is flexible enough to allow staff to experiment with different pedagogical approaches, and adapt programmes to local conditions and demand . . . Nordic guidelines are formulated on a consultative basis, and receive the critical analysis and consent of the major stakeholders before becoming statutory.
>
> (Bennett 2004: 7)

(An account of the process of developing such guidelines is provided in Broström 2001).

Meanwhile, Bennett argues, those countries with a *pre-primary* approach (as in China) hold the view that readiness for primary school is important and curricula are strongly influenced by a primary or elementary school model of education and learning. This model requires that children are assessed (usually against national guidelines) and formal quality control is implemented through inspections. Countries in which readiness for school is an important aim tend to adopt the *pre-primary* approach:

> a conception of early education much influenced by the primary (elementary) school model . . . The achievement or performance of children is often benchmarked or assessed.
>
> (Bennett 2004: 7–8)

The countries categorized in this *pre-primary* group by the OECD research include Belgium, France, Ireland, Netherlands and the UK. In this model opportunities for play and choice are limited; although practitioners may lead activities which they hope will be attractive and playful for children, they are not true play.

Bennett (2004) claims that poor investment (*structural* failure) results in poor quality curricula, and inadequate pedagogical theory and practice (*orientation* failure) results in a host of inadequacies, such as poor understanding of how children learn from each other, a failure to reflect on practice, and either too great an emphasis on academic goals or the reverse. As a result of the paucity of cross-cultural research exploring and comparing the *social pedagogic* and the *pre-primary* traditions, Bennett suggests that the tradition espoused in itself is perhaps less important than *structural* and/or *orientation* failures. However, we would argue that the traditions may arise out of different economic and cultural climates, with different constructions of childhood and their consequences (see also Anning *et al.* 2004; and Chapter 1 of this book).

Interpretations of learning through play and their consequences

The ways in which educators interpret learning through play can often mean that the teacher presents the children (who have first been told they are to take part, rather than having chosen to participate) with a playful activity. Clearly, the ability of a teacher to engage in freely chosen, child-directed play with a group or with individual children will be more challenging when adult–child ratios are high, when they have a large number of pre-set targets for each child to be achieved, or external pressures (from parents, teachers of older children, inspectors, and so on) include particular expectations about what the children will be capable of when they reach the primary school phase. Achieving an appropriate and sensitive balance between child-directed play and adult-directed playful activities will depend on a practitioner's understandings, training, and confidence (see Neil Kitson's observations in Chapter 8 of this book). External endorsement (from inspectors where they operate, but mainly from superiors and parents) will impact on practice. Practitioners' own appreciation of each child, as an individual and as a member of their learning community, and their values concerning children will also affect how they teach (see BERA 2003).

In England, for example, play is emphasized in the *Curriculum Guidance for the Foundation Stage* (QCA DfEE 2000) as the main medium for teaching/learning. However, other demands and constraints mean that many practitioners find it hard to understand the difference between play and playful adult-directed activities, and to have the confidence to assert the value of play (BERA Early Years SIG 2003; Siân Adams, Chapter 15 of this book). Edwards (2004: 87–9) argues that in England today early childhood is seen as a period of social investment, 'expected to pay dividends'. She claims that this is indicative of a modernist search for certainty through a 'normalizing' education system. In such a system, play cannot be allowed to go on simply because it is beneficial and enjoyable.

Variations within countries

While national assumptions and national guidelines may create the climate in which one model prevails over others, as cross-cultural research in China, Japan and the USA by Tobin *et al.* (1989) suggests, one cannot conclude that all early childhood settings in a particular country will operate in a particular way. Local cultural differences and individual teachers and their teams will interpret learning through play in their own ways. For example, Hartley (1993) found that children in different nurseries in the same location and country were treated very differently as staff interpreted the futures of the children according to their families' current socio-economic statuses. The children's opportunities for play and for choice and the shared understandings were subtly tailored to staff assumptions about the children in each setting. Lubeck (1986) found similar differences between the interpretations of learning through play in two groups, one in a disadvantaged black neighbourhood and one a more privileged white neighbourhood in an American city. Her ethnographic study demonstrated that the three staff in the disadvantaged area setting organized more whole-group activities and modelled mutual support on a regular basis. Meanwhile, the three staff in the more affluent area encouraged the children in individualistic tasks and rarely interacted with each other during the play sessions. She concluded that if only each staff team could learn from the other, all the children would learn how to be cooperative yet also brave and capable of thinking and acting alone; independent yet also interdependent. In other words different behaviours were valued and modelled despite learning through play being the educational approach espoused in both settings.

In a similar way, other research in the UK has indicated the paramount importance of ECEC educators' cultural understandings of children's home lives (BERA 2003). Such understandings mean they can build on the knowledge children have acquired at home or in earlier settings, and they can mediate learning, ensuring a mismatch is not caused as a result of cultural differences between home learning patterns and those of the setting.

Several key publications (for example Edwards *et al.* 1998; Shonkoff and Phillips 2000) have emphasized the view that the central task of the earliest years is the establishment of relationships and the interface between the cognitive, affective and social aspects of development (see Broadhead and English, Chapter 5 of this book). Children learn to participate, to adapt and fit in, to be accepted by their cultural group *by participating*, as Strandell's (2000) research about a group of boys playing demonstrates.

However, research evidence also demonstrates the potential difficulties that may arise when there is a cultural mismatch between contexts in which individuals participate, for example for young children between their homes and early childhood settings (BERA 2003). In describing the development of cultural identities, Bhabha proposes the existence of *liminal* spaces (between cultural groups), which may or may not allow for the emergence of hybrid cultural identities. Such spaces are vital for those in multicultural societies and relationships (whether adult–adult, adult–child or child–child), especially if, as Bhabha (1998: 2) says:

the exchange of values, meanings and priorities may not always be collaborative and dialogical, but may be profoundly antagonistic, conflictual and even incommensurable.

Players and power

The children now attending ECEC settings are being educated for a future world we can only try to imagine. Kane (2004: 13) argues that the work ethic is ill-equipped to deal with the world we now inhabit, let alone the future one. He adds that in order to feel more in control of their own lives and to enjoy them, both adults and children in our culturally complex, work-dominated society need to adopt a play ethic – to become *players*. He states that living as a player is precisely about embracing ambiguity and revelling in uncertainty and paradox, energized by that knowledge. So when particular play approaches are advocated or adopted in early years settings in a culture, what are the reasons for doing so? Is play being hijacked to achieve certain specified ends that are supposed to benefit the children and their culture in the long term? Or is there a belief in play (the importance of being *players*) as a way of living and learning for its own sake, in the here and now? Players choose, have power over their own time and space. So above all, when exploring different cultures and play, we need to ask ourselves where the ideas about play have come from. Who are the players (the children, parents, practitioners, policy-makers)? Who directs the play, why, and what does this tell us about that culture?

Questions to set you thinking

1 What similarities and differences can you identify between your own early nursery or school experience and that in a setting you have observed? Can you explain the similarities and/or differences in cultural terms? (This might be a *subcultural* phenomenon, such as David Hartley identified in his research.)
2 Examine recent government documents covering the Foundation Stage (such as the QCA's Early Learning Goals, the Literacy Strategy) and try to decide what they tell us about the importance (or otherwise) of child-initiated play in English early years settings?
3 In a similar way to Question 3 above, examine documents from a government concerning provision for children from birth to 3. What messages are embedded in the document about the role of play in that culture and what assumptions are made about babies and toddlers?

Note

[1] Produced by Beijing Shifan Daxue and entitled 'You'eryuan Kuaile yu Fazhan Kecheng', Laoshi Zhidao Yongshu (3 books).

18 Play, the universe and everything!

Tina Bruce

Summary

This chapter begins with a brief introduction to the possible links between childhood play scenarios and future adult life. Many examples are given of children playing. Traditional principles of early learning are outlined, updated in the light of recent developments. The twelve features of play (Bruce 1991) are linked with these new initiatives. Diversity and inclusion in play are shown to be of central importance, and the chapter emphasizes the value of cross-cultural aspects of play, and the developments in including children with complex needs, disabilities and special educational needs.

Introduction

When I was a child, I played schools. Erikson (1963) argues that through our childhood play we are partners with our future. Perhaps, after all, there is sense in the traditional saying that we should give sitting babies a box of objects and that, depending on what they select, their future will be divulged! Through observing and becoming part of a child's play, we discover an individual child's personal play style and 'tune in' to what we, as practitioners, can do to help that child develop the dispositions that support active learning through play.

This chapter is about 'tuning in' to the processes of children's play, and how adults are crucial in encouraging children to participate in the social group and culture. Children are active agents in their own play but they need adults who are informed advocates, promoting and protecting free flow play not only for children but for adults too. The sociocultural environment is important in establishing individual children's sense of agency in developing their play. Research into brain development (Damasio 2004) is showing that nurture triggers, shapes and influences nature. Our environments – social, cultural, physical and material – serve as an extension of our brains, it seems (as we have also seen in the previous chapter by Tricia David and Sacha Powell).

Observing free-flow play in action

Tom, age 2, spent an afternoon cracking a bowl of nuts with two types of nutcracker: a corkscrew model and a pincer model. He was involved in forces, holes and broken parts. He shared this experience with his mother, engaging in shared and sustained conversations as he played (Siraj-Blatchford *et al.* 2002). By the age of 3, he was making paper aeroplanes. He was completely fascinated when shown by an older child that he could cut bits off the wing to make flaps, which speed up and slow down flight and vary the direction of the aeroplane. Vygotsky (1978) has emphasized the importance of children spending time with people who are more skilled than they are if learning is to be effectively developed.

During his play, he loved to throw sticks into bushes in the garden and into water. He, in Europe, is doing what a group of three children (aged 2, 4 and 7) are doing on the banks of the River Nile on the African continent.

Photograph 18.1   Children are active agents in their own play

They are making boats that will sail in particular directions and float with cargoes. Tom is playing with forces, crashes and splashes, just as they are as they throw sticks and stones into the Nile around the boats that they have made. This kind of free-flow play is happening all over the world. There are ubiquitous aspects of play that resonate wherever children are growing up. Ubiquity is about the common core of play, which has a universal dimension.

Hannah at 14 is choreographing a solo dance for her GCSE course. This is the culmination of the dance play she has maintained from the age of ten months, when she began the 'knees-bend' swaying to music indulged in by children in cultures throughout the world (Davies 2003). At 6 she danced for hours on end with her 4-year-old friend, Ming, using dressing-up clothes, music on a tape recorder and homemade instruments, playing at dancing and using everything she knew about dance.

In Cairo, a different mixed-age group comprising three boys (one 12-year-old and two 15-year-olds) free-flow play-dance on a patch of park between two busy roads. They have brought a ghetto-blaster, play Arabic music and all do their own thing. Gradually, one echoes what another does. For an hour they increasingly coordinate their movements until they are dancing together. Their improvised dancing is influenced by Arabic folk-dance styles. One of the important features of play involving dance or music is that it does not require talking. Those participating simply need to remain sensitive to what is difficult for each other. In free-flow play, one of the features is that the players are sensitive to each other's personal agendas as well as a feeling of group sensitivity emerging.

At an international conference in England, Nigel Kennedy spoke of the way musicians found they could improvise and literally 'play' music together, which was of a high standard and respected the different cultural backgrounds from which they came. They found they could allow one style of music to emerge and subside, letting another form become dominant at different points. This kind of free-flow playing respects individuals and encourages group sensitivity. There are resonances with the processes involved in creativity here, since improvisation and making connections are key aspects of creativity (Bruce 2004a; Duffy, Chapter 13 of this book). Free-flow play is about functioning at a high level, and also leads to quality in the way individuals interact with the sciences, as is apparent in the following example.

Seven-year-old Chris goes to stay for a week on a cabin cruiser boat holiday on the River Thames with William (11) and Ayo (13). It is his first experience of boat life. Here is another mixed-age group, again untypical of those found in formal schools. The older children teach him to work a lock, tie a knot, move safely on to land, light a barbecue, put up a tent, strip a stick, make an arrow, make a bow from willow, fish, swab the deck and sweep the stairs. He is learning in a very practical way key elements of science and technology as well as geography and history. He sees the older children settle to an hour's homework each day, and spends that time choosing to sketch, play, read and practise, becoming, for example, skilled in lighting his own barbecue. As he plays, he wallows in using the bow and arrow and celebrates his skill in shooting at a target of his making. This resonates with the play of children and adults in the Hadza tribe in Tanzania who spend time in bow and arrow practice play.

Different children and different cultural expectations influence the play of children (see Chapter 17 of this book). It is the Hadza boys who play with bows and arrows. Similarly, it is Tom, not Ayo, who initiates this kind of play. Characteristically, if Ayo had played this at age 7, she would probably have 'become' Boudicca or someone like her. Girls seem to be drawn into narrative more easily than boys (Paley 1986; Holland 2003; Kalliala 2005; Jane Hislam in Chapter 7 of this book).

Chris, like William, loves to 'play' scientifically. His imagined world is to do with alternative hypotheses for what will happen to the arrow when he does this, that or the other (Howe and Davies explore further examples of science, technology and play in Chapter 11 of this book). Adults are around, but he can take responsibility and control and is proud of himself. When he needs help, he asks, or an adult notices and comes to offer help. He is told (or read) a story each evening sitting by the camp fire. In particular he loves King Arthur stories. There is no competition with other 7-year-olds. He is the only one. He goes at his own speed and sets himself high standards, encouraged by the admiration of others, but influenced to learn by the leadership of the older children.

Play is a concept that embraces diversity, but it is also inclusive. Both adults and children have the propensity for play in any culture or community. Children with special educational needs, disabilities and complex requirements are now seen as participators in their communities, and the encouragement of their play development is now recognized as being of great importance (see Theodora Papatheodorou's discussion in Chapter 3 of this book).

Daniel, from the age of 3, thoroughly enjoyed dressing-up clothes. It was a tradition at family gatherings to play charades, which involved one group acting out words – titles of books, films or famous names – whilst the others try to guess who/what they are. Because of his disabilities, Daniel had great difficulty in reading, writing and breaking words down into components. For years, the joy of charades for him was in choosing his dressing up clothes and trying to get the group to act a story he told. The rest of the family group worked gently around his play agenda, acting out phrases like 'Footballer's Wives'. By the time he was about 12, he was thinking about the costumes others would wear, rather than simply planning his own. He began to join in thinking what roles they would adopt, although the storyline and characters still revolved around him. Everyone felt the effort was for him and respected his hard work in trying to do this.

Suddenly, at the age of about 14, he made a huge step forward. He saw that a phrase like 'Footballer's Wives' could be acted out in four parts, according to the number of syllables. He realized, in a quantum leap forward in his thinking, that the group could then make a story out of the whole phrase. He no longer needed to be the centre of attention. The first syllable had a hospital operating theatre with people with bad feet having surgery. The second was a football match with the ball going into the goal. The third had children in a lesson at school not knowing the answer to a teacher's questions, saying 'Erh' all the time. Then came a party and he needed to introduce his wife. The whole word was then acted out, echoing a scene from the programme on television. He was now participating in a group event without needing to dominate the play.

The years from 3 to 14 of dressing up in imitation of characters, leading into the becoming of characters, with gentle but sustained and relentless encouragement to think of other people's parts in stories and themes acted out, and in what makes a storyline that helps the audience to see the point of the acting, had helped Daniel to develop part–whole relationships (Piaget 1947; Clay 1975; Ferreiro and Teberosky 1983). Play in a social context has made a huge contribution to his development. We often see a slower development in children with special educational needs and disabilities, but this helps to illuminate and show clearly why play is so important in developing learning as a whole person.

The bedrock principles of early childhood practice

We need to reflect further on the experience Chris has on the boat trip, and to consider what schools ought to be like for children at least until the end of the English Key Stage 1. Chris helps with chores that are essential to living on a boat. Not all the tasks are pleasant or exciting but he does them willingly and dutifully and is proud of his contribution. He can see the point of doing them. He is involved in a little formal learning relating to shopping (number and money) and literacy (stories, reading and writing). He plays for nearly half of his day, sometimes alone, but also with William and Ayo. He socializes a great deal, participating in ball games with William. He is with adults who are able to give him attention when he seeks or needs it, or just to be around them watching as they work. He is encouraged to use what is essential and universal to being a human – his possibility to relate to others, and to act symbolically and through narrative in a number of ways. He can represent experiences through number, language and free-flow play. He is also encouraged to be himself and to develop his free-flow play according to his own temperament. As Brazelton (1969: 281) points out, young children 'show a resistance to being pushed into habits that are not sympathetic to their style, a resistance backed up by all the strength inherent in an well-organized personality, infant or adult'.

The great pioneer educators were aware of the delicate balance between what is universal to being human, and the unique way in which every individual is human. For example, Froebel (1782–1852) was constantly aware of certain aspects that human beings have in common, which bind them together as a species across the world. He considered free-flow play to be an important one of these, seeing every child as a unique individual who needs sensitive and appropriate help in order to develop and learn optimally. In this way, we can see that play is an integrating mechanism in a child's development, and perhaps into adulthood too.

In Bruce (1987), I extrapolated ten principles from the literature and philosophy of the heritage left by pioneers such as Froebel, Rudolf Steiner (1861–1925) and Maria Montessori (1869–1952). These are:

1 Childhood is seen as valid in itself, as part of life and not simply as preparation for adulthood.
2 The whole child is considered to be important. Health, physical and mental well-being, is emphasized together with the importance of feelings, having ideas, thoughts and spiritual aspects.
3 Learning is not compartmentalized, because everything is linked.
4 Intrinsic motivation, resulting in child-initiated self-directed activity, is valued.
5 Self-discipline is emphasized (4 and 5 lead to autonomy).
6 There are especially receptive periods of learning at different stages of development.
7 What children can do (rather than what they cannot do) is the starting point in the child's education.
8 There is an inner structure in the child which includes the imagination and which emerges especially under favourable conditions.
9 The people (both adults and children) with whom the child interacts are of central importance.
10 The child's education is seen as an interaction between the child and the environment the child is in – including, in particular, other people and knowledge itself.

While in the UK there is considerable agreement about the principles which guide early childhood education, as set out in the core reference document *Curriculum Guidance for the Foundation Stage* (QCA/DfES 2000), now enshrined in law and part of the English National Curriculum, there is also great variation in the way principles are interpreted in practice by those working with young children and their families. There are those who choose to package them into an identifiable method (Montessori, High/Scope, Reggio Emilia) and those who instead emphasize the importance of quality training, embedded in sound general principles, as the most effective long-term strategy to encourage reflective practice (Moyles *et al.* 2002; Pascal and Bertram 2001; Bennett 2004).

These principles, which as Moyles *et al.* (2002) point out operate in the complex framework they outline, help us to explore what humans have in common wherever they live. It is not possible for people to step outside their culture, society or upbringing, but examining commonalities between human beings is useful. It brings together what we know of how children develop according to brain research in biological terms and the sociocultural dimension of development (Bruce 2004b). We know that humans have the potential to function symbolically (Athey 1990; Trevarthen 1998). They do this in many ways, for example through language and literacy (Whitehead 2002; Broadhead and English, Whitebread and Jameson, Chapters 5 and 4 of this book respectively), visual representation (Matthews 2003), dance and movement (Davies 2003), mathematically (Worthington and Carruthers 2003; Griffiths, Chapter 12 of this book), and through play (Bruce, 1991, 2004c; Moyles 1989).

There are commonalities in children's play and the contribution of free-flow play to the learning process that are outlined in Bruce (1991). This involved examining the triangle that makes up a quality curriculum (child, context and content):

- the *child*: this involves the process of free-flow play as an integrated part of the child's biological and sociocultural aspects of development;
- the *context*: this involves people, culture and environment and access to play;
- the *content*: what the child knows, wants to know and is interested in, as well as what the child needs and is expected to learn, and the role of play in facilitating the content.

Because there is widespread confusion about what play is, 'free-flow play' was adopted as a term because it expresses a view of play supported by twelve features extrapolated from the literature, as follows:

Twelve features of free-flow play

1 It is an active process without a product.
2 It is intrinsically motivated.
3 It exerts no external pressure to conform to rules, pressures, goals, tasks or definite direction. It gives the player control.
4 It is about possible, alternative worlds, which lift players to their highest levels of functioning. This involves being imaginative, creative, original and innovative.
5 It is about participants wallowing in ideas, feelings and relationships. It involves reflecting on, and becoming aware of, what we know – meta-cognition.
6 It actively uses previous first-hand experiences, including struggle, manipulation, exploration, discovery and practice.
7 It is sustained and, when in full flow, helps us to function in advance of what we can actually do in our real lives.
8 During free-flow play, we use technical prowess, mastery and competence we have previously developed, and so can be in control.

9 It can be initiated by a child or an adult, but if by an adult he/she must pay particular attention to 3, 5 and 11 of the features.
10 Play can be solitary.
11 It can be in partnership or groups, with adults and/or children who will be sensitive to each other.
12 It is an integrating mechanism, which brings together everything we learn, know, feel and understand.

These twelve features can be summed up through the equation, 'Free-flow play = Wallow in past experiences + Technical prowess, competence, mastery and control acquired.'

Simpler texts of the features can be found in Bruce (2001b) in relation to the English documents *Curriculum Guidance for the Foundation Stage* (QCA/DfEE 2000) and in the *Birth to Three Matters* Framework (DfES 2002) and, in relation to the latter, in Langston and Abbott, Chapter 2 of this book. The features are used by some practitioners to help them observe and identify play and to inform them both as they make assessments for learning in the Foundation Stage Profile (QCA 2003b) and for 'well-planned play' (QCA/DfEE 2000: 25).

Commonalities and differences in free-flow play across cultures

It is helpful to begin studying how play develops in children (and adults) by looking at the ubiquitous aspects such as the features common to play. It is also important to look at sociocultural differences in the way that children play in different families and communities trans-globally, if we are to respond to and value the uniqueness of each human being and the rich diversity of different cultures, emphasized by David and Powell in the previous chapter. Theodora Papatheodorou (Chapter 3 of this book) also helps us to consider the ways in which children with disabilities and complex needs engage in play, providing for their particular needs in a spirit of inclusion.

Free-flow play is found among children in all parts of the world, as well as in ancient civilizations. It is part of being human. However, those who study play view it through a variety of different lenses, which result in it being encouraged, discouraged, constrained or valued in widely differing ways, which have a great impact on the child's access and opportunities for free-flow playing.

There is a tendency among some to see free-flow play as a privilege enjoyed mainly by middle-class children in Europe and North America, and yet in reality this is unlikely to be so. It is 'misguided to characterize the middle classes as historical pinnacles of indulgent concern for children's needs' (Konner 1991: 196). It may even be that those in the 'fast lane' of complex industrialized societies are in danger of losing, or at least damaging and seriously eroding, aspects of traditional childhood which are in fact central to being truly successful human adults. 'More haste and less speed' is the dilemma (Angela Anning shares some of this dilemma in Chapter 1 of this book).

In complex industrialized life there is so much that children need to know. In the UK since the late 1980s there has been slippage into the earlier introduction of formal schooling with an emphasis on direct teaching and the transmitting of a particular culture. This is typically presented to children through highly pre-structured experiences in a predominantly 'tell and write' mode. However, this may not produce the kind of adult who can survive the future nearly so well as the adaptive intelligence, imagination and creativity required of children brought up to actively experience and learn in real-life situations, with opportunity and access to free-flow play (Blakemore 2000). As the English Foundation Stage becomes increasingly embedded, this trend should be reversed, with more balance between adult-led, directly taught experiences and child-initiated, indirectly structured and taught experiences for children. Many writers within this volume see this as a major way forward.

It is not a question of those in complex industrialized societies trying to return to a romantically perceived view of the hunting and gathering or agricultural community, where children play, socialize and learn from being with adults as they work each day. It is much more a question of not discarding what is central to humanity (Huizunga 1949) by throwing the baby out with the bath water in an attempt to keep a place in the 'fast lane'. Those who study children free-flow playing do not see romance but a highly effective mechanism giving access to symbolic and physical functioning of a high level, crucial for the future of humanity both as individuals and as participants in their communities and cultures.

Children's play is sometimes used and taken over by adults as a way of gaining access to guiding and structuring children's learning so that they are, it is argued, adequately prepared for adult life, and helped to learn in ways that are appropriate to childhood. This 'preparation for life' view of play is supported by modern theorists such as Bruner and has gained great influence in England and North America, although not so much in the Nordic countries and other countries of Western Europe.

It is interesting to examine figures produced by Whiting and Whiting's *Six Cultures Project* (Konner 1991). Five agricultural societies in Kenya, Mexico, the Philippines, Japan and India were studied together with a town called 'Orchardtown' in Pennsylvania, New England, USA. The children in Orchardtown were involved in household and garden chores for 2 per cent of their time. They were engaged in casual social interactions, watching adults, chatting and so on, for about 52 per cent of the time. Formal school-type learning took up 16 per cent of the time. From these figures, we could perhaps argue that these urban children are playing for a healthy and appropriate part of their day. However, there is more to this as we shall see later.

We know from Donaldson's (1978) pioneering studies that children perform better on embedded tasks, which make what she calls 'human sense' to them. When the tasks are in the context of their own everyday lives and have purpose and function, and when children are able to learn through their senses with freedom of movement, they learn with more breadth, depth and permanence. Their well-being and sense of self is stronger. They are more confident. They are more engaged and take pride in what they do. They want to participate and make a good contribution. They have the dispositions needed for life-long learning.

Konner (1991: 309) suggests that we have seen a massive switch in developed industrial societies so that children are now in compulsory schooling in contrast to performing compulsory chores or labour. Using figures from the *Six Cultures Project*, he shows that in agricultural societies children tend to work at chores for their parents for 17 per cent of the time, in fields or in the home. They play for 44 per cent of their time. They are involved in casual social interactions, chatting, watching adults and so on for 34 per cent of their time, and in formal learning for only 5 per cent of the time.

When we speak of child labour being an abuse of children's rights, we need to be clear what we are talking about. Putting children to work in coalmines and factories with the growth of industrialization is not the same as children helping in the home or on the family farm. Konner argues (1991: 309) that 'Despite their hardships, chores give children skills they are proud of all their lives, and can bring parents and children closer together.'

In hunting and gathering societies, such as the Kung or Hadza (BBC 1999), children learn through watching, socializing, playing and slowly doing, with virtually no formal teaching. In agricultural societies children are required to do more of the essential chores which arise through living in one place rather than moving on. Pretty Shield (in Niethammer 1977: 27), a member of the Crow tribe, remembering her childhood at the turn of the century, describes the 'chores' element in her education:

> Indian girls were gently led into the art of motherhood, and their introduction to other womanly tasks was gradual, too, at least for the littlest girls. They accompanied their mothers and big sister while they gathered foods, weeded gardens, and went for water and wood. As the girls grew older more was expected of them. A Fox woman, living in the area of what is now Wisconsin and Illinois, told how she was encouraged when she was about nine to plant a few things and to hoe the weeds. Then she was taught to cook what she had raised, and was lavishly praised for her efforts.

Pretty Shield also remembers the importance of free-flow play during her childhood (Niethammer 1977: 25):

> Learning the role of woman by playing was the pervading method of

education for young girls, and mothers often took pains to see that their daughters had accurate miniatures of real household equipment to use in playing house. In some of the Plains tribes such as the Cheyenne, Omaha, Arapaho and Crow, daughters of the more well-to-do families even had their own skin tents as play-houses, and when time came to pack up camp to follow the buffalo, the girls got their own household – tipe, toys and clothes – packed and ready to move.

Kalliala (in press 2005) discusses gender issues in young children's play today, and the changes since the 1950s. Her research resonates with the reminiscences of Pretty Shield from the 1900s.

Children in both hunting and gathering societies and agricultural societies learn through watching, playing, socializing and slowly doing according to an apprenticeship model. Children do not have to tell or write what they learn. They have to show their learning by doing (for example weaving in the context of everyday life). In their play, they reflect on these active experiences and wallow in them, demonstrating the technical prowess they have been struggling to master. Play is about wallowing in what has been experienced and dealing with mastering, facing, and controlling what is experienced emotionally, socially, bodily, in movement, thoughts and ideas. It is, in the main, about the application of what is known, using the skill and competence that has been developed. We can see this clearly in Pretty Shield's memory of her childhood as well as in more modern times.

This contrasts with industrial societies, in which household chores are replaced with child labour in factories and mines, or with formal schooling with children following adult-set and led tasks for long hours of the day. Konner argues (1991: 310) that school 'attempts to turn children into a workforce with skills that society needs. In these senses it exploits children just as much as work does.'

Conclusion

Recently there has begun to be a realization in the UK that play *is* important. There has been a surge of initiatives funded by government, such as Arts Council projects on creativity in schools and communities, the publication of *Excellence and Enjoyment* by the National Primary Strategy (DfES 2003) and the appointment of the first Senior National Director for the Foundation Stage. This is putting a major emphasis on the importance of embedding the Foundation Stage and the *Birth to Three Matters* Framework in the work of local authorities across the maintained, voluntary and private sectors. In developing the Green Paper, *Every Child Matters* (DfES 2004a), the English government has also a priority in its 'transitions' project so that children in Key Stage 1 are offered a more appropriate learning environment indoors and outdoors (see Chapter 16 of this book). More appropriate forms of assessment are being pioneered through the *Foundation Stage Profile* (QCA 2003b), and leading local authorities in the field of early childhood work (such as Peterborough) are integrating this with records from birth to 6, integrating the *Birth to Three Matters* Framework and working closely with primary schools, daycare and other settings in doing so.

All these developments mean that play has been re-established on an official level at the heart of the way practitioners need to work with children in setting up and working in appropriate learning environments indoors and outdoors for children from birth to at least the age of 6. Both the traditional philosophical principles supporting play, with its emphasis on experienced intuition and practice wisdom handed down from generation to generation (Bruce 1987, 2004c) and the theories giving high value to childhood play and beyond into adulthood remain important. These are confirmed through recent research evidence from major research projects such as *Effective Provision of Preschool Education* (EPPE) (Sylva *et al.* 2003) and the *Study of Pedagogical Effectiveness in Early Learning* (SPEEL) (Moyles *et al.* 2002), which give clear evidence of the importance of play in the development and learning of young children.

This is not to argue that young children do not benefit from education. It does suggest that it is crucial for parents and practitioners to help children to develop and learn effectively and appropriately according to the way the young brain develops. Practitioners working with groups of other people's children need to be educated, mature, highly trained and qualified so that they can support and extend children's play in an informed way, with the sophistication and sensitivity required to do so. Play needs committed adult advocates.

Societies which neglect their infrastructure are likely to hit problems, producing adults who are not able to problem solve, persevere, concentrate, be imaginative or creative, make connections, improvise, be flexible and adaptive, read the body movements and language of others, see things from different points of view, or tune into the thoughts and feelings of other people or situations. Free-flow play is part of the infrastructure of any civilization (Huizinga 1949; Kalliala in press 2005).

Play is, it seems, about the universe and everything. It often has to function in a hostile environment, but when it is encouraged, supported and extended, it makes a major contribution to, and sophisticated impact on the development of individuals and humanity as a whole.

Questions to set you thinking

1 What actions in your life constitute free-flow play?
2 How do you take account of children from different cultural backgrounds within your context?
3 How could you use the 12 features of free-flow play to help you understand children's play in your setting?
4 How do you encourage children with special educational needs to engage fully in play in your setting?

Afterword

Janet Moyles

There you have it: the arguments for the 'excellence of play'. Beginning as we did with some scepticism in relation to researchers' abilities to prove the value of play in children's learning and development, we have moved forward convincingly, I believe, to end with the concept of full free-flowing play – and covered a whole world of play in between, all of it based within children's development, learning and natural dispositions.

Although many of the contributors' views are clearly compatible with each other, differences in emphasis and challenges of definition remain – there is always the need to agree to differ on constructs of play because of the formidable prospect of 'proving' anything so potentially and actually ephemeral. Vandenberg's words are still true today:

> The aspiration for a precise definition of play is an admirable impulse which will lead to further refinements in our conceptualization of the term . . . the belief that airtight definitions are ultimately possible may lead us to be impatient with imprecise definitions and cause us to throw the playful baby out with the bathwater . . . what is needed are efforts aimed at linking the abstract definition with its concrete manifestations, and an analysis of how the perturbating factors influence the specific form of play.
>
> (Vandenberg 1986: 19–20)

This is exactly what all of us, the writers of this book, are advocating and offering as the way forward. We can be certain if we observe children's play that much is happening. But it is practitioners who are in the position daily of seeing how much value there is in children's play and how it can be channelled into a very powerful, meaningful and child-oriented learning medium. It takes courage and confidence in one-self as a practitioner as we have seen in many chapters. But we have never had such a well-educated workforce as we are now developing, so surely this is the time to grasp play and make it succeed for adults and children? Those now teaching and caring for birth to 6-year-olds have the support of *Birth to Three Matters* and the *Curriculum Guidance for the Foundation Stage*. Children *will* play despite adult approval or otherwise. It is surely better to approve of it, and strive to understand it when children are young rather than to allow the harsher elements of play potentially to surface later in anti-social acts (Sutton-Smith and Kelly-Byrne 1984). A curriculum that sanctions and utilizes play is more likely, as several con-tributors have argued, to produce well-balanced, happier, more self-confident and self-sufficient children.

Playing and responding playfully means taking some risks both for adults and for children. Both have in the recent past succumbed to work-ing and playing in 'safe' conditions: adults to work within perceived boundaries of curriculum and government prescription; a generation of children in becoming 'couch potatoes' and losing out on the excitement of learning how to cope with taking risks safely (see for example Smith 1998; Lindon 1999). There are serious physical and mental health con-sequences for children (Ouvry 2003). But we also know that adults who feel autonomous, 'in control' (of their own lives) and knowledgeable are happier, more self-confident and motivated in their work (see Chapter 15 of this book). It seems that a watershed has now been reached in curric-ulum thinking (certainly in England) and the time appears ripe to step back a pace and ask what is this curriculum for? Practitioners should now take whatever curriculum they are working within and evaluate it in relation to how children are actually *receiving* it, not just performing within in: having information in itself is not enough: it has to be *used* in meaningful ways to become 'knowledge', both by children and by practi-tioners! Galton *et al.* (1999) suggest that the best contexts for developing lasting and worthwhile learning are in the more informal situations of early years and lower primary practices. Instead of sidelining play prac-tices in order to 'deliver' a curriculum, we should be taking the best play-ful practices and raising their profile together with the children's profiles and test scores! If this is done, children and adults can learn together through play for the benefit of both (Beardsley 1998; Moyles and Adams 2001).

A frequently expressed political vision is for a 'learning society', yet it seems unlikely that this will be a reality unless the earlier play-learning suggests to children that learning and understanding is something excit-ing, with which they can cope and which has some meaning for them as individuals. All the writers in this book are firmly committed to such a learning society. This requires practitioners committed to adult engage-ment and interaction in children's play, be it as models, providers, enhancers, initiators, advocates or contributors, as a way of ensuring quality provision, greater understanding and, above all, a well-conceived and justifiable commitment to creating the most 'excellent' play and learning environments.

Photograph 19.1   Play requires practitioners committed to adult engagement and interaction with children

References

Adams, S. and Moyles, J. (2005) *Images of Violence*. Market Harborough: Feather-stone Publications.

Adams, S., Alexander, E., Drummond, M.J. and Moyles. J. (2004) *Inside the Foundation Stage. Re-creating the Reception Year*. London: Association of Teachers and Lecturers.

Adams, S., Medland, P. and Moyles, J. (2000) Supporting play-based teaching through collaborative practice-based research, *Support for Learning*, 15(4), 159–64.

Alexander, R., Rose, J. and Woodhead, C. (1992) *Curriculum Organisation and Class-room Practice in Primary Schools*. London: HMSO.

Alvarez, A. (1992) *Live Company Psychoanalytic Psychotherapy with Autistic Borderline, Deprived and Abused Children*. London: Routledge.

Anning, A. (1997) *The First Years at School*, 2nd edition. Buckingham: Open University Press.

Anning, A. and Ring, K. (2004) *Making Sense of Children's Drawings*. Maidenhead: Open University Press.

Anning, A., Cullen, J. and Fleer, M. (eds) (2004) *Early Childhood Education, Society and Culture*. London: Sage Publications.

Arthur, L. (2001) Popular culture and early literacy learning, *Contemporary Issues in Early Childhood*, 2(3), 295–307.

Arts Council of England (2002) *Culture and Learning: Creating Arts and Heritage Education Projects*. London: Arts Council of England.

Athey, C. (1990) *Extending Thought in Young Children: A Parent–Teacher Partnership*. London: Paul Chapman.

ATI (American Toy Institute) (2000) *The Power of Play*. Factsheet. New York: ATI.

Attenborough, L. (2003) *Parents Sometimes Need Help with Preschool Preparation*. Press Release: The National Literacy Trust and the Royal College of Speech and Language Therapists, 2 September. Available online at http://www.literacytrust.org.uk. Accessed 5 January 2005.

Aubrey, C. (1997) *Mathematics Teaching in the Early Years*. London: Falmer.

Axline, V. (1947) *Play Therapy: The Inner Dynamics of Childhood*. Boston, MA: Houghton Mifflin.

Axline, V. (1990) *Play Therapy*. New York: Churchill Livingstone.

Barber, N. (1991) Play and energy regulation in mammals, *Quarterly Review of Biology*, 66, 129–47.

Barrett, G. (1986) *Starting School: An Evaluation of the Experience*. London: Assistant Masters and Mistresses Association.

Barrs, M. (1988) Maps of play, in M. Meek and C. Mills (eds) *Language and Literacy in the Primary School*. Lewes: Falmer Press.

Bateson, G. (1979) *Mind and Nature: A Necessary Unity*. New York: Dutton.

BBC (British Broadcasting Corporation) World Service (1999) *My Century*. Broadcast 8 September.

Beardsley, G. (with Penelope Harnett) (1998) *Exploring Play in the Primary Classroom*. London: David Fulton.

Beijing Shifan Daxue (2004) *You'eryuan Kuaile Yu Fazhan Kecheng*, Laoshi Zhidao Yongshu (3 books). Beijing: Beijing Normal University Press.

Bennett, J. (2004) Curriculum issues in national policymaking. Keynote address, European Early Childhood Education Research Association International Conference, Malta, September.

Bennett, N. and Kell, J. (1989) *A Good Start? Four-year-olds in Infant Schools*. Oxford: Blackwell.

Bennett, N., Wood, E. and Rogers, S. (1997) *Teaching Through Play: Teachers' Thinking and Classroom Practice*. Buckingham: Open University Press.

BERA (British Education Research Association) Early Years Special Interest Group (2003) *Review of Early Years Research: Pedagogy, Curriculum and Adult Roles*. Southwell: British Educational Research Association.

Berenbaum, S.A. and Snyder, E. (1995) Early hormonal influences on childhood sex-typed activity and playmate preferences: implications for the development of sexual orientation, *Developmental Psychology*, 31, 31–42.

Berlak, A., Berlak, H., Bagantos, N. and Midel, E. (1975) Teaching and learning in the English primary schools, *School Review*, 83, 215–44.

Berlyne, D. (1960) *Conflict, Arousal and Curiosity*. New York: McGraw-Hill.

Bertram, T., Pascal, C., Bokjari, J., Gasper, M. and Holterman, S. (2002) *Early Excellence Centre Pilot Programme Second Evaluation Report 2000–2001*. London: DfES.

Bhabha, H. (1998) *The Location of Culture*. London: Routledge.

Bjorklund, D. and Green, B. (1992) The adaptive nature of cognitive immaturity, *American Psychologist*, 47, 46–54.

Black, P. and Hughes, S. (2003) Using narrative to support young children's learning in science and D&T, in D. Davies and A. Howe (eds) *Teaching Science and Design Technology*. London: David Fulton.

Blakemore, S.J. (2000) *Early Years Learning*, Report No. 140 (June). London: Parliamentary Office of Science and Technology.

Blank-Grief, E. (1976) Sex role playing in preschool children, in J.S. Bruner, A. Jolly and K. Sylva, *Play and its Role in Evolution and Development*. Harmondsworth: Penguin.

Blatchford, P. and Sharp, S. (eds) (1994) *Breaktime and the School: Understanding and Changing Playground Behaviour*. London and New York: Routledge.

Blenkin, G. and Kelly, A. (1994) *The National Curriculum and Early Learning: An Evaluation*. London: Paul Chapman.

BMEC (Beijing Municipal Education Commission) (2003): *Draft Guidelines for Kindergarten Education*. BMEC Publishing House.

BMEC/British Council Beijing (2004) *Terms of Reference for Training Programme for Chinese Early Years Educators*, July 2004. Beijing: The British Council.

Bolton, G. (1979) *Towards a Theory of Drama in Education*. London: Longman.

Boulton, M.J. (1991) A comparison of structural and contextual features of middle school children's playful and aggressive fighting, *Ethology and Sociobiology*, 12, 119–45.

Bourdieu, P. (2001) *Language and Symbolic Power*. Cambridge, MA: Harvard University Press.

Bowman, W. (2004) Cognition and the body: perspectives from music education, in L. Bresler (ed.) *Knowing Bodies, Moving Minds: Towards Embodied Teaching and Learning*. Dordrecht, The Netherlands: Kluwer Academic Publishers.

Brazelton, T. Berry (1969) *Infants and Mother: Differences in Development*. New York: Delacorte Press.

Breer, P. and Locke, E. (1965) *Task Experience as a Source of Attitudes*. Homewood, IL: Dorsey Press.

Broadhead, P. (1997) Promoting sociability and co-operation in nursery settings, *British Educational Research Journal*, 23(4), 513–31.

Broadhead, P. (2001a) Investigating sociability and cooperation in four- and five-year-olds in Reception class settings, *International Journal of Early Years Education*, 9(1), 23–35.

Broadhead, P. (2001b) Learning from play for grown ups – observing young learners socialise and cooperate, *Early Education*, 33, 3–4.

Broadhead, P. (2003). *Early Years Play and Learning: Developing Social Skills and Cooperation*. London: RoutledgeFalmer.

Bromley, H. (2003) Playing with the Literacy Hour, *Primary English Magazine*, October 2003.

Bronfenbrenner, U. (1979) *The Ecology of Human Development: Experiments by Nature and Design*. Cambridge, MA: Harvard University Press.

Bronfenbrenner, U. and Morris, P.A. (1998) The ecology of developmental process, in R. Lerner (ed.) *Handbook of Child Psychology, Vol. 1: Theoretical Models of Human Development*, 5th edition. New York: John Wiley and Sons.

Bronowski, J. (1958) *The Ascent of Man*. London: BBC Publications.

Brooker, L. (2002) *Starting School: Young Children Learning Cultures*. Buckingham: Open University Press.

Broström, S. (2001) Constructing the early childhood curriculum: the example of Denmark, in T. David (ed.) *Promoting Evidence-based Practice in Early Childhood Education*. Oxford: Elsevier.

Broström, S. (2002) Communication and continuity in the transition from kindergarten to school, in H. Fabian and A.-W. Dunlop (eds) *Transitions in the Early Years. Debating Continuity and Progression for Young Children*. London: Routledge Falmer.

Browne, N. and Ross, C. (1991) Girl's stuff, boys' stuff: young children talking and playing, in N. Browne (ed.) *Science and Technology in the Early Years*. Milton Keynes: Open University Press.

Bruce, T. (1987) *Early Childhood Education*. London: Hodder and Stoughton.

Bruce, T. (1997) *Early Childhood Education*, 2nd edition. London: Hodder and Stoughton.

Bruce, T. (2005) *Early Childhood Education*, 3rd edition. London: Hodder Arnold.

Bruce, T. (1991) *Time to Play in Early Childhood Education*. London: Hodder and Stoughton.

Bruce, T. (1994) Play, the universe and everything!, in J. Moyles (ed.) *The Excellence of Play*. Buckingham: Open University Press.

Bruce, T. (2001a) *Helping Young Children to Learn through Play*. London: Hodder and Stoughton.

Bruce, T. (2001b) *Learning through Play: Babies, Toddlers and the Foundation Years*. London: Hodder and Stoughton Educational.

Bruce, T. (2004a) *Cultivating Creativity: Babies, Toddlers and Young Children*. London: Hodder and Stoughton.

Bruce, T. (2004b) *Developing Learning in Early Childhood*. London: Paul Chapman/ Sage Publications.

Bruce (2004c) Play matters, in L. Abbott and A. Langston (eds) *Birth to Three Matters: Supporting the Framework of Effective Practice*. Maidenhead: Open University Press.

Bruer, J. (1997) Education and the brain: A step too far?, *Educational Researcher*, 26(8), 4–16.

Bruner, J.S. (1962) *On Knowing: Essays for the Left Hand*. Cambridge MA: Harvard University Press.

Bruner J.S. (1966) *Towards a Theory of Instruction*. Cambridge, MA: Harvard University Press.

Bruner, J.S. (1972a) Functions of play, in Bruner *et al.* (1976) *On Knowing: Essays for the Left Hand*, 2nd edition. New York: Atheneum.

Bruner, J.S. (1972b) The nature and uses of immaturity. *American Psychologist*, 27, 687–708.

Bruner, J.S. (1972c) *The Relevance of Education*. London: Allen and Unwin.

Bruner, J.S. (1986) *Actual Minds, Possible Worlds*. Cambridge, MA: Harvard University Press.

Bruner, J.S. (1996) *The Culture of Education*. Cambridge, MA: Harvard University Press.

Burningham, J. (1993) *Avocado Baby*. New York: Harper Collins.

Burton, J. (1980) The beginning of artistic language, *School Arts*, September.

Campbell, R. and Neill, S. St J. (1991) *Thirteen Hundred and Thirty Days: Final Report of a Pilot Study of Teacher Time in Key Stage 1*. Commissioned by the Assistant Masters and Mistresses Association, Coventry: University of Warwick.

Campbell-Clark, S. (2000) Work/family border theory: a new theory of work/ family balance, *Human Relations*, 53(6), 747–70.

Cannella, G.S. (1997) *Deconstructing Early Childhood Education*. New York: Peter Lang.

Carr, M. (2001) *Assessment in Early Childhood Settings*. London: Paul Chapman Publishing.

Carson, J., Burks, V. and Parke, R.D. (1993) Parent–child physical play: determinants and consequences, in K. MacDonald (ed.) *Parent–child Play*. New York: SUNY Press.

Claxton, G. (1999) *Wise Up: The Challenge of Lifelong Learning*. London: Bloomsbury.

Claxton, G. (2000) A sure start for an uncertain future, *Early Education*, 30, Spring. Unnumbered centrefold pullout.

Claxton, G. and Carr, M. (2004) A framework for teaching and learning: the dynamics of disposition, *Early Years*, 24(1), 87–97.

Clay, M. (1975) *What Did I Write?* London: Heinemann.

Cole-Hamilton, I. and Gill, T. (2002) *Making the Case for Play – Building Policies and Strategies for School-aged Children.* London: National Children's Bureau.

Collaer, J. and Hines, M. (1995) Human behavioural sex differences: a role for gonadal hormones during early development, *Psychological Bulletin*, 118, 55–107.

Connolly, P (2004) *Boys and Schooling in the Early Years.* London: Routledge Falmer.

Corsaro, W.A. and Molinari, L. (2000) Priming events and Italian children's transition from preschool to elementary school: representations and action, *Social Psychology Quarterly*, 63(1), 16–33.

Craft, A. (2000) *Creativity Across the Primary Curriculum.* London: Routledge.

Craft, A. (2001) Little c creativity, in A. Craft, B. Jeffrey and M. Leibling (eds) *Creativity in Education.* London: Continuum.

Craft, A. (2002) *Creativity and Early Years Education: A Lifewide Foundation.* London: Continuum.

Csikszentmihalya, M. (1979) The concept of flow in play, in B. Sutton-Smith (ed.) *Play and Learning.* New York: Gardner Press.

Csikszentmihalya, M. (1996) *Creativity flow and the psychology of discovery and invention.* New York: HarperCollins.

Cullumbine, H. (1950) Heat production and energy requirements of tropical people, *Journal of Applied Physiology*, 2, 201–10.

Curtiss, V.S., Mathur, S.R. and Rutherford, R.B. (2002) Developing behavioural intervention plans: a step-by-step approach, *Beyond Behavior* (Winter Issue), 28–31. Available online at http//www.ccbd.net/documents/bb/developing_a_BIP_winter_02.pdf (accessed 12 April 2004).

Dahlberg, G., Moss, P. and Pence, A. (1999) *Beyond Quality in Early Childhood Education and Care.* London: Falmer Press.

Damasio, A. (2004) *Looking for Spinoza.* London: Vintage, Random House Press.

Dansky, J. and Silverman, I. (1975). Play: a general facilitator of associative fluency, *Developmental Psychology*, 11, 104.

D'Arcy, S. (1990) Towards a non-sexist primary classroom, in E. Tutchell (ed.) *Dolls and Dungarees: Gender Issues in the Primary School Curriculum.* Buckingham: Open University Press.

David, T. (ed.) (1993) *Educating Our Youngest Children: European Perspectives.* London: Paul Chapman.

David, T. (ed.) (1998) *Researching Early Childhood Education: European Perspectives.* London: Paul Chapman.

David, T. (ed.) (1999) *Teaching Young Children.* London: Paul Chapman.

David, T., Curtis, A. and Siraj-Blatchford, I. (1992) *Effective Teaching in the Early Years: Fostering Children's Learning in Nurseries and Infant Classes.* An OMEP (UK) Report. Organization Mondial Pour L'Education Prescholaire.

David, T., Goouch, K. and Jago, M. (2001) Cultural constructions of childhood and early literacy, *Reading*, 35(2), 47–53.

David, T., Goouch, K., Powell, S. and Abbott, L. (2003) *Birth to Three Matters: A Review of the Literature.* Nottingham: DfES Publications.

David, T., Raban, B., Ure, C., Goouch, K., Jago, M., Barrière, I. and Lambirth, A. (2000) *Making Sense of Early Literacy.* Stoke-on-Trent: Trentham Books.

Davies, B. and Banks, C. (1992) The gender trap: a feminist poststructuralist analysis of primary school children's talk about gender, *Journal of Curriculum Studies*, 24(1), 1–25.

Davies, J. (1991) Children's adjustment to nursery class: how to equalize opportunities for a successful experience, *School Organisation*, 11(3), 255–62.

Davies, M. (1995) *Helping Children to Learn Through a Movement Perspective*. London: Hodder and Stoughton.

Davies, M. (2003) *Movement and Dance in Early Childhood*, 2nd edition. London: Paul Chapman/Sage Publications.

Dawson, J. (2003) Reflectivity, creativity, and the space for silence, *Reflective Practice*, 4(1), 33–9.

DCMS (Department for Culture, Media and Sport) (2001) *Culture and Creativity – The Next Ten Years*. London: DCMS.

DES (Department of Education and Science) (1982) *Mathematics Counts*. Report of the Cockcroft Committee. London: HMSO.

DES (1990) *English in the National Curriculum: Programmes of Study*. London: HMSO.

Devereux, P. (2001) *Stone Age Soundtracs*. London: Channel 4 Productions.

Devi, S. (1990) *Figuring*. London: Penguin.

Devon Curriculum Services (1998) Science: *Writing Frames for Investigations for KS1, 2, 3 and Beyond*. Exeter: Devon County Council.

DfE (Department for Education) (1990) *Starting with Quality*. London: HMSO.

DfE (1995) *English in the National Curriculum*. London: HMSO.

DfE (1996) *The Education Act 1996*. London: HMSO.

DfEE (Department for Education and Employment) Standards and Effectiveness Unit (1999) *The National Literacy Strategy: Framework for Teaching*. London: DfES.

DfEE (2001) *Special Educational Needs Code of Practice*. London: DfEE.

DfEE/QCA (Qualifications and Curriculum Authority) (1999) *The National Curriculum*. London: DfEE/QCA.

DfES (Department for Education and Skills) (2001) *Schools Building on Success*. Norwich: The Stationery Office.

DfES (2002) *Birth to Three Matters: A Framework to Support Children in their Earliest Years*. London: DfES.

DfES (2003) *Excellence and Enjoyment: A Strategy for Primary Schools*. London: DfES.

DfES (2004a) *Every Child Matters: Change for Children*. London: DfES/HM Government.

DfES (2004b) *Removing Barriers to Achievement: The Government's Strategy for SEN*. Nottingham: DfES Publications.

DfES/DoH (Department of Health) (2004) *Disabled Child: National Services Framework for Children, Young People and Maternal Units*. London: DoH.

DfES/QCA (2003) *Foundation Stage Profile Handbook*. London: DfES/QCA.

DiPietro, J.A. (1981). Rough-and-tumble play: A function of gender. *Developmental Psychology*, 17, 50–58.

DoH/DfEE/HO (Home Office) (2000) *Framework for the Assessment of Children in Need and their Families*. Norwich: DfEE/HO.

Donaldson, M. (1978) *Children's Minds*. London: Fontana.

Donnachie, I. (2000) *Robert Owen: Owen of New Lanark and New Harmony*. East Linton: Tuckwell Press.

Dowling, M. (2000) *Young Children's Personal, Social and Emotional Development*. London: Paul Chapman.

Driver, R. (1983) *The Pupil as Scientist?* Milton Keynes: Open University Press.

Duffy, B. (1998) *Supporting Creativity and Imagination in the Early Years*. Milton Keynes: Open University Press.

Duffy, B. (2004) Creativity matters, in L. Abbott and A. Langston (eds) *Birth to Three Matters: Supporting the Framework of Effective Practice*. Maidenhead: Open University Press.

Dunlop, A.-W. (2003) Bridging early educational transitions in learning through children's agency, *Transitions: European Early Childhood Education Research Journal, Themed Monograph*, 1, 67–86.

Dunlop, A.-W. (2004) Curricular and pastoral continuity and progression in the transition from preschool to primary education. PhD final draft. Glasgow: University of Strathclyde.

Dunlop, A.-W. and Fabian, H. (2003) (eds) *Transitions. European Early Childhood Education Research Journal, Themed Monograph*, 1.

Dunn, S. and Morgan, V. (1987) Nursery and infant school play patterns: sex-related differences, *British Educational Research Journal*, 13(3), 271–81.

Early Childhood Research Institute on Inclusion (ECRII) (1999) *Me, Too! Inside Preschool Inclusion*, Modifications ECRII Brief #13. Available online at http://www.fpg.unc.edu/#ecrii.

Eaton, W.C. and Enns, L. (1986) Sex differences in human motor activity level, *Psychological Bulletin*, 100, 19–28.

Eaton, W.C. and Yu, A. (1989) Are sex differences in child motor activity level a function of sex differences in maturational status?, *Child Development*, 60, 1005–11.

Edgington, M. (1998) *The Nursery Teacher in Action: Teaching 3-, 4- and 5-year-olds*. London: Paul Chapman.

Edgington, M. (2004) *The Foundation Stage Teacher in Action – Teaching 3-, 4- and 5-year-olds*. London: Paul Chapman.

Education and Employment Committee (2000) *Early Years. The Report and the Proceedings of the Education Sub-Committee Relating to the Report*. London: The Stationery Office.

Edwards, A. (2004) Understanding context, understanding practice in early education, *European Early Childhood Education Research Journal*, 12(1), 85–102.

Edwards, C., Gandini, L. and Forman, G. (eds.) (1998) *The Hundred Languages of Children. The Reggio Emilia Approach – Advanced Reflections*. London: Ablex Publishing.

Egan, K. (1988) *Primary Understanding: Education in Early Childhood*. London: Routledge.

Egan, K. (1997) *The Educated Mind: How Cognitive Tools Shape our Understanding*. Chicago, IL: University of Chicago Press.

Eisner, E. (1982) *Cognition and Curriculum*. New York: Longman.

Eliot, L. (1999) *Early Intelligence*. London: Penguin.

Ellis, B. and Bjorklund, B. (eds) (2005) *Origins of the Social Mind: Evolutionary Psychology and Child Development*. New York: Guilford Press.

Ellis, M. (1973) *Why People Play*. Hemel Hempstead, Englewood Cliffs, NJ: Prentice-Hall.

Erikson, E. (1950) *Childhood and Society*. London: Aber.

Erikson, E. (1963) *Childhood and Society*, 2nd edition. London: Routledge and Kegan Paul.

Exley, H. (1991) *Music Lovers' Quotations*. Watford: Exley.

Eyles, J. (1993) Play – a trivial pursuit or meaningful experience?, *Early Years*, 13(2), 45–9.

Fabian, H. (2002) *Children Starting School*. London: David Fulton Publishers.

Fabian, H. and Dunlop, A.-W. (2002a) (eds) *Transitions in the Early Years. Debating Continuity and Progression for Young Children*. London: Routledge Falmer.

Fabian, H. and Dunlop, A.-W. (2002b) InterconneXions, *Early Years Matters*. Glasgow: Learning and Teaching Scotland.

Fagen, R. (1981) *Animal Play Behavior*. New York: Oxford University Press.

Fagot, B. (1974) Sex differences in toddlers' behaviour and parental reaction, *Developmental Psychology*, 10, 554–8.

Fein, G. (1978) *Child Development*. Englewood Cliffs, NJ: Prentice-Hall.

Fein, G. (1981) Pretend play: an integrative review *Child Development*, 52, 1095–18.

Fein, G. and Wiltz, N. (1998) Play as children see it, in D. Fromberg and D. Bergen *Play from Birth to Twelve and Beyond*. London: Garland Publishing Inc.

Ferreiro, E. and Teberosky, A. (1983) *Literacy before Schooling* (translated by K. Goodman Castro). London: Heinemann.

Fernald, A. (1992) Human maternal vocalisations to infants as biologically relevant signals: an evolutionary perspective, in J. Barklow, I. Cosmides and J. Toobly (eds) *The Adapted Mind: Evolutionary Psychology and the Generalisation of Culture*. Oxford: Oxford University Press.

Feurstein, R. with Rand, Y. and Hoffman, M.B. (1979) *The Dynamic Assessment of Retarded Performers. The Learning Potential Assessment. Theory, Instruments and Techniques*. Baltimore MD: University Park Press.

Filer, A. and Pollard, A. (2000) *The Social World of Pupil Assessment*. London: Continuum.

Fisher, J. (2002) *Starting from the Child*, 2nd edition. Buckingham: Open University Press.

Fisher, R. (1990) *Teaching Children to Think*. Cheltenham: Nelson Thornes Ltd.

Fisher, R. (2003) *Understanding Creativity: A Challenging Concept*, Primary Leadership Paper 10, September. London: National Association of Head Teacher.

Foulds, K., Gott, R. and Feasey, R. (1992) *Investigative Work in Science: A Report Commissioned by the National Curriculum Council*. York: NCC.

Freud, S. (1961) *Beyond the Pleasure Principle*. London: Hogarth Press and the Institute of Psycho-analysis.

Fry, D.P. (1987) Differences between play fighting and serious fights among Zapotec children, *Ethology and Sociobiology*, 8, 285–306.

Galton, M., Gray, J. and Ruddock, J. (1999) *The Impact of Transitions and Transfers on Pupils' Attitudes to Learning and Progress*. Nottingham: DfEE Publications.

Gardner, H. (1983) *Frames of Mind: The Theory of Multiple Intelligences*. New York: Basic Books.

Gardner, H. (1989) *To Open Minds*. New York: Basic Books

Gardner, H. (1993a) *Creating Minds*. New York: Basic Books.

Gardner, H. (1993b) *The Unschooled Mind: How Children Think and How Schools Should Teach*, London: Fontana.

Gardner, H. (1999b) *Intelligence Reframed*. New York: Basic Books.

Gardner, H. (1999a) *The Disciplined Mind*. New York: Simon and Schuster.

Garvey, C. (1976) Some properties of social play, in J.S. Bruner, A. Jolly and K. Sylva, *Play: Its Role in Evolution and Development*. Harmondsworth: Penguin.

Ghaye, A. and Pascal, C. (1988) Four-year-old children in Reception classrooms: participant perceptions and practice, *Educational Studies*, 14(2), 187–208.

Gillen J. and Hall, N. (2004) The emergence of early childhood literacy, in N. Hall,

J. Marsh and J. Larson (eds) *Handbook of Early Childhood Literacy*. London: Sage Publications.

Gimpel, G.A. and Holland, M. L. (2003) *Emotional and Behavioral Problems of Young Children. Effective Interventions in the Preschool and Kindergarten Years*. New York: The Guilford Press.

Gipps, C. and MacGilchrist, G. (1999) Primary school learners in P. Mortimore (ed.) *Understanding Pedagogy and its Impact on Learning*. London: Paul Chapman.

Goddard-Blythe, R. (2000) First steps to the most important ABC, *Times Educational Supplement*, 7 January.

Goldsworthy, A. and Feasey, R. (1997) *Making Sense of Primary Science Investigations*, 2nd edition. Hatfield: Association for Science Education.

Goodfellow, J. (2000) Knowing from the inside: reflective conversations with and through the narratives on once co-operating teacher, *Reflective Practice*, 1(1), 25–41.

Goouch, K. (2004) Pedagogical transplants. Unpublished presentation delivered for the Beijing Early Years Training Programme, October.

Gopnik, A., Melzoff, A. and Kuhl, P. (1999) *How Babies Think: The Science of Childhood*. London: Weidenfeld and Nicolson.

Greenfield, S. (1996) *The Human Mind Explained*. London: Cassell.

Greenfield, S. (1997) *The Human Brain: A Guided Tour*. London: Weidenfeld and Nicolson.

Greenfield, S. (2004) *The Human Brain: A Guided Tour*. Phoenix, AZ: Phoenix Mass Marker Publications.

Greenfield, S. (2000) *Brain Story*. London: BBC Books.

Griebel, W. and Niesel, R. (1999) From kindergarten to school: a transition for the family, Paper presented at 9th European Early Childhood Education Research Association European Conference on Quality in Early Childhood Education, 1–4 September, Helsinki.

Griffiths, N. (1997) *Storysacks: A Starter Information Pack*. Bury: Storysacks Ltd.

Griffiths, R. (1988) *Maths through Play*. London: Macdonald.

Griffiths, R. (2004) *Extra Help in Maths, Ages 5 to 7*. Leamington Spa: Scholastic.

Groos, K. (1898) *The Play of Animals*. New York: Appleton.

Groos, K. (1901) *The Play of Man*. New York: Appleton.

Guha, M. (1988) Play in school, in G.M. Blenkin and A.V. Kelly (eds) *Early Childhood Education: A Developmental Curriculum*, London: Paul Chapman.

Hall, G. Stanley (1908) *Aspects of Child Life and Education*. Boston MA: Ginn.

Hall, N. and Robinson, A. (2003) *Exploring Writing and Play in the Early Years*, 2nd edition. London: David Fulton.

Handy, C. (1997) Schools for life and work, in P. Mortimore and V. Little (eds) *Living Education: Essays in Honour of John Tomlinson*. London: Paul Chapman.

Hannon, P. and Hirst, K. (2004) *Shared Beginnings External Evaluation*. http://www.rif.org.uk/aboutrif/sbgexternalevaluation.htm. Accessed 22 December.

Harding, S. (1999) What's happening with the bikes? Unpublished MA Assignment, MA Early Education and Care, University of North London/Pen Green Research Base, Corby.

Harding, S. (2000) How can I tell you? Valuing the non-verbal skills of three and four year olds with particular reference to proxemics and kinesics. Unpublished MA Dissertation, MA Early Education and Care, University of North London/Pen Green Research Base, Corby.

Harding, S. (2004) The Magic Mountain and beyond: our journey to maintaining and managing the pedagogic garden. Paper submitted for a Leadership Research Bursary, Pen Green Leadership and Research Centre, Corby.

Hargreaves, D. (2004) Keynote Lecture, National Association of Music Educators Conference London, 17–19 September.

Harlen, W. (2000) *The Teaching of Science in Primary Schools*, 3rd edition. London: Paul Chapman Publishing.

Harrison, C. and Pound, L. (1996) Talking music: empowering children as musical communicators, *British Journal of Music Education*, 33(3), 233–42.

Harrold, M. (2004) A case study of B. Unpublished report, Earlham Early Years Centre, Norwich.

Hartley, D. (1993) *Understanding the Nursery School*. London: Cassell.

Heathcote, D. (1984) *Collected Writings*. London: Hutchinson.

Hereford, W. H. (1901) *The Student's Froebel*. London: Isbister and Company Ltd.

Hewitt, K. (2001) Blocks as a tool for learning: historical and contemporary perspectives, *Young Children*. 56(1), 6–13.

Hildebrandt, C. (1998) Creativity in music and early childhood, *Young Children*, 53(6), 68–74.

Hines, M. and Kaufman, F.R. (1994) Androgen and the development of human sex-typical behaviour: rough-and-tumble play and sex of preferred playmates in children with Congenital Adrenal Hyperplasia (CAH), *Child Development*, 65, 1042–53.

Hislam, J. (1994) Sex-differentiated play experiences and children's choices, in J. Moyles (ed.) *The Excellence of Play*. Buckingham: Open University Press.

Hislam, J. (2002) Telling the whole story: developing children's oral skills and imagination within the Literacy Hour, in J. Moyles and G. Robinson, *Beginning Teaching: Beginning Learning in Primary Education*, 2nd edition. Buckingham: Open University Press.

Holland, P. (2003) *We Don't Play With Guns Here: War, Weapons and Superhero Play in the Early Years*. Maidenhead: Open University Press.

Holt, J. (1991) *Learning All the Time*. Ticknell, Derbyshire: Education NOW.

Home Office, DfEE and DoH (1989) *The Children Act 1989* (c.41). Norwich: The Stationery Office. Available online at http://www.hmso.gov/uk/acts/acts1989/Ukpa_19890041_en_2.htm#nsmdiv1 (Accessed 8 October 2004).

Hord, S., Rutherford, W., Huling-Austin, L. and Hall, G. (1998) Taking Charge of Change. Austin, TX: South West Educational Development Laboratory.

Horner, R.H., Sugai, G.A. and Todd, A.W. (2001) 'Data' need not be a four-letter word: using data to improve schoolwide discipline, *Beyond Behavior*, (Fall), 20–2. Available online at http//ccbd.net/documents/bb/datanotbe4letterword.pdf. Accessed 12 April 2004.

Howe, A. (2004) *Play with Natural Materials*. London: David Fulton.

Howe, A., Davies, D. and Ritchie, R. (2001) *Primary Design and Technology for the Future: Creativity, Culture and Citizenship in the Curriculum*. London: David Fulton.

Hughes, M. (1986) *Children and Number*. Oxford: Basil Blackwell.

Hughes, M., Desforges, C. and Mitchell, C. (2000) *Numeracy and Beyond: Applying Mathematics in the Primary School*. Buckingham: Open University Press.

Hughes, M., Pinkerton, G. and Plewis, I. (1979) Children's difficulties on starting infant school, *Journal of Child Psychology and Psychiatry*, 20, 187–96.

Huizinga, J. (1949) *Homo Ludens: A Study of the Play Element in Culture*. London: Routledge and Kegan Paul.

Humphreys, A. and Smith, P.K. (1987) Rough and tumble, friendship and dominance in school children: evidence for continuity and change with age, *Child Development*, 58, 201–12.

Humphreys, A.P. and Smith, P.K. (1984) Rough-and-tumble play in preschool and playground, in P.K. Smith (ed.) *Play in Animals and Humans*. Oxford: Blackwell.

Hurst, V. (1994a) *The Implications of the National Curriculum and Early Learning: An Evaluation*. London: Paul Chapman.

Hurst, V. (1994b) Observing play in early childhood, in J. Moyles (ed.) *The Excellence of Play*. Buckingham: Open University Press.

Hutt, S.J., Tyler, S., Hutt, C. and Christopherson, H. (1989) *Play, Exploration and Learning: A Natural History of the Preschool*. London: Routledge.

Inch, S. and MacVarish, J. (2003) Across the divide, *Reflective Practice*, 4(1), 1–10, 1470–103.

Isaacs, S. (1929) *The Nursery Years*. London: Routledge and Kegan Paul.

James, W. (1890) *The Principles of Psychology*. London: Macmillan.

Jensen, M., Foster, E. and Eddy, M. (1997) Locating a space where teachers can locate their voices and develop their pedagogical awareness, *Teaching and Teacher Education*, 13(8), 863–75.

Jin, L. and Cortazzi, M. (1998) Dimensions of dialogue: large classes in China, *International Journal of Educational Research*, 29, 739–61.

Johnston, J. (1996) *Early Explorations in Science*. Buckingham: Open University Press.

Kalliala, M. (in press 2005) *Children's Play Culture in a Changing World*. Maidenhead: Open University Press.

Kane, P. (2004) *The Play Ethic*. London: Macmillan.

Karmiloff, K. and Karmiloff-Smith, A. (2001) *Pathways to Language*. Cambridge, MA: Harvard University Press.

Kent Schools' Advisory Service (2003) *Writing in the Air: Nurturing Young Children's Dispositions for Writing*. Maidstone: Kent County Council.

Kitson, N. and Spiby, I. (1997) *Drama 7–11*. London: Routledge.

Konner, M. (1991) *Childhood*. Boston, MA: Little, Brown.

Kress, G. (1997) *Before Writing: Rethinking the Paths to Literacy*. London: Routledge.

Lancaster, P. (2003) *Listening to Children*. Maidenhead: Open University Press.

Langlois, J. and Downs, C. (1980) Mothers, fathers and peers as socialisation agents of sex-typed play behaviour in young children, *Child Development*, 7, 1237–47.

Lave, J. and Wenger, E. (1991) *Situated Learning. Legitimate Peripheral Participation*. Cambridge: Cambridge University Press.

Leavers, F., Vandenbussche, E., Kog, M. and Depondt, L. (undated) *A Process-oriented Child Monitoring System for Young Children*, Experiential Education Series, No. 2. Belgium: The Centre for Experiential Education.

Lever, J. (1978) Sex differences in the complexity of children's play and games, *American Sociological Review*, 43, 471–83.

Lewis-Williams, D. (2002) *The Mind in the Cave*. London: Thames and Hudson.

Li, G. (2002) *East is East, West is West? Home Literacy, Culture and Schooling*. New York: Peter Lang.

Lieberman, J.N. (1977) *Playfulness: Its Relation to Imagination and Creativity*. New York: Academic Press.

Lillard, A. (2002) Pretend play and cognitive development, in U. Goswami (ed.) *Blackwell Handbook of Childhood Cognitive Development*. Oxford: Blackwell.

Lindon, J. (1999) *Too Safe for Their Own Good? Helping Children Learn about Risk and Life Skills*. London: National Early Years Network.

Lobman, C. (2003) What should we create today? Improvisational teaching in play-based classrooms, *Early Years*, 23(2), 131–42.

Lubeck, S. (1986) *Sandbox Society*. London: Falmer.

Lubeck, S. and Jessup, P. (2001) Globalisation and its impact on early years funding and curiculum, in T. David (ed.) *Promoting Evidence-based Practice in Early Childhood Education*. Oxford: Elsevier.

Maccoby, E.E. (1998) *The Two Sexes: Growing Up Apart, Coming Together*. Cambridge, MA: Harvard University Press.

MacDonald, K. (1993) Parent–child play: an evolutionary perspective, in K. MacDonald (ed.) *Parent–child Play*. New York: SUNY Press.

MacDonald, K. and Parke, R. (1986) Parent–child physical play, *Sex Roles*, 15, 367–78.

McDougall, W. (1933) *An Outline of Abnormal Psychology*. London: Methuen.

MacGregor, H. (1998) *Tom Thumb's Musical Maths*. London: A. and C. Black.

McLane, J. and Spielberger, J. (1996) Play in early childhood development and education: issues and questions. Playing for keeps: supporting children's play topics, *Early Childhood Education*, 2(10), 5–10.

Macmillan, M. (1919) *The Nursery School*. London: J.M. Dent and Sons.

MacNaughton, G. (2003) *Shaping Early Childhood*. Maidenhead: Open University Press/McGraw-Hill.

Manning, K. and Sharp, A. (1977) *Structuring Play in the Early Years at School*. Cardiff: Ward Lock Educational.

Manning-Morton, J. and Thorp, M. (2003) *Key Times for Play*. Maidenhead: Open University Press.

Marsh, J. (2000) But I want to fly too! Girls and superhero play in the infant classroom, *Gender and Education*, 12(2), 209–20.

Marsh, J. and Millard, E. (2000) *Literacy and Popular Culture: Using Children's Culture in the Classroom*. London: Paul Chapman.

Matthews, J. (2003) *Drawing and Painting: Children and Visual Representation*, 2nd edition. London: Paul Chapman/Sage Publications.

Medlicott, M. (1996) Word of mouth, *Nursery World*, 24 October, 23.

Meggitt, C. (2001) *Baby and Child Health*. Oxford: Heinemann Educational Publishers.

Meisels, S.J. and Atkins-Burnett, S. (2000) The elements of early childhood assessment, in J.P. Shonkoff, and S.J. Meisels (eds) *Handbook of Early Childhood Intervention*. Cambridge: Cambridge University Press.

Ministry of Education of the PRC (People's Republic of China) (1981) *Draft National Curriculum for the Preschool*. Beijing: Ministry of Education. English translation available in R. Liljeström, E. Néren-Björn, G. Schyl-Bjurman, B. Öhrn, L. Gustafsson, L and O. Löfgren (1983) *Young Children in China*. Clevedon: Multilingual Matters.

Ministry of Education of the PRC (2001) *You'eryuan Jiaoyu Zhidao Gangyao (shixing) – (Draft) Guidelines (National) for Kindergarten Education*. Beijing: Ministry of Education of the PRC.

Moyles, J. (1989) *Just Playing? The Role and Status of Play in Early Childhood Education*. Buckingham: Open University Press.

Moyles, J. and Adams, S. (2001) *StEPS: Statements of Entitlement to Play*. Buckingham: Open University Press.

Moyles, J., Adams, S. and Musgrove, A. (2002) *SPEEL: Study of Pedagogical Effectiveness in Early Learning*, Research Report 363. London: DfES.

Moyles, J., Hargreaves, L., Merry, R., Paterson, A. and Esarte-Sarries, V. (2003) *Interactive Teaching in the Primary School: Digging Deeper into Meanings*. Maidenhead: Open University Press.

Murray, L. and Andrews, L. (2000) *The Social Baby*. Richmond: CP Publishing.

National Advisory Committee on Creativity and Cultural Education (NACCCE) (1999) *All Our Futures: Creativity, Culture and Education*. London: DfEE.

National Children's Bureau (2004) *Childhood Bereavement: Developing the Curriculum and Pastoral Support*. London: NCB.

Neelands, J. (1984) *Making Sense of Drama*. London: Heinemann.

Neisworth, J.T. and Bagnato, S.J. (1988) Assessment in early childhood special education. A typology of dependent measure, in S.L.Odom, and M.B. Karnes (eds) *Early Intervention for Infants and Children with Handicaps: An Empirical Base*, 2nd edition. Baltimore, MD: Paul H. Bookes Publishing.

Nicholls, G. (1999) Young children investigating: adopting a constructivist framework, in T. David (ed.) *Teaching Young Children*. London: David Fulton.

Niethammer, C. (1977) *Daughters of the Earth: The Lives and Legends of American Indian Women*. New York: Collier/Macmillan.

Norman, D. (1978) Notes towards a complex theory of learning, in A.M. Lesgold (ed.) *Cognitive Psychology and Instruction*. New York: Plenum.

Nutbrown, C. (1994) *Threads of Thinking: Young Children Learning and the Role of Early Education*. London: Paul Chapman.

Nutbrown, C. (1999) *Threads of Thinking: Young Children Learning and the Role of Early Education*, 2nd edition. London: Paul Chapman.

Odam, G. (1995) *The Sounding Symbol*. Cheltenham: Stanley Thornes.

Odom, S.L., Vitztum, J., Wolery, R., Lieber, J., Sandall, S., Hanson, M.J. *et al.* (2004) Preschool inclusion in the United States: a review of research from an ecological systems perspective, *Journal of Research in Special Educational Needs*, 4(1), 17–49.

Office for Standards in Education (Ofsted) (2003) *The Child at the Centre – Report on the Early Excellence Centre Pilot*. London: HMSO.

Office for Standards in Education (Ofsted) (2004) *Special Educational Needs and Disability. Towards Inclusive Schools*. London: Ofsted Publication Centre.

Oldfield, L. (2001) *Free to Learn*. Stroud: Hawthorn Press.

O'Shea, M. (2002) *The Brain: A Very Short Introduction*. Oxford: Oxford Paperbacks.

Ouvry, M. (2003) *Exercising Muscles and Minds: Outdoor Play and the Early Years Curriculum*, 2nd edition. London: NCB.

Page, J. (2000) *Re-framing the Early Childhood Curriculum*. London: Routledge Falmer.

Paley, V.G. (1984) *Boys and Girls: Superheroes in the Doll Corner*. Chicago, IL: Chicago University Press.

Paley, V.G. (1986) *Mollie is Three*. Chicago, IL: University of Chicago Press.

Paley, V.G. (2004) *A Child's Work: The Importance of Fantasy Play*. Chicago, IL: Chicago University Press.

Palmer, J. (1994) *Geography in the Early Years*. London: Routledge.

Pan, H.L.W. (1994) Children's play in Taiwan, in J.L. Roopnarine, J.E. Johnson and F.H. Hooper (eds) *Children's Play In Diverse Cultures*. Albany, NY: State University of New York Press.

Papatheodorou, T. (2005) *Behaviour Problems in the Early Years*. London: Routledge Falmer.

Papert, S. (1980) *Mindstorms*. Brighton: Harvester Press.

Papousek, H. (1994) To the evolution of human musicality and musical education, in I. Deliege (ed.) *Proceedings of the 3rd International Conference for Music Perception and Cognition*. Liege: ESCOM.

Papousek, H. and Papousek, M. (1994) Early musicality and caregivers' infant-directed speech, in I. Deliege (ed.) *Proceedings of the 3rd International Conference for Music Perception and Cognition*. Liege: ESCOM.

Pappas, C. (2003) Listen to my story, *Nursery World*, 20 March, 12.

Parke, R.D. and Suomi, S.J. (1981) Adult male infant relationships: human and nonhuman primate evidence, in K. Immelman, G.W. Barlow, L. Petronovitch and M. Main (eds) *Behavioural Development*. New York: Cambridge University Press.

Parker-Rees, R. (2004) Moving, playing and learning: children's active exploration of their world, in J. Willan, R. Parker-Rees and J. Savage, *Early Childhood Studies*. Exeter: Learning Matters.

Pascal, C. and Bertram, T. (2001) *Effective Early Learning: Case Studies in Improvement*. London: Paul Chapman.

Pellegrini, A.D. (1985) The narrative organisation of children's fantasy play, *Educational Psychology*, 5, 17–25.

Pellegrini, A.D. (1988) Elementary school children's rough-and-tumble play and social competence, *Developmental Psychology*, 24, 802–6.

Pellegrini, A.D. (1994) The rough play of adolescent boys of differing sociometric status, *International Journal of Behavioral Development*, 17, 525–40.

Pellegrini, A.D. (1995) *School Recess and Playground Behaviour*. Albany, NY: State University of New York Press.

Pellegrini, A. D. (2002) Rough-and-tumble play from childhood through adolescence: development and possible functions, in P.K. Smith and C. Hart (eds) *Blackwell Handbook of Social Development*. Oxford: Blackwell.

Pellegrini, A.D. and Bjorklund, D.F. (1997) The role of recess in children's cognitive performance, *Educational Psychologist*, 31, 181–7.

Pellegrini, A.D. and Davis, P. (1993) Relations between children's playground and classroom behaviour, *British Journal of Educational Psychology*, 63, 86–95.

Pellegrini, A.D. and Smith, P.K. (1998) Physical activity play: the nature and function of a neglected aspect of play, *Child Development*, 69, 577–98.

Pellegrini, A.D. and Smith, P.K. (2005) (eds) *The Nature of Play: Great Apes and Humans*. New York: Guilford Press.

Pellegrini, A.D., Huberty, P.D. and Jones, I. (1995) The effects of recess timing on children's playground and classroom behaviours, *American Educational Research Journal*, 32, 845–64.

Peters, M. and Sherratt, D. (2002) *Developing Play and Drama in Children with Autistic Spectrum Disorders*. London: David Fulton.

Peters, R.S. (1981) *Moral Development and Moral Education*. London: Allen and Unwin.

Piaget, J. (1929) *The Child's Conception of the World*. New York: Harcourt Brace.

Piaget, J. (1947) *The Psychology of Intelligence* (translated by M. Piercy and D. Berlyne). London: Routledge and Kegan Paul.

Piaget, J. (1951) *Play, Dreams, and Imitation in Childhood*. London: Routledge and Kegan Paul.

Pollard, A. and Filer, A. (1996) *The Social World of Children's Learning*. London: Cassells.

Pollard, A., Broadfoot, P., Croll, P., Osborn, M. and Abbott, D. (1994) *Changing English Primary Schools? The Impact of the Education Reform Act at Key Stage One.* London: Cassell.

Post, J. and Hohmann, M. (2000) *Tender Care and Early Learning: Supporting Families and Toddlers in Childcare Settings.* Ypsilanti, MI: High/Scope Press.

Potts, P. (2003) *Modernising Education in Britain and China.* London: Routledge Falmer.

Pound, L. (2002) Breadth and depth in early foundations, in J. Fisher (ed.) *The Foundations of Learning.* Buckingham: Open University Press.

Pound, L. (2003) Creativity, musicality and imagination. Symposium paper presented at the 13th Annual EECERA Conference, 3–6 September.

Pound, L. and Harrison, C. (2003) *Supporting Musical Development in the Early Years.* Buckingham: Open University Press.

Powell, S. (2001) Constructions of early childhood in China: a case study of contemporary Shanghai. Unpublished doctoral thesis, University of Kent.

Pramling-Samuelsson, I. (2004) Can play and learning be integrated in a goal oriented preschool? Paper given at the International Froebel Society Conference, Froebel in the Twenty First Century: Challenges and Uncertainties, Froebel College, University of Surrey, Roehampton, 2 July.

Prentice, R. (2000) Creativity: a reaffirmation of its place in early childhood education, *The Curriculum Research Journal,* 11(2), 145–58.

Pretti-Frontczack, K. and Bricker, D. (2001) Use of embedding strategy during daily activities by early childhood education and early childhood special education teachers. Infant-toddler intervention, *The Transdisciplinary Journal,* 11(2), 111–28.

Qualifications and Curriculum Authority (QCA) (2001) *English Tasks Teacher's Handbook.* London: QCA/DfES.

QCA (2002) *Arts Alive.* London: QCA.

QCA (2003a) *Creativity: Find It, Promote It.* London: QCA.

QCA (2003b) *The Foundation Stage Profile Handbook.* London: QCA.

QCA (undated) CD Rom. *Observing Children – Building the Profile.* London: QCA.

QCA/Department for Education and Employment (2000) *Curriculum Guidance for the Foundation Stage.* London: QCA/DfEE.

Quinn, M.M., Gable, R.A., Rutherford, R.B., Nelson, C.M. and Howell, K.W. (1998) *Addressing Student Problem Behavior. An IEP's Team Introduction to Functional Behavioral Assessment and Behavior Intervention Plans.* The Center for Effective Collaboration and Practice. Available online at http://cecp.air.org/fba/problembehavior/funcanal.pdf. Accessed 26 February 2004.

Raver, S. A. (2003) Monitoring child progress in early childhood special education settings, *Teaching Exceptional Children,* 36(6), 52–7.

Roberts, R. (1995) *Self-esteem and Successful Early Learning.* London: Hodder and Stoughton.

Robinson, K. (2001) *Out of our Minds – Learning to Be Creative.* Oxford: Capstone.

Rogoff, B., Paradise, R., Arauz, R.M., Correa-Chavez, M. and Angelillo, C. (2003) Firsthand learning through intent participation, *Annual Review of Psychology,* 54, 175–203.

Roopnarine, J.L., Hooper, F.H., Ahmeduzzaman, M., and Pollack, B. (1993) Gentle play partners: mother–child and father–child play in New Delhi, India, in K. MacDonald (ed.) *Parent–child play.* New York: SUNY Press.

Rosen, M. and Oxenbury, H. (1993) *We're Going on a Bear Hunt*. London: Walker Books.

Rosenquest, B. (2002) Literacy-based planning and pedagogy that supports toddler-language development, *Early Childhood Education Journal*, 29(4), 241–9.

Rosenthal, M. (2000) Quality in early childhood education, Paper presented at University of Malta International Symposium on Curricula, Policies and Practices in Early Childhood Education, Malta, 28 November to 3 December.

Roskos, K. and Christie, J. (2001) Examining the play–literacy interface: a critical review and future directions, *Journal of Early Childhood Literacy*, 1(1), 59–89.

Ross, J. (2004) The instructable body: student bodies from classrooms to prisons, in L. Bresler (ed.) *Knowing Bodies, Moving Minds: Towards Embodied Teaching and Learning*. Dordrecht: Kluwer Academic Publishers.

Rosser, R. (1994) *Cognitive Development: Psychological and Biological Perspectives*. Needham Heights, MA: Allyn and Bacon.

Routh, D., Schoeder, C. and O'Tuama, L. (1974) Development of activity levels in children, *Developmental Psychology*, 10, 163–8.

Sammons, P., Taggart, B., Smees, R., Sylva, K., Melhuish, E., Siraj-Blatchford, I. and Elliot, K. (2003) *The Early Years Transition and Special Educational Needs (EYTSEN) Project*, Research Report No. 431. Nottingham: DfES.

Sanders, B. (2004) Childhood in different cultures, in T. Maynard and N. Thomas (eds) *An Introduction to Early Childhood Studies*. London: Sage Publications.

Sayeed, Z. and Guerin, E. (2000) *Early Years Play. A Happy Medium for Assessment and Intervention*. London: David Fulton.

Schafer, M. and Smith, P.K. (1996) Teachers' perceptions of play fighting and real fighting in primary school, *Educational Research*, 38, 173–81.

Schwartzman, H. (1978) *Transformations: The Anthropology of Children's Play*. New York, London: Plenum Press.

Schweinhart, L.J. and Weikart, D.P. (1998) Why curriculum matters in early childhood education, *Educational Leadership*, 55(6), 57–60.

Sha, J. (1998) Chinese parents' and teachers' perceptions of preprimary school children's play. Unpublished Master's thesis, University of Wyoming.

Sheridan, M.K., Foley, G.M. and Radlinski, S.H. (1995) *Using the Supportive Play Model: Individualized Intervention in Early Childhood Practice*. New York: Teachers College Press.

Shi, H. (1989) Young people's care and education in the People's Republic of China, in P. Olmsted and D. Weikart (eds) *How Nations Serve Young Children*. Ypsilanti, MI: High/Scope Press.

Shonkoff, J. and Phillips, D. (eds) (2000) *From Neurons to Neighbourhoods: The Science of Early Childhood Development*. Washington, DC: National Academy Press.

Siegel, D. (1999) *The Developing Mind*. New York: Guilford Press.

Sigel, I.E. (1993) Educating the young thinker: A distancing model of preschool education, in J. Roopnarine and J. Johnson (eds) *Approaches to Early Childhood Education*. New York: Macmillan.

Simmons, J., Sparks-Langer, G., Starko, A., Pasch, M., Colton, A. and Grinberg, J. (1989) Exploring the structure of reflective pedagogical thinking in novice and expert teachers: the birth of a developmental taxonomy. Paper presented at the Annual Meeting of the American Educational Research Association, San Francisco, in D. Kagan (1990) Ways of evaluating teacher cognition. Inferences concerning the Goldilocks principles, *Review of Educational Research*, 60(3), 419–69.

Singer, D. and Singer, J. (1990) *The House of Make Believe*. Cambridge, MA: Harvard University Press.

Singer, J. (1973) *The Child's World of Make-Believe: Experimental Studies of Imaginative Play*. London: Academic Press.

Siraj-Blatchford, I. and Sylva, K. (2004) Researching pedagogy in English preschools, *British Educational Research Journal*, 30(4), 713–30.

Siraj-Blatchford, J. and MacLeod-Brudenell, I. (1999) *Supporting Science, Design and Technology in the Early Years*. Buckingham: Open University Press.

Siraj-Blatchford, J. and Siraj-Blatchford, I. (2001) A content analysis of pedagogy in the new DfEE/QCA Guidance, *Early Education*, 35, 7–8.

Siraj-Blatchford, I., Sylva, K., Muttock, S., Gilden, R. and Bell, D. (2002) *Researching Effective Pedagogy in the Early Years*, Research Report No. 356. London: DfES.

Small, C. (1998) *Musicking: The Meaning of Performing and Listening*. New England: Wesleyan University Press.

Smilansky, S. (1968) *The Effects of Socio-dramatic Play on Disadvantaged Preschool Children*. New York: Wiley.

Smilansky, S. (1990) Socio-dramatic play: its relevance to behaviour and achievement in school, in E. Klugman and S. Smilansky, *Children's Play and Learning Perspectives and Policy Implications*. New York: Teachers College Press.

Smilansky, S. and Shefatya, L. (1990) *Facilitating Play: A Medium for Promoting Cognitive, Sociocultural and Academic Development in Young Children*. Gaithersburg, MD: Psychosocial and Educational Publications.

Smith, A. (1998) *Accelerated Learning in Practice: Brain-based Methods for Accelerating Motivation and Achievement*. Stafford: Network Educational Press.

Smith, P.K. (1982) Does play matter? Functional and evolutionary aspects of animal and human play, *The Behavioural and Brain Sciences*, 5, 139–84.

Smith, P.K. (1988) Child's play and its role in early development: A re-evaluation of the 'play ethos', in A. Pellegrini (ed.) *Psychological Bases for Early Education*. Chichester: Wiley.

Smith, P.K. (1990) The role of play in the nursery and primary school curriculum. In C. Rogers and P. Kutnick (eds) *The Social Psychology of the Primary School*, London: Routledge.

Smith, P.K. (1997) Play fighting and real fighting: perspectives on their relationship, in A. Schmitt, K. Atswanger, K. Grammar and K. Schafer (eds) *New Aspects of Ethology*. New York: Plenum Press.

Smith, P.K. (2005) Play: types and functions in human development, in B. Ellis and D. Bjorklund (eds) *Origins of the Social Mind: Evolutionary Psychology and Child Development*. New York: Guilford Press.

Smith, P.K. and Connolly, K. (1980) *The Ecology of Preschool Behaviour*. Cambridge: Cambridge University Press.

Smith, P.K. and Hagan, T. (1980) Effects of deprivation on exercise play in nursery school children, *Animal Behaviour*, 28, 922–8.

Smith, P.K. and Lewis, K. (1985) Rough-and-tumble play, fighting, and chasing in nursery school children, *Ethology and Sociobiology*, 6, 175–81.

Smith, P.K., Smees, R. and Pellegrini, A.D. (2004) Play fighting and real fighting: using video playback methodology with young children, *Aggressive Behavior*, 30, 164–73.

Smith, S. (1998) *Risk and our Pedagogical Relation to Children: On the Playground and Beyond*. Albany, NY: State University of New York Press.

Snow, C.P. (1959) *The Two Cultures: A Second Look.* Cambridge: Cambridge University Press.

Spencer, B. (1873) *Recent Discussion in Science, Philosophy and Morals.* New York: Appleton.

Spencer, H. (1898) *The Principles of Psychology*, 3rd edition. New York: Appleton.

Steedman, C. (1985) Listen how the caged bird sings, in C. Steedman, C. Urwin and V. Walkerdine (eds) *Language, Gender and Childhood*, History Workshop Series. London: Routledge and Kegan Paul.

Stern, D.N. (1985) *The Interpersonal World of the Infant.* New York: Basic Books.

Stevens, J. (2002) Windy day activities, *Practical Pre-School*, 31, 11–12.

Storr, A. (1989) *Solitude.* London: Collins.

Strandell, H. (2000) What is the use of children's play: preparation or social participation?, in H. Penn (ed.) *Early Childhood Services.* Buckingham: Open University Press.

Sutton-Smith, B. (1966) Piaget on play: a critique, *Psychological Review*, 73(1), 104–10.

Sutton-Smith, B. (1976) *How to Play with your Child and When Not To.* New York: E.P. Dutton.

Sutton-Smith, B. (1979) *Play and Learning.* New York: Gardner/Halsted Press.

Sutton-Smith, B. (1997) *The Ambiguity of Play.* Cambridge, MA: Harvard University Press.

Sutton-Smith, B. and Kelly-Byrne, D. (1984) The idealization of play, in P.K. Smith (ed.) *Play in Animals and Humans.* Oxford: Basil Blackwell.

Sylva, K., Bruner, J. and Genova, P. (1976) The role of play in the problem solving of children aged 3–5 years, in J. Bruner, A. Jolly and K. Sylva (eds) *Play: Its Role in Development and Evolution.* Glasgow: Penguin.

Sylva, K., Roy, D. and Painter, M. (1980) *Childwatching at Playgroup and Nursery School.* Oxford: Blackwell.

Sylva, K., Melhuish, E., Sammons, P., Siraj-Blatchford, I., Taggart, B. and Elliot, K. (2003) *The Effective Provision of Preschool Education (EPPE) Project: Findings from the Preschool Period.* London: Institute of Education.

Sylwester, R. (1997) *A Celebration of Neurons: An Educators' Guide to the Human Brain.* Alexandria, VA: Association for Supervision and Curriculum Development.

Symons, D. (1978) *Play and Aggression: A Study of Rhesus Monkeys.* New York: Columbia University Press.

Thelen, E. (1979) Rhythmical stereotypies in normal human infants, *Animal Behaviour*, 27, 699–715.

Thelen, E. (1980) Determinants of amounts of stereotyped behaviour in normal human infants, *Ethology and Sociobiology*, 1, 141–50.

Thomas, F. (2004) How can we sustain and support learning in the nursery garden? Paper submitted for a Leadership Research Bursary, Pen Green Leadership and Research Centre, Corby.

Thyssen, S. (1997) The child's beginning in daycare, Paper presented at the European Early Childhood Education Research Association, 7th European Conference on the Quality of Early Childhood Education. Munich, 3–6 September.

Tizard, B., Blatchford, P., Burke, J., Farquhar, C. and Plewis, I. (1988) *Young Children at School in the Inner City.* Hove: Lawrence Erlbaum.

Tobin, J. (2004) The disappearance of the body in early childhood education, in L.

Bresler (ed.) *Knowing Bodies, Moving Minds: Towards Embodied Teaching and Learning*. Dordrecht: Kluwer Academic Publishers.

Tobin, J.J., Wu, D.Y.H. and Davidson, D.H. (1989) *Preschool in Three Cultures*. London: Yale University Press.

Trevarthen, C. (1987) Sharing makes sense: intersubjectivity and the making of an infant's meaning, in R. Steele and T. Treadgold (eds) *Essays in Honour of Michael Halliday*, Amsterdam/ Philadelphia, PA: John Benjamin.

Trevarthen, C. (1998) The child's need to learn a culture, in M. Woodhead, D. Faulkner and K. Littleton (eds) *Cultural Worlds of Early Childhood*. London: Routledge/The Open University.

Trevarthen, C. and Aitken, K.J. (2001) Infant intersubjectivity: research, theory, and clinical applications, *Annual Research Review. The Journal of Child Psychology and Psychiatry and Allied Disciplines*, 42, 1, 3–48.

Turner-Bissett, R. (1999) The knowledge bases of the expert teacher, *British Educational Research Journal*, 25(1), 39–55.

United Nations (UN) (1989) *United Nations Convention on the Rights of the Child*. New York: UN.

Vacc, N.A. and Ritter, S.H. (1995) *Assessment of Preschool Children*. ERIC Digest (REIC identifier: ED389964).

Vandenberg, B. (1986) Mere child's play, in K. Blanchard (ed.) *The Many Faces of Play*. Association of the Anthropological Study of Play, Vol. 9. Champaign, IL: Human Kinetics.

Vandenberg, D. (1991) *Being and Education: An Essay in Existential Phenomenology*. Englewood Cliffs, NJ, Hemel Hempstead: Prentice-Hall.

Van Gennep, A. ([1908] 1960) *The Rites of Passage*. London: Routledge and Kegan Paul.

Van Hoorn, J., Monighan-Nouret, P., Scales, B. and Rodriquez-Alward, K. (2003) *Play at the Center of the Curriculum*. New Jersey, NJ: Merrill, Prentice-Hall.

Vasta, R., Haith, M.M. and Miller, S.A. (1999) *Child Psychology: The Modern Science*, 3rd edition. New York: Wiley.

Vygotsky, L. S. ([1933] 1966) Play and its role in the mental development of the child, *Voprosy Psikhologii*, 12, 62–76.

Vygotsky, L. (1978) *Mind in Society: The Development of Higher Psychological Processes* (translated by M. Cole, V. John-Steiner, S. Scribner and E. Souberman). Cambridge, MA: Harvard University Press.

Walkerdine, V. (1997) *Daddy's Girl: Young Girls and Popular Culture*. Basingstoke: Macmillan.

Walsh, D. (2004) Frog Boy and the American Monkey: the body in Japanese early schooling, in L. Bresler (ed.) *Knowing Bodies, Moving Minds: Towards Embodied Teaching and Learning*. Dordrecht: Kluwer Academic Publishers.

Wei, Z. and Ebbeck, M. (1996) The importance of preschool education in the People's Republic of China, *Journal of Early Years Education*, 4(1), 27–34.

Wells, G. (1985) *Language Learning and Education*. Windsor: NFER/Nelson.

Wenger, E. (1999) *Communities of Practice. Learning, Meaning, and Identity*. Cambridge: Cambridge University Press.

Whitebread, D. (2000) Teaching children to think, reason, solve problems and be creative, in D. Whitebread (ed.) *The Psychology of Teaching and Learning in the Primary School*. London: Routledge Falmer.

Whitebread, D. and Jameson, H. (2003) The impact of play on the oral and written storytelling of able 5–7 year olds. Paper presented at the 33rd Annual Meeting of the Jean Piaget Society, Chicago.

Whitehead, M. (2002) Developing Language and Literacy with Young Children 2nd edition. London: Paul Chapman/Sage Publications.

Wilson, R. (1998) *Special Educational Needs in the Early Years*. London: Routledge.

Wolfberg, P. (1998) *Autism and Play*. London: Jessica Kingsley.

Wong, L.Y. (1992) *Education of Chinese Children in Britain and the USA*. Clevedon: Multilingual Matters.

Wood, E. (1999) The Impact of the National Curriculum on Play in Reception Classes, *Educational Research*, 41(1), 11–22.

Wood, E. (2004a) A new paradigm war? The impact of national curriculum policies on early childhood teachers' thinking and classroom practice, *Teaching and Teacher Education*, 20, 361–74.

Wood, E. (2004b) Developing a pedagogy of play, in A. Anning, J. Cullen, and M. Fleer, *Early Childhood Education*. London: Sage Publications.

Wood, L. and Attfield, J. (1996) *Play, Learning and the Early Childhood Curriculum*. London: Paul Chapman.

Woodhead, M. (1989) School starts at five . . . or four years old? The rationale for changing admission policies in England and Wales, *Journal of Education Policy*, 4(1), 1–21.

Wordsworth, W. ([1803–6] 1919) 'Intimations of Immortality', from *Recollections of Early Childhood*, in A.T. Quiller-Couch (ed.) *The Oxford Book of English Verse*. Oxford: Clarendon.

Worthington, M. and Carruthers, E. (2003) *Children's Mathematics*. London: Paul Chapman/Sage Publications.

Wu, D.Y.H. (1996) Parental control: psycho-cultural interpretations of Chinese patterns of socialization, in Sing Lau (ed.) *Growing up the Chinese Way*. Hong Kong: Chinese University Press.

Xinhua News Agency (2001) Beijing Issues Regulations on Preschoolers. Education. *Xinhua News Agency*, 31 July 2001.

Young, J. and Glover, S. (1998) *Music in the Early Years*. Milton Keynes: Open University Press.

Index

MAKING SENSE OF CHILDREN'S DRAWINGS
Angela Anning and Kathy Ring

If you know and love young children, find a way to read this book. Here you will discover the hidden talents of young children for complexity, design, and tenacity for learning . . . This book is a wonderful addition to the too-small library of quality books on young children's learning through art.

Shirley Brice Heath, Professor Emerita, Stanford University
and Professor at Large, Brown University USA

This book is unique in giving an in-depth account of the way young children approach drawing at home and at school. It shows the cognitive value of drawing in children's intellectual and emotional development and sets out the truly extraordinary range of drawing types that are used and understood by three to six year olds . . . It is an invaluable experience.

Professor Ken Baynes, Department of Design and Technology,
Loughborough University

This book explores how young children learn to draw and draw to learn, both at home and at school. It provides support for practitioners in developing a pedagogy of drawing in Art and Design and across the curriculum, and provides advice for parents about how to make sense of their children's drawings.

Making Sense of Children's Drawings is enlivened with the real drawings of seven young children collected over three years. These drawings stimulated dialogues with the children, parents and practitioners whose voices are reported in the book. The book makes a powerful argument for us to rethink radically the role of drawing in young children's construction of meaning, communication and sense of identity. It provides insights into the influence of media and consumerism, as reflected in popular visual imagery, and on gender identity formation in young children. It also offers strong messages about the overemphasis on the three Rs in early childhood education.

Key reading for students, practitioners and parents who want to encourage young children's drawing development without 'interfering' with their creativity, and who need a novel approach to tuning into young children's passions and preoccupations.

Contents
Preface – Acknowledgements – Young children making meaning at home and school – Young children learning to draw – Overview of the project – Luke's story – Simon's story – Holly's story – Lianne's story – Themes from the seven children's drawings – Implications – References – Index.

152pp   0 335 21265 4 (Paperback)   0 335 21266 2 (Hardback)